HEALING AND CREATIVITY IN ECONOMIC ETHICS

The Contribution of Bernard Lonergan's Economic Thought to Catholic Social Teaching

Stephen L. Martin

Studies in Religion and the Social Order

University Press of America,® Inc.
Lanham · Boulder · New York · Toronto · Plymouth, UK

University Press of America,® Inc.
4501 Forbes Boulevard
Suite 200
Lanham, Maryland 20706
UPA Acquisitions Department (301) 459-3366

Estover Road
Plymouth PL6 7PY
United Kingdom

Printed in the United States of America
British Library Cataloging in Publication Information Available

Library of Congress Control Number: 2007926939
ISBN-13: 978-0-7618-3765-7 (paperback : alk. paper)
ISBN-10: 0-7618-3765-5 (paperback : alk. paper)

∞™ The paper used in this publication meets the minimum requirements of American National Standard for Information Sciences—Permanence of Paper for Printed Library Materials, ANSI Z39.48—1984

Studies in Religion and the Social Order

TABLE OF CONTENTS

LIST OF FIGURES

ACKNOWLEDGMENTS

For my wife Elaine who never let up in her constant encouragement and undying support and sacrifice toward my completing this work. Without her and our two daughters Kara and Jessica's support, I wouldn't have had the solid foundation needed to write this book.

Next to my family, my highest appreciation is to Dr. Christine Firer Hinze who as director of my dissertation in theology and society at Marquette University helped shepherd this book through its first incarnation. Dr. William Shea, Director of the Center for Religion, Ethics, and Culture, Holy Cross University, was instrumental, along with Dr. Jacob Neusner, Bard College, in accepting this book in the Religion and Social Order Series at University Press of America.

I wish to thank those also who have also have assisted me along the way in my study of Bernard Lonergan and onto the frontier of understanding and interpreting his economic thought. Fr. Peter Drilling, Christ the King Seminary, East Aurora, NY, not only introduced me to Lonergan's thought, but also to an early unpublished manuscript of Lonergan's economics manuscript. Frederick Crowe, S.J., Fr. Robert Croken, S.J., and Robert Doran, S.J. of the Toronto Lonergan Research Centre, and Kerry Cronin and Patrick Byrne of the Lonergan Institute at Boston College provided me access to other published and unpublished primary and secondary materials in Lonergan. I gratefully acknowledge The University of Toronto and the Lonergan Estate for permission to quote from Lonergan's works. Philip McShane, probably the most knowledgable scholar of Lonergan's economics, kindly and helpfully read over my chapters on Lonergan's economic methodology and economics. Anthony Sciglitano, my colleague in the Department of Religious Studies at Seton Hall University was gracious enough to read through my final draft and made several valuable suggestions. I also benefited from a University Research Council Summer Research Grant from Seton Hall University.

Finally, I wish to express a great debt of appreciation to Robin Linstromberg, my professor in undergraduate courses in the history of economic Thought and economics senior seminar at Bradley University, who raised questions about economics in these classes that were never answered to my satisfaction (and I don't think his either) within my study of orthodox economics. But these questions started me on the pursuit that only through studying Catholic social teaching, alternative schools in economics, and especially Bernard Lonergan has allowed me to come to some sort of satisfactory perspectives which I seek to share in this book.

INTRODUCTION

HEALING AND CREATIVITY IN ECONOMIC ETHICS

Christian economic ethics is a relatively new field within the broader field of Christian social ethics.[1] Although the social teachings of the Christian churches have traditionally dealt with such economic issues as the proper use of wealth, the moral status of usury, etc., it is only since the middle of the 19th century with the American social gospel, social Catholicism in Europe, Anglican social teaching, and the beginning of the Catholic social encyclical tradition with Pope Leo XIII's *Rerum Novarum* in 1891 that Christian social ethics has dealt with the prospect and reality of institutionalized economic systems grounded in political economic theories.[2]

Due to both historical and theoretical factors Catholic social teaching (CST) has always seemed to tread between the proverbial rock and a hard place: the Charybdis of unregulated capitalism which leads to a situation little better than human slavery and the Scylla of socialism, rejected also by Leo XIII as leading to consequences also inhumane. Just a few examples of dichotomies involved in this dialectical maneuvering are:

- competition vs. cooperation
- self-regulated markets vs. state regulation
- capital vs. labor
- centralization vs. decentralization
- innovation vs. tradition
- productive justice vs. distributive justice
- social harmony vs. conflict

However, this prototypical Catholic "both/and" approach leads to both theoretical and practical difficulties. For example, Paul Lakeland takes CST to task for the fact that the same encyclical can be spun many different ways.[3] This was confirmed when Pope John Paul II's *Centesimus Annus* (1991) was seen at the same time as both confirming the victory of the market-directed economy and of placing strict limitations on the market. As discussed extensively in Chapter 2, Mary Hobgood notes that in its dialogue with capitalism, socialism and its own tradition, CST has three competing paradigms at work—the orthodox, liberationist, and organic. This competition undermining its effectiveness.[4]

In harsher tones, while he appreciates CST's attempt to cut out a social and economic "sacred space," John Milbank writes that due to its dismissal of the possibility of Christian socialism, "Catholic social teaching becomes in consequence a grotesque hybrid: liberal, Lockean understandings of property rights, and [Adam] Smithian construals of supposed 'contribution' of capital to production are freely incorporated, and yet upon them is superimposed an organicist, patriarchal vision of society."[5] As a result, many find it hard to locate practical implications resulting from CST's both/and approach to these dichotomies; a desired "third way" is hard to contemplate in concrete terms. As Christian Duquoc points out, "moral precepts that are not technically specific turn out to be quite ineffectual."[6]

Adopting a different approach, I take a cue from Bernard Lonergan and Pope John Paul II and argue that instead of offering a 'third way,' Catholic social thought provides primarily a necessary "healing" function in respect to disorders in modern economic society. For example, to evaluate where humanity should locate itself within the dichotomies mentioned above, CST has incorporated central criteria such as human dignity and capacity for self-transcendence; the reality and value of human interrelatedness; a substantive conception of freedom ("freedom to" vs. merely "freedom from"; the preferential option for the poor; and the principle of subsidiarity. These aspects I argue are not incorporated sufficiently into capitalist or socialist social theory and therefore help constitute Catholic social teaching as an original social, but not economic, theory.

But as Lonergan points out, healing is not sufficient. Without the concomitant task of creating alternative economic models, he argues that Christian teaching on specific pastoral issues is a "soul without a body." For example, while early Christianity had the pastoral power to help ameliorate some of the social decline after the fall of the Roman Empire, this effort was unaccompanied by the natural complement of creating. As a result the church lived on after the decay and disintegration of the Roman empire, "not in a civilized world, but in a dark and barbarous age in which, as a contemporary reported, men devoured one another as fishes in the sea."[7] Therefore the tasks of Christian social ethics, and a reconstructed economics, are to incorporate two distinct but interrelated aspects of human concern: respect for the human person in all her dimensions, and to investigate and provide explanatory and normative theories of economic interrelatedness, including macroeconomic theories, to help manage the economy in an efficient and just manner.[8]

Creativity and healing then are the two "vectors" of human intelligence and love. Healing seeks to break "the bonds of psychological and social determinisms with the conviction of faith and the power of hope," while creating moves,

> from experience to growing understanding, from growing understanding to balanced judgment, from balanced judgment to fruitful courses of action, and from fruitful courses of action to the new situations that call forth further understanding, profounder judgment, richer courses of action.[9]

Truly interdisciplinary research in economic ethics, versus approaches that mainly just accommodate the results of the other discipline and thus corrupt one's own, must incorporate both healing and creativity.

Lonergan provides an excellent specification of this interdisciplinary approach:

> [W]e must demand that two requirements are met. The first regards economic theorists, the second regards moral theorists. From economic theorists we have to demand, along with as many other types of analysis as they please, a new and specific type that reveals how moral precepts have both a basis in economic process and so an effective application to it. From moral theorists we have to demand, along with their other various forms of wisdom and prudence, specifically economic precepts that arise out of economic process itself and promote its proper functioning.[10]

Writing this in 1975, Lonergan was not only sending out a call for such collaboration. Going beyond not only theoretical, practical and moral difficulties in mainstream capitalism and socialism, but also what he perceives as deficiencies in CST's approach to economics, Lonergan is building on two manuscripts he had already written that developed a new macroeconomics. These seek to reveal how "moral precepts have both a basis in economic process and so an effective application to it." Originally written from 1930-1944, they were updated by Lonergan up until his death in 1984, and recently published as *Towards a New Political Economy* and *Macroeconomic Dynamics: An Essay in Circulation Analysis.*[11] While disagreeing with the moralistic approach of the just wage, Lonergan's view of the economic agent coheres with that of Catholic social teaching on the role of freedom and morality in economic process vs. that of neoclassical economics. As he writes: "to put the same points in negative terms, when physicists can think on the basis of indeterminacy, economists can think on the basis of freedom and acknowledge the relevance of morality."[12]

To help link economics and morality, Christian economic ethics requires interdisciplinary study in order to integrate and critique economic and social theory. There are four current approaches to this task 1) those that utilize either mainstream[13] or Marxian economic theory[14] to criticize predominant Christian economic ethical views; 2) those that criticize already existing economic paradigms from a Christian point-of-view and then seek to incorporate elements from those paradigms cohering best with Christian ethical principles (the most conspicuous example being Catholic social teaching);[15] 3) those that go beyond finding flaws and seek to incorporate existing alternative economic paradigms[16] or even to formulate new alternative economic paradigms;[17] and 4) those that reject an interdisciplinary approach altogether, relying instead on a purely "theological economics." The emerging school of "Radical Orthodoxy," developed primarily by the aforementioned John Milbank, is the most influential and cogent of this last approach.[18]

The main argument of this book is that one particular example of an alternative economics, Bernard Lonergan's economic thought, closely aligned with "social economics,"[19] provides a necessary dimension to Christian economic ethics hitherto not adequately provided. This is because Christian ethicists' collaboration with alternative traditions to capitalism and socialism share one flaw that mars these traditions themselves: their inability as of yet to come up with an alternative macroeconomic paradigm to that of Marxism and orthodox economic theory. One of my arguments is that Lonergan's macroeconomics more effectively explains economic process than do orthodox and socialist macroeconomic theory.

If my assessment is correct, then Lonergan's work is crucial to human flourishing because only through effective economic understanding of macroeconomic process, can we help political systems avoid the destructive effects of capitalist and state-socialist ideologies and institutionalizations in history. On a more differentiated level, although the economic system is only one system of social interaction, it is clearly linked to other systems, especially the political system. While it is up to the social and political systems to decide upon such economic related questions such as proper income distribution, market regulation, etc., government and social policy in regards to these questions needs to take into account the economic ramifications and limits to possible policies. Lonergan does not follow the Catholic economic theologian Michael Novak's strict distinction among the economic, political and moral realms. Rather, as will be shown, questions about the common good and appropriate moral action fall *within* economics, as I am envisioning adequate economic theory. On the other hand, no amount of purely moral and/or theological analysis of existing economic understandings/arrangements will fully address the challenges of Christian economic ethics: to diagnose economic injustice, to heal victimization and oppression, and to help create new theoretical understandings of economics process toward eliminating the injustices of current political-economic arrangements.

To accomplish this, we must first take a truly radical approach. The root of the word "radical" means to turn back to the roots of an issue. I argue that a focus on economic methodology is crucial to this task. The first section delves into Christian economic ethics by concentrating on Catholic social teaching and its relationship to economic theory. The second section presents Lonergan's economic methodology as extrapolated from his cognitive and social theory (found mainly in his seminal works, *Insight* [1957] and *Method in Theology* [1972]), and then his macroeconomic theory itself. Each of these sections has two chapters: the first chapter in each section concentrates on the healing function of interdisciplinary economic ethics; the second investigates efforts to creatively correlate economic theory with the "healing" insights found in the first chapter of each section.

The scope of the book, following the dialectic between healing and creativity, moves from existential-problem, to the methodological-theoretical, to the existential-practical that the combination of healing and creativity in economic ethics can bring. The content moves from 1) establishing the crucial place that economic anthropology plays in both treatment of the human person in economic life, and economic theorizing—this is done through an analysis and critique of Catholic social teaching and alternative visions; to 2) the links between the economic anthropology explicit in Catholic social teaching and Lonergan's economic anthropology—by elucidating Lonergan's implicit economic methodology from his major writings and economic manuscripts; to 3) how that foundation allows for a new macroeconomic paradigm, grounded in a realistic view of the human person and essential for truly democratic and responsible guidance of the economy by all economic agents.

In sum, I seek to show not only that Lonergan's economics is in line with the humanistic, religious, anthropological, and philosophical perspectives of Christian economic ethics and Catholic social teaching, but also provides a cogent, concrete, explanatory perspective on economic process to replace what Lonergan sees as scientific flaws in orthodox macroeconomic theory, flaws which lead continually to great, unnecessary human suffering. In my conclusion, I elucidate some implications of *Macroeconomic Dynamics: An Essay in Circulation Analysis* for Christian economic ethics and Catholic social teaching.

NOTES

1. Joseph F. Gower, "Introduction," in *Religion and Economic Ethics*, ed. Joseph F. Gower (Lanham, MD.: University Press of America, 1990), [ix]-xxvi.

2. On the growth of social ethics in general in response to the development of the social sciences which in turn followed the rapid growth of technology and economic development see Gibson Winter, "Introduction," in *Social Ethics: Issues in Ethics and Society*, ed. Gibson Winter (New York: Harper & Row, 1968), 4.

3. Paul Lakeland, *Theology and Critical Theory* (Nashville: Abingdon Press, 1990).

4. Mary E. Hobgood, *Catholic Social Teaching and Economic Theory: Paradigms in Conflict* (Philadelphia: Temple University Press, 1991).

5. John Milbank, "On Complex Space" in *The Word Made Strange: Theology, Language, and Culture* (Cambridge, MA: Blackwell Publishers, 1997), 283.

6. Christian Duquoc, *Ambiguité des theologies de la secularization: Essai critique* (Gembloux: Ducolot, 1972), 103-112 and 113-128 (on Vatican II's *Gaudium et Spes).* Quoted in Bernard Lonergan, "Healing and Creating in History," in *Third Collection,* ed. Frederick E. Crowe, S.J. (New York/Mahwah, NJ: Paulist Press, 1985), 108. The Radical Orthodox theologian D. Stephen Long points out related criticisms of Catholicism's both/and approach for its "formal vacuousness" and for tempting "us to tolerate competing allegiances without recognizing we are doing so," in his *The Goodness of God: Theology, Church and the Social Order* (Grand Rapids, MI: Brazos, 2001), 57-58. As an example of its harmful effect on the socio-political order, he cites Michael Budde's severe criticism of the Catholic Church's "ineffectiveness in preventing Christians by Christians in Rwanda, 'the most Catholic Country in Africa'" (Michael Budde, "Pledging Allegiances: Reflections on Discipleship and the Church in Rwanda," in *Church as Counterculture*, ed. Michael L. Budde and Robert W. Brimlow [Albany, NY: SUNY Press, 2000], 214.)

7. Lonergan, "Healing and Creating," 108.

8. As Daniel Maguire makes clear, we must know "what" we are talking about in matters of moral inquiry: "The *is* is parent to the *ought,*" (Daniel Maguire, *The Moral Choice* [Garden City, NY: Doubleday: 1978], 129). Consonant with the argument of this book, Maguire also addresses the need to avoid uncritically accepting the judgments of "experts" in scientific matters, including economics (301-304).

9. Lonergan, "Healing and Creating," 106.

10. Lonergan, "Healing and Creating," 108.

11. *The Collected Works of Bernard Lonergan*, ed. Frederick E. Crowe and Robert M. Doran, vol. 21, *For a New Political Economy*, ed. Philip McShane (Toronto: University of Toronto Press, 1998) and vol. 15, *Macroeconomic Dynamics: An Essay in Circulation Analysis*, ed. Frederick Lawrence, Charles Hefling and Patrick Byrne (Toronto: University of Toronto Press, 1999).

12. Lonergan, "Healing and Creating," 108.

13. See for example, Michael Novak, *The Spirit of Democratic Capitalism* (New York: Simon & Schuster/American Enterprise Institute, 1982); Robert Benne, *The Ethic of Democratic Capitalism: A Moral Reassessment* (Philadelphia: Fortress Press, 1981); Brian Griffiths, *The Creation of Wealth: A Christian's Case for Capitalism* (Downers Grove, IL: Intervarsity Press, 1984).

14. See Hobgood, *Catholic Social Teaching and Economic Theory*; Beverly W. Harrison, "The Role of Social Theory in Religious Social Ethics," in *Making the Connections: Essays in Feminist Social Ethics*, ed. Carol S. Robb (Boston: Beacon Press, 1985) and "The Fate of the Middle Class in Late Capitalism," in *God and Capitalism*, ed. J. Mark Thomas and Vernon Visick (Madison, WI: A-R Editions, 1991), 53-71.

15. Along with the Catholic social teaching found for example in David J. O'Brien and Thomas A. Shannon, Editors, *Catholic Social Thought: The Documentary Heritage* (Maryknoll, NY: Orbis Books, 1992); J. Philip Wogaman, *The Great Economic Debate: An Ethical Analysis* (Philadelphia: Westminster Press, 1977); Gary Dorrien, *The Democratic Socialist Vision* (Towata, NJ: Rowman & Littlefield, 1986); Ronald H. Preston, *Religion and the Persistence of Capitalism* (London: SCM Press, 1979) and *Religion and the Ambiguities of Capitalism* (Cleveland: The Pilgrim Press, 1979); John Atherton, *Christianity and the Market: Christian Social Thought for Our Times* (1991); and Craig M. Gay, *With Liberty and Justice for Whom?: The Recent Evangelical Debate Over Capitalism* (Grand Rapids, MI: William P. Eerdmans, 1991).

16. One such alternative tradition is "social economics," which predates Adam Smith by about 40 years. Thomas Nitsch offers an extensive history of social economics in "Social Economics: The First 200 Years" in *Social Economics: Retrospect and Prospect*, ed. Mark A. Lutz (Boston: Kluwer Academic

Publishers, 1990), 5-90.

17. Besides the example of Bernard Lonergan's economics which is the focus of this book, see Prentiss L. Pemberton and Daniel Rush Finn, *Toward a Christian Economic Ethic* (Minneapolis: Winston Press, 1985); John P. Tiemstra, et. al., *Reforming Economics: Calvinist Studies on Methods and Institutions*, vol. 48 of *Toronto Studies in Theology*, ed. John P. Tiemstra (Lewiston, NY: The Edwin Mellen Press, 1990); Donald Hay, *Economics To-day: A Christian Critique* (Grand Rapids, MI: William P. Eerdmans, 1989); Bob Goodzwaard, *Capitalism and Progress: A Diagnosis of Western Society*, trans. J. van Zylstra Nuis (Grand Rapids, MI: William P. Eerdmans, 1979); Gregory Baum, *Karl Polanyi: On Ethics and Economics* (Montreal: McGill Queens University Press, 1996); John B. Cobb, Jr., "Christianity, Political Theology and the Economic Future," in *Civil Religion and Public Theology*, ed. Leroy C. Rouner (Notre Dame, IN: University of Notre Dame Press, 1986), 207-23; and Herman Daly and John B. Cobb, Jr., *For the Common Good: Redirecting the Economy Toward Community, the Environment and a Sustainable Future* (Boston: Beacon Press, 1989).

18. Along with the Radical Orthodoxy manifesto *Theology and Social Theory* (Oxford, ENG: Basil Blackwell, 1990), Milbank critiques Catholic social teaching in "Against the Resignations of the Age" in *Things Old and New: Catholic Social Teaching Revisited*, ed. Francis P. McHugh and Samuel M. Natale (Lanham MD: University Press of America, 1993), 1-39; and Milbank, "On Complex Space." D. Stephen Long prescribes an almost purely theological approach to economics in *Divine Economy: Theology and The Market* (London/New York: Routledge, 2000), and "Catholic Social Teaching and the Global Market" in *Wealth, Poverty and Human Destiny*, ed. Doug Bandow and David L. Schindler (Wilmington, DE: ISI Books, 2003), 77-102.

19. An early title of Lonergan's *Macroeconomic Dynamics* was "Towards a Pure Theory of Social Economics."

CHAPTER 1

HEALING IN CHRISTIAN ECONOMIC ETHICS: CATHOLIC SOCIAL TEACHING AND ECONOMIC ANTHROPOLOGY

As an influential and important tradition of Christian social ethics, Catholic social teaching has sought to address moral and ethical issues in the development and application of modern social and economic practice and science. The first part of this chapter provides an overview of these issues within Catholic social thought, with attention to the context of the social and economic developments they address. The documents discussed (in chronological order) will be Leo XIII's *Rerum Novarum* (1891; hereafter referred to as RN); Pius XI's *Quadragesimo Anno* (1931; QA); *Mater et Magistra* (1961; MM) and *Pacem in Terris* (1963; PT) of John XXIII; Vatican II's *Gaudium et Spes* (1965; GS); Paul VI's *Populorum Progressio* (1967; PP) and *Octogesima Adveniens* (1971; OA); John Paul II's *Laborem Exercens* (1981; LE), *Sollicitudo Rei Socialis* (1987; SRS), and *Centesimus Annus* (1991; CA), and *Economic Justice for All* (1982; EJA), a pastoral letter written by the United States Catholic Bishops.[1]

The purpose of this overview is to examine the Christian "economic anthropology" utilized by these documents as alternatives to those they associate with reigning capitalist and socialist economic paradigms. The aim of this chapter and the next is to show that despite its inconsistencies and even internal contradictions, this economic anthropology provides the basis for Catholic social teaching's original social theory and its alternative economic ethic to those of liberal capitalism and socialism. This is because, as the social economist Giuseppe Gaburro rightly claims, "Every economic theory is conceived in a particular philosophical context, and is based on a particular anthropological concept. The validity of the theory is conditioned by the validity of the anthropological concept."[2]

Overview of Catholic Social Teaching from Economic Anthropological Perspectives

It is the intent of this overview is to use these critiques to make explicit the (dis)connection between CST's economic anthropology and secular economic theory. In my view this often adversarial relationship is not sufficiently treated in many commentaries on the social encyclicals. For example, David Hollenbach, in locating the coherence of the encyclical tradition in its defense of human rights, pays only indirect attention to the encyclicals' treatment of human agency in economic matters.[3] My emphasis on economic anthropology concentrates on the relationship between self and society within economic theory.

Rerum Novarum

The Roman Catholic encyclical approach to political economy has arisen within particular economic, political and social contexts. It has applied an approach necessarily in line with its own particular resources such as scripture, tradition, and natural law, in an attempt to provide a social theory that avoids the limitations and deleterious consequences of the approaches of liberal capitalism and socialism. Leo XIII's *Rerum Novarum* (RN) is the first attempt by a pope to address the modern "social question" by providing alternatives to the reigning social order beyond the political responses as favored by his predecessors such as Pius IX. As noted in my Introduction, RN is a response, if somewhat belated, to the impact of industrial capitalism upon the working class. They had moved to the cities, enjoyed less community and government support, and became subject to the "iron laws" of 19th century political economics that led to subsistence wages or worse. Despite the democratic ideals expounded by the founders of liberal capitalistic theory, Leo XIII is moved to proclaim instead that, "a small number of very rich men have been able to lay upon the masses of the poor a yoke little better than slavery itself" (RN 2).

But RN is also, and in some commentators' judgments mainly, a rejoinder to 19th century socialist movements which themselves had arisen in response to the misery of the masses. Leo XIII clearly interprets socialism as both a threat to the institutional influence of the Catholic church and to the material and spiritual well-being of the proletariat whom socialist movements so ardently wanted to serve: "If they [socialist programs] were carried out, the workingman himself would be among the first to suffer" (RN 3).

The response of *Rerum Novarum* to the "problems of the age" grew out of movements already present within the church that sought to remedy the individualistic basis and economic practices of liberalism. The wage-contract system replaced the medieval guild systems as the dominant organizer of capital and labor. In so doing it significantly shifted the balance of power to capital owners and thus was singled out by early

Catholic opponents to liberal capitalism.[4] Those favoring a return (somehow) to the guild system have been accused of doing so mainly out of their nostalgia for a simpler, more organic economic life, built around a predominantly agricultural milieu, with clearly defined roles among the state, the church, the owners and the workers. While certainly this sentiment played a part, Catholic social theorists and activists were also concerned with the erosion of social and communal bonds between peoples uprooted from the land by the Industrial Revolution. Simultaneously, workers were conceptually cut free from these bonds by liberal contract theory and liberal individualism, and treated as mere commodities in modern economic thought. One very limited way to accomplish a restoration of these bonds were the somewhat paternalistic efforts by Catholic factory owners, such as Leon Harmel, who gave their employees wages, benefits and participation over and above what the wage contract system would have afforded them. Other writers still argued for a more systematic return to the guild system.[5]

Thus, RN ends up as a "middle position" in two ways. It seeks to create a "space" between capitalism and socialism. But it also maneuvers between the extreme positions of those who advocated a return to the guild system, and economic theorists such as Charles Perin who advocated mainly private charity as the Christian response to the ill effects of capitalism.[6]

In addressing this intra-church tension centering around constructing alternatives to capitalism and socialism, Leo ends up taking the way of Bishop Emmanuel von Ketteler of Mainz (1811-1877), Leo's "*notre grand predecesseur*."[7] Originally in favor of the guild system, Ketteler became a pioneer of the ameliorative or "reform" approach to the problems posed by socialism and capitalism. Thus instead of proposing any sort of third way, Leo advocates such measures as a just wage, state intervention and worker's associations (although limited) that sought to remedy the deleterious affects of liberal capitalism and avoid socialist revolution by improving the welfare of the masses.[8] While Leo seems to regret the passing of the guild system, he does not advocate a return to it. Instead, he wishes somehow to incorporate into modern social economy the social and communal bonds provided by this system. The fundamental economic anthropological point is Leo's counterpoising the Christian view of the human as social and individual over against capitalist individualism and socialist collectivism. By using this anthropology to directly argue against the anthropological assumptions of liberal capitalism and Marxian socialism, he proposes a foundation for any alternative economic paradigm to these dominant approaches. Thus RN addresses contemporary economic theory on the basis of morality, ethics, and a rudimentary Christian economic anthropology. That Christian economic anthropology becomes more explicit and more developed in Pius XI.

Unfortunately, while avoiding a move to return to the past in economic organizations, Leo couches this anthropology within an organic framework that maintained strong links to medieval economic arrangements. This version of organic social theory stressed the hierarchical ordering of spiritual and material realities and the importance of stability and order in society.[9] This causes Leo for example to misinterpret his philosophical hero, Thomas Aquinas, whose medieval thought Leo called upon in *Aeterni Patris* (1879) to help solve modern problems, on some key points. For instance, while Aquinas argued that the institution of private property was a socially-constructed addition to divine law because of its empirical benefits to the common good, Leo states that private property was itself divinely instituted and therefore an absolute right (RN 7).[10]

Moreover, Leo's stress on the organic hierarchical conception of society with its corresponding support for the status quo served to undermine his prescriptions for social change. This can be clearly seen in Leo's limited support of worker's associations, or trade unions. While Leo advocates that workers form associations (as long as they were Catholic) to gain more economic power, he stops short of granting them the right to strike to gain this power, arguing that this would disrupt the common good. On the other hand, Leo correctly points out the power that the wealthy had achieved over the poorer classes. This power granted them political capacity to prevent any change in the status quo favorable to workers and poor, when such a change would disfavor their economic position. To overcome this, Leo puts too much faith in the church's role of convincing the rich to be charitable to the poor.

While it reflects a non-radical, hierarchical view of social change, *Rerum Novarum* does challenge the dominant economic theories of the time. Underpinning Leo's claim that neo-classical "laws" of supply and demand were not in fact laws, is his conviction that morality should and does play a role in day-to-day economic functioning. This emphasis upon morality against mechanism is reflected in Leo's view that economics should regard labor "not [as] a commodity to be bought at market prices." As he points out, that often means no more than slave labor. Rather, wages should be set to take in consideration the needs of the workers, a living or just wage which would be enough to enable workers to save to buy their own personal property (a divine right). Because the state had the responsibility to protect both the human rights of the workers and the property rights of the owners of capital, Leo sees at least a moderate interventionist role for the state. While this view is not radical, it caused some of his contemporaries to conclude that the pope had "gone over to socialism."[11]

Donal Dorr is correct then that while RN stops short of adopting an explicit "option for the poor," it helped to support church activism on the side of the poor, and set modern Catholic social teaching in tension with liberal economic theory and practice over the treatment of the working class in the market system.[12] This tension is heightened in Pius XI's *Quadragesimo Anno* (QA), which deepens Leo's structural critique of capitalism and Leo's critique of the moral, ethical, and anthropological foundations of capitalism and socialism.

Quadragesimo Anno

Quadragesimo Anno (1931) was written to mark the fortieth anniversary of *Rerum Novarum.* The primary drafter was Oswald von Nell-Breuning, a student in a circle of Jesuit economic thinkers around Heinrich Pesch, all influenced strongly by Rerum Novarum. Changed economic circumstances since RN, including a worldwide economic depression and even greater concentration of wealth in the hands of the few, causes Pius XI to be even more critical of capitalism than Leo XIII, especially the economic individualism which Pius and the drafters of QA maintained lay behind it. Pius credits Leo's insistence on the legitimacy of state intervention and the subsequent influence of clerics seeking to apply Leo's teaching with helping to create "a new branch of jurisprudence concerned with the soul: the energetic defense of the workingman, with particular regard to women and children."[13] Pius was influenced by both the economic circumstances of the depression and Pesch's theory of corporatism, which sought to integrate ethical, moral and anthropological issues within concrete political economic arrangements. QA ends up putting forth a strong structural, even radical, analysis of liberal capitalism and goes beyond Leo by advocating concrete structural alternatives to capitalism and socialism.[14]

Pius XI (and corporatism) does not reject capitalism *per se*, favoring a large measure of free enterprise. But he has strong words for that type of capitalism that rests ideologically on the principle that the proper ordering of economic life be left to free competition—that market forces should be the determining factor in the economic order, regulating prices, profits and wages, and thus who succeeds and who fails (QA 109). Ironically, but in

Pius' view typically, unrestrained competition leads to the end of free-competition due to the emergence of monopolies and oligopolies in the struggle for control of finance, markets and even governments themselves (QA 105-108).

Pius reiterates Leo XIII's defense of private property, but at the same time moves away from Leo's view of it as divine and absolute. When natural law fails to determine the precise freedoms and limits of private ownership, government has the responsibility to do so, "specifying more accurately what is licit and what is illicit for property owners in the use of their possessions" (QA 9). Thus, as David Hollenbach points out, for Pius the right of private property is not absolute but should be determined in accordance with personal freedom and "social strategies for fulfilling basic human needs."[15] Here he begins the move away from divine right of property initiated by Leo toward viewing property as more of a socially constructed right as maintained by each subsequent social encyclical as shown below. These views are more consistent with Aquinas' view and with Lonergan's economics' view of surplus profits as a "social dividend," not 'belonging' to one class.

In this vein, Pius comes out strongly against the capitalist practice of seizing all of the profits from an enterprise, leaving all but the minimum necessary for workers. Here he criticizes the liberalist Manchester school of neo-classical economists who had argued this is the result of inexorable economic laws. This determinism or even worse fatalism clearly goes against the Catholic Christian role of free human (and divine) agency in constructing the social order. On the other hand, he argues against Marx's view that workers deserve surplus income because they are the ones who toil to produce it.[16] Also, natural law demonstrates that distribution of wealth and property should attain the end intended by God, by ministering to the needs of all, so that "one class is forbidden to exclude the other from a share in the profits" (QA 57). Therefore wealth must be distributed among various individuals and classes for the common good of all, each class receiving its due share.

To achieve just distribution in which the propertyless will have enough to own property and thus guard against "agitators of revolution disrupting public order and peace and tranquility of human society," wages must be increased. The best way of achieving this is by modifying the wage contract, so that "workers and executives become sharers in ownership and management or else participate in some way in the profits" (QA 65).

However, Pius XI's proposal for achieving universal worker ownership differs from Leo XII's. In Leo's scheme, through the Church's moral suasion employers were to grant workers more of the profits from an enterprise, so that they might, through thrift, one day own property and participate in the economic system. Pius' solution to the conflict between the classes caused by the unequal distribution of goods and the poverty of the working classes was to deal directly with the social order by reforming social and economic institutions and correcting morals. While reiterating Leo's stress on the need for a just wage, the right to organize and the economic role of government, Pius also contributes the important concept of social justice to incorporate this structural aspect of justice.

As Hollenbach explains, social justice is "a conceptual tool by which moral reasoning takes into account the fact that relationships between persons have an institutional or structural dimension."[17] One way of achieving social justice was through corporatism. This solution, successful in certain areas, but in Italy and other places ending up supporting fascism, involved grouping similar occupations together in an attempt to reach back beyond the industrial revolution and the wage system to craft unions made up of both employees and employers. In this scheme, the economy would not be ruled by the free play of rugged competition (which Pius points out has been replaced anyway in practice by economic imperialism), but by justice and charity.[18]

Pius XI reiterates Leo's condemnation of socialism, although he does admit of some distinctions between types of socialism. While moderate socialists condemned bloody revolutions and abolition of private property (in this way approaching the ameliorative thrust of the encyclicals), Pius found their conception of society so different from the Christian one that he still finds Christian socialism a contradiction in terms (QA 120). This is because socialists maintain that living in community is for the sake of advantages which it can bring to humanity, in contrast to the Christian belief that social life is for "people to use faculties to praise and glory of the creator" (QA 118). According to Pius, socialists also maintain that even liberty must be subordinated to exigencies of efficient production for the economic health of the community. The concomitant loss of human dignity is (unfairly for Pius) compensated for by the abundance of goods in socialist production (QA 119).

Mater et Magistra

Due to the post-World War II affluence of post-Great Depression welfare-capitalism which used Keynesian fiscal and monetary policies to guide market economies, John XXIII abandons the corporatism that influenced Leo and characterized much of Pius' solution to the social problem. In the spirit of *aggiornamento* (updating the church) that characterized his call for the Second Vatican Council, John seeks to update Catholic social teaching in light of the exigencies of a new economic situation. World War II had ended most attempts at corporatism (which in much practice had tended to follow not the model proposed in QA, but Mussolini's fascist model). Also, the economic conditions in the 1950's and early 1960's did not require in John's view such a radical critique as presented by Pius XI. The return of prosperity to Europe after the war and the rising affluence of most of Western society caused John to be more hopeful about the prospects of welfare or social-assistance forms of reformed capitalism evolving in many democratic nations. Instead of the failure of capitalism of the Great Depression that pushed Pius XI toward social reform, it was the wealth-creation abilities and attention to economic equity as exhibited in the post-World War II boom of welfare capitalism that John sees as the means of extending justice, freedom and prosperity to undeveloped nations and greater economic democracy to workers in the developed countries.

One of Pope John XXIII's major contributions to Catholic social teaching, developed in *Mater et Magistra*, is to relate Catholic social thought to the greater complexity of social structures in the modern era.[19] Through greater *socialization*, there had been a multiplication of social relationships, and thus an expansion of services provided by both the public and private sector.[20] However, this increasing organization of human freedom threatens to subordinate human dignity to social institutions. Therefore, the restriction of individual freedom in this new situation requires that there be a balance between social restrictions and the free action of individuals. The principle for judging this balancing is the common good, which for John "embraced the sum total of conditions of social living, whereby men are enabled more fully to achieve their own perfection" (MM 65). John actually sees this ideal as possible within reformed capitalism tempered by justice and charity, and his optimism leads him to assert that with the proper tools and concerns, political economics can lead to greater economic and political freedom and inclusiveness.

Within this optimism as to the ability of liberal reform or welfare capitalism to raise worldwide standards of living (MM 48, 67, 155-165, 170-171), John XXIII couches his social and economic recommendations within the dialectic between private initiative and public intervention. While he holds that first place should be given to private initiative (describing the benefits of economic enterprise as constituting "productive justice"),[21] he also stresses that public authorities should take active interest in justice and charity.[22] The solution to this dialectic is as follows. First, John reiterates Leo XXIII and Pius XI's insistence upon a just wage but with consideration for particular enterprises and for the common good. Second, political economy as a whole should not be unregulated free competition. He agrees with Pius XI that this ends in economic domination and the corruption of politics. But neither can political economy be built on class warfare and moderate socialism because although the aims of moderate socialism may closely resemble those of Catholic social teachings, the former still stresses material welfare over spiritual welfare; plus the liberty of workers is sacrificed in state socialism.

Although John turns away from corporatist solutions, he still considers the optimum solution where workers and employers can be co-owners and partners in economic enterprise. Ultimately, John's prescriptions are based upon *Quadragesimo Anno*'s principle of subsidiarity.[23] In making sure that the right level of government action is initiated, this principle is a double-edged sword against both unregulated capitalism and over-bureaucratization: public action can increase freedom of private citizens to provide for themselves and their families, but where private initiative is lacking, political tyranny and stagnation prevails.

In order to best provide for the common good in this new situation of reform capitalism, where economic productivity, tempered by charity and inclusiveness, is seen as an engine of economic justice, John argued that economic development and social progress have to be balanced. Part of this balancing act was to be accomplished by companies sharing the wealth that results from their rapid growth by granting money to employees, especially if they are not now receiving a just wage, instead of continuing to put all excess revenues into replacement and plant expansion. This conforms to John's conception of the common good in that when full-employment is gained, there is a better balance between wages and prices, and goods and services are made more accessible for a better life for all. This type of inclusive economic development would eliminate or limit inequalities among the social classes and between the classes of nations as well (MM 79, 92).

Pacem in Terris

John's other major encyclical, *Pacem in Terris*, is not as explicitly an economic encyclical as *Mater et Magistra*. However, it does stress MM's themes regarding the rights proper to each individual and the development of the common good. It also added to these rights, for example, the right to work. Taken together MM and PT argue for the right to life and a worthy standard of living. PT reiterates Leo XIII's teaching on the just wage as being allowing families a standard of living in keeping with dignity of the human person (PT 20). The state has the duty of promoting the rights of individuals, social as well as economic progress, proper work for all and a just wage. However, John reiterates his teaching of MM 109, that "the balance between private and public-state intervention in the economic field ought not be exercised in such a way as to curtail individual freedom of personal initiative" (PT 65).

Among the popes studied thus far, John XXIII, despite the optimism expressed concerning welfare capitalism in MM, shows the most open attitude toward Marxism and socialism, allowing that Catholics can work together for social and economic justice with other groups without compromising their religion or morals. Nonetheless, John argued that one can make a distinction between philosophical positions of socialism that run counter to Christian theological anthropology, and the spirit motivating the movements. Indeed these movements (specified only by John as "non-Catholic") "contain elements that are positive and deserving of approval" (PT159).[24] Pope Paul VI will further extend this opening to socialism and Pope John Paul II in *Laborem Exercens* enters into explicit dialogue with Marx on the condition of labor.

Gaudium et Spes

Gaudium et Spes (1965), a document of the Second Vatican Council incorporates five central elements: "personalism, the social nature of person, the relation between church and world, justice, and development."[25] Hollenbach points out the significance of GS' consolidating these previously circumscribed elements in CST, transforming them into a new model for church-society interaction.[26] This not only incorporates a new dimension for Catholic social teaching, but is also a key development in the Church's theology.[27]

The position of GS toward the socioeconomic order is that technical progress, a spirit of initiative, eagerness to create and expand must be fostered, and methods of production contributing toward development must be adopted, not for profit or domination, but for the service of humanity. Consequently, economic activity is to be carried out according to its own methods and laws but within the limits of morality so that God's plan for humanity can be realized. This crucial Catholic contribution based on the relative independence of the natural from the supernatural order is a central feature of Lonergan's autonomous, yet not secularist, economic theory. Development should not be left up to the judgment of a few powerful people or groups, but rather the largest possible number of people should have an active share in its direction. Development thus should not be allowed to follow a course solely resulting from economic activity of individuals, nor be solely directed by government authority. At the same time, theories which obstruct necessary reforms in the name of a false liberty must be branded as erroneous.

GS holds that private ownership is good for the development of personality and provides the occasion for persons to exercise their roles in society and in the economy. However, private property must not hurt the common good. Private property has a social quality deriving from the law of the communal purpose of created goods. If the social quality of property is overlooked, property often becomes the occasion of greed and of serious disturbances (GS 71).

Dorr argues that a primary issue of GS is the extent to which the church was prepared to take a radical or prophetic stance that challenged the current values of society. Because the emphasis was still on Western liberal thought, there is missing the view of economic development from third-world based theology. Nevertheless, GS represents an advancement over earlier views, even those of John XXIII, on the autonomy of culture and history, and problems of the third-world. GS adopts a more dialectical strategy that recognizes that reality is marred by social evil, reflecting a more nuanced approach than that of John (GS 69). What is original in GS is the view that because the balance in society tips very often against the poor and powerless, the right to private property is relative to the need at times to expropriate property to empower the poor. Dorr finds in GS a deep compassion for the poor but still not the option for the poor because it advocates a top-down approach to social change. Despite these reservations, Dorr judges correctly that GS provides a solid basis for such documents as Medillin and *Populorum Progressio*, especially in GS' stress that capitalistic "development" is not adequate and that "authentic" development must be undertaken by the poor themselves.

Populorum Progressio

Paul VI's *On the Development of Peoples* (PP; 1967) follows John XXIII's and Vatican II's initiatives toward placing the social question in a worldwide context and widening the window for church dialogue with Marxism in the quest for economic justice. Like his predecessors from Pius XI on, Paul VI rejects the basic precepts of liberal capitalism such as unrestricted private property, the centrality of the profit motive and the argument that free trade in a world economy always benefits all countries involved. The political, social and economic ends of the authentic or "integral development" prescribed by Paul VI are greater assurance of finding subsistence, health and stable employment. Beyond these economic goods, integral development means an increased share of responsibility without oppression, greater political freedom for the third-world vis-à-vis first and second world countries, more autonomous growth. In sum, Paul believes that integral development is a surer route to needed economic, political and social improvements and full human enhancement and equality with developed nations than the neo-colonialist development model that mainly benefits the more "developed" nations.[28]

As Paul writes, while development solely at the direction of developed countries has improved the technological and scientific stock of knowledge in developing countries, diminished sickness and improved living conditions, poorer economies have also been hurt by certain practices of "colonial" powers (PP 7). These include developing single-crop economies too dependent upon fluctuations of the market, and choosing means of development that weaken cultural supports. The economic situation must be addressed because according to the pope, left to itself, the gap between developing and developed countries in economic well-being and political power will widen even further.

Paul instead promotes a Christian vision of development that is not limited to mere economic growth, because the economic cannot be separated from the human in a true scale of values. Mere economic development *may* provide an improved material standard of living goods. But for integral development rather than mere industrialization to occur, it cannot be achieved through promotion of oppressive social structures involving abuses of ownership and power, exploitation of workers, or unjust transactions between rich and poor countries (PP 14-21).

Because Paul views the solution as mainly a matter of redistribution of wealth from the rich to the poor, "for the universal purpose of created things," Dorr argues that the papacy again promotes a "top-down" approach to social change.[29] However, when Paul does advocate sacrifice by the wealthy on behalf of the poor, Dorr claims on the economic anthropological level that:

> Paul's inclusion of self-sacrifice in the definition of development challenges in two ways the assumption of Western economists and development planners that people are motivated mainly by self-interest. Firstly the pope believes that a human being can be fulfilled personally by a willingness to cooperate with others even when this imposes a personal cost on the individual; therefore self-interest is not opposed to concern with others. Secondly, and equally significantly, the pope sees frugality not as a limitation to personal development but as a positive element within it.[30]

Following my emphasis on economic anthropology, this suggests a model of development not necessarily tied to charity by the rich; rather, a way to authentic development can be found embedded within economic systems, adequately understood and responsibly guided. This is exactly the route taken by Lonergan's economics, both regarding the domestic economy and international trade.

Regarding industrialization as an engine for authentic development, Paul is highly appreciative of its contributions toward economic and human growth; it "is a sign and contributes to authentic human development" (PP 25).[31] He also praises the entrepreneurial taste for research and discovery, the ability to take calculated risks, boldness in enterprise and generosity and responsibility for the fruits of the process that modern industrialism has often evidenced.[32] However, as shown above, he does not unequivocally endorse industrial capitalism. On the contrary, Paul condemns the profit system as the key motive for economic development, competition as the supreme law of economics, and private ownership of means of production as an absolute right that has no limits and carries no corresponding social obligation.[33] This latter element produces "an international imperialism of money." Instead, the economy should be at the service of humanity, "but because certain types of capitalism have been the source of excessive suffering, it would be wrong to attribute to industrialization itself evils that belong on the woeful system that accompanies it" (PP 26, paraphrasing QA 109). Therefore, there is a need for public bodies to stimulate forces engaged in common activity because individual initiative and "mere play of competition" left alone could "never assure successful development" (PP 33). In this social action, Paul VI encourages involvement with non-Christians (PP 82).

Octogesima Adveniens

Pope Paul VI's apostolic letter *Call to Action* (1971), promulgated on the eightieth anniversary of RN, represents a shift in Paul's social teaching from the *economics* of development to the *politics* of authentic human and economic development (OA 46). Urgent questions that he sought to respond to were increased urbanization and other rapid economic changes. Paul continues to question the Western model of development, consciously striving to bring Christians into the arena of political activity. Paul argues that social decisions are made in the political order. But, politics is not ultimate for Paul either: "[The] Christian who wishes to live his faith in a political activity which he thinks of as service cannot without contradicting himself adhere to ideological systems which radically or substantially go against his faith and his concept of man" (OA 26).

It is on this basis that Christians must discern among competing ideologies to guide their political activity. Neither Marxist nor liberal ideology are compatible with Paul VI's Christian understanding of the human person. To aid in this discernment, Paul offers his view of the essence of Christian political activity: "[it] should be the projection of a plan of society which is consistent in its concrete means and in its inspiration, and which spring from a complete conception of man's vocation and of its differing social expressions" (OA 25). Paul sees this as activity or praxis, not ideology, wishing to avoid the imposition by any party of an ideology which would lead to a dictatorship of minds. He also sought to warn Christians of the limitations of Marxist and liberal ideologies. The Christian "cannot adhere to the Marxist ideology, to its atheistic materialism, to its dialectic of violence and to the way it absorbs individual freedom in the collectivity, at the same time denying all transcendence to man and his personal and collective history." According to Paul, neither can a Christian "adhere to the liberal ideology which believes it exalts individual freedom by withdrawing it from every limitation, by stimulating it through exclusive seeking of interest and power, and by considering social solidarities as more or less automatic consequences of individual initiatives, not as an aim and a major criterion of the value of social organization" (OA 26).

While continuing John XIII's openness to Christians working with non-Christians, even Marxists, in pursuit of social and economic justice, Pius warns also of the attraction of socialism because it remains conditioned by the (false) ideologies from which they originated. Also, while differentiating more than any of his predecessors the different strains of

Marxism and the work of Marxist analysis, he stresses that this analysis, no matter how fruitful, cannot be finally severed from Marxist ideology which inevitably leads to a totalitarian and violent society. On the other hand, Christians who tend toward liberal ideology are also in danger of ideological overreach—philosophical liberalism's defense of individual freedom "against the overwhelming hold of organizations, and as a reaction against the totalitarian tendencies of political powers." While Paul wishes to uphold personal initiative, he saw the danger of idolizing "an erroneous affirmation of the autonomy of the individual" (OA 35).

There are two contemporary movements that Paul did appreciate, as long as they are approached from a Christian point-of-view. The first is the "rebirth of utopias." While an appeal to utopia can be negative if it encourages people to "escape from concrete tasks in order to take refuge in an imaginary world," their 'eschatological horizon' have an important role in criticizing modern concrete political systems. This role is to provoke the "forward-looking imagination both to perceive in the present the disregarded possibility hidden within and to direct itself toward a fresh future; it thus sustains social dynamism by the confidence that it gives to the inventive powers of the human mind and heart" (OA 37).

The second is the pursuit of the human sciences toward a truer picture of the human. Despite warranted suspicion of actual human sciences, the "Church has confidence in this research also and urges Christians to play an active part in it." If Christians are motivated by their faith and the desire to know humanity better in a scientific way within a particular scientific discipline, they will be able to grasp a true, if partial, understanding of the human person (OA 40).

The necessity for political action discloses for Paul VI "a radical limitation to economics." While economic activity is necessary and if at the service of humanity is a "source of brotherhood and sign of providence" (OA 86) it has many limitations. It is often a field of confrontation and domination, and it runs the risk of taking up too much strength and curtailing freedom. Here Paul changes the emphasis of social action from *Populorum Progressio* from economic activity to political activity. This is because, in the social and economic field, "the ultimate decision rests with political power" (OA 46), which for Paul is the arena for the achievement of the common good.

Laborem Exercens

John Paul II's *Laborem Exercens* reflects not so much new economic and social conditions in the world, as it does his attempt to place his stamp on Catholic social teaching. John Paul brings to this task an extensive philosophical background, including published works on Christian personalism in dialogue with Marxism, as well as his background as a bishop in the Polish collectivist state. Although his thought clearly arises from his personal experience of being priest and bishop in communist Poland, his view is both more philosophical and abstract than previous social encyclicals.

John Paul II's contention in LE is that the central conflict of our time, the major cause of oppression, alienation, wars and dehumanization, is the conflict between labor and capital. Nevertheless, this is not a necessary conflict. Rather, from the primary definition of the human person as laborer and the correct understanding of capital, it can be seen that capital and labor are not inherently opposed to each other and any social theory that attempts to postulate a fundamental antagonism between the two is wrong. The present conflict between capital and labor according to John Paul is a contingent one, arising primarily from human ignorance and sinfulness.

Refining CST's economic anthropology, John Paul II defines humans as laborers. Although he explicitly states that this definition is not the only one possible, he makes the strong claim that "human work is a key, probably the essential key, to the whole social question" (LE 11). Through labor, humans build society. Through our labor, we are transformed, "either suffering damage or becoming more authentically human."[34] The point of this present analysis of John Paul II is not necessarily his view of labor, but how this view provides a lens into socioeconomics as furthering human dignity. As John Paul II writes, "The only chance there seems to be for radically overcoming this error [the priority of capital or things over labor] is through adequate changes both in theory and in practice, changes in line with the definite conviction of the primacy of the person over things and of human labor over capital as a whole collection of means of production" (LE 62).

Central to this emphasis on labor as primary activity of humans and individuals as originators of themselves and society is John Paul's idea that work has both subjective and objective dimensions. Humanity, being made in the "image of God," acts intentionally on his or her environment, with a tendency to self- realization; "these actions must all serve to realize his humanity, to fulfill the calling to be a person that is his by reason of his very humanity" (LE 23). As Baum notes, work involves an essential subjective dimension because as "an essential form of self- expression, work actualizes and transforms human beings." The objective dimension is the product of labor, that is, capital. Therefore, capital is simply the accumulation of labor. Although this objective dimension is important, "what is more important is the personal engagement, personal transformation, and actualization of the working persons."[35] Thus labor is always to be given priority over capital and capital is meant always to serve labor (LE 65).

Because in our current socioeconomic conditions capital is given priority over labor, the conflicts, poverty and misery of the world have arisen. This has occurred not of necessity but because of historical actions by capitalists and laborers, especially since the beginning of the industrial revolution—actions legitimized later by liberal economists and the system of free-market capitalism. Capitalists violated the principle of the priority of labor over capital by exploiting workers mainly by seeking to minimize costs and maximize profits by paying workers as low a wage as possible. Laborers (whether willingly or out of necessity, John Paul is not clear) "cooperated" by offering their services at these low wages. Only later did economists justify this by establishing the principle that wages are best determined by the "laws" of supply and demand, where labor (as well as land) are to be seen as commodities on the level of material products. This materialism John Paul labels "economism" (LE 13). Even with modern ethically motivated modifications of the free-market system toward the welfare state, capital continues to dominate labor through the transnational corporations.

According to LE, this inversion of the priority of labor over capital is not restricted to Western capitalism. Soviet collectivism also gave priority to capital by giving power to state bureaucracies which deny proper subjectivity to the laborers. Thus it is interesting that the term capitalism is given an entirely pejorative redefinition in this encyclical by the Pope. *Any* system that inverts this priority, whether free-market or collectivist, is negatively termed "capitalism" by John Paul II (LE 30).

Although John Paul II claims that his analysis is derived from the Bible and not Marxism, Gregory Baum finds that John Paul "Follows the Marxist perspective in understanding society and history very largely in terms of human labor."[36] Also, when the pope says that capital is wholly the product of human labor, he uses almost the same terminology as Marx's doctrine of capital as "congealed labor." According to Baum, these commonalities can be attributed to the fact that both John Paul and Marx write from a humanist perspective in their reaction to industrial capitalism. However, there are important differences. First, the pope does not follow Marx's exclusion of both the poor and non-industrial workers from belonging to the category of labor. Instead the Pope includes all people as laborers. This disagreement is important in noting the differences between Marx's social ethics and the Christian social ethics proposed by John Paul II: "Marx himself had little sympathy for marginal people, the unemployable. . . He called them '*Lumpen*,' the German word for hoodlum." In contrast, "the call for solidarity of the poor and with the poor is a truly radical Christian principle."[37]

Instead the pope includes all people as laborers. This stems from the facts that a) the unemployed are potential workers and b) not only industrial laborers are created in God's image and thus called to be co-creators: all except the idle rich belong to "labor," including agricultural workers, managers, government administrators, lawyers, etc. Second, as discussed above, there is no necessary conflict between labor and capital, only a historical one based on sin and misunderstanding, thus no "class conflict" between laborers and capitalists. Third, John Paul finds that Marx followed the same errors of economism as liberal capitalism. That is, despite Marx's early humanism, Marxism follows capitalism in viewing humans as economic units who follow deterministic, "scientifically" grounded laws based on individual self-interest. Fourth, John Paul II's emphasis on the subjective dimension (according to Baum, Marx paid scarce attention to subjectivity) "allows the Pope to assign a dignity and importance to the human person that is not found in Marxism."[38]

John Paul II de-reifies "rigid" Marxism (as opposed to some forms of "revisionist Marxism") as well as "rigid" capitalism (LE 66). However, he integrates some key Marxist concepts such as class struggle and laws of history, while at the same time de-reifying them in light of Christian principles. Baum thus claims that John Paul "explodes Marxism, or better he transcends Marxism from within—but not in the direction of political theories popular in capitalist countries." In the struggle for justice, progress and change come not from class conflict between the proletariat and capitalists and the resulting abolition of private property, but from the solidarity of "people themselves, freely discovering who they are and what their oppression is, freely organizing in the name of justice. . . ."[39]

Instead of emphasizing who owns the means of production, John Paul locates the current priority of capital over labor as the source of oppression. Rather than class conflict, the goal of the struggle to end oppression is to make capital serve labor. In other words, *contra* Marxism, he sees the question of ownership as morally irrelevant: as long as capital serves labor. Although the best way to encourage this may be through worker ownership, there are at least two other means to achieve this goal 1) increasing greater workplace democracy where labor have more of a say in decisions (greater decentralization away from economic elites having control), and 2) greater national planning (this time greater centralization but again away from economic elites making key decisions). Both of these efforts are directed toward true participatory economic democracy. Although the priority of labor is primary, it is always of the highest concern that workers receive just remuneration, a family living wage, enough to support a family in a dignified way (LE 68).

Sollicitudo Rei Socialis

Concentrating as it does on the development dilemma (commemorating the 20th anniversary of Paul VI's *Populorum Progressio*), *Sollicitudo Rei Socialis* does not engage socioeconomic theory as extensively as LE. Rather it concentrates on the effect of the East-West struggle of capitalism vs. collectivism on third-world countries. However, in continuity with LE and Catholic social teaching, SRS continues criticisms of both liberal capitalism and Marxist collectivism. Again, John Paul II stresses that certain faults of Marxist theory are shared by the theory of liberal capitalism. Both theories rely exclusively on enlightened self-interest (personal and collectively). Both entertain an economistic view of human beings: that economic behavior follows certain laws and hence is determined (economics as exact science); and both reject entry of traditional values such as justice and solidarity into the economy. Both sides cling to their respective ideologies in an inflexible manner and by forcing third-world countries to accept their ideology as a grounds for receiving support, they tragically commit these countries to generating economic projects on a purely "scientific" basis, and disregard the cultural and religious values of third-world peoples. In his words, "the entire world civilization becomes one destined to lead us more quickly towards death" (SRS 24).

As in LE, the solution is for economic systems to be reformed in order that they be based on an appropriate understanding of human beings, including the cultural-spiritual dimension. Instead of being guided by a strict internal logic, these systems "should operate through concrete mechanisms and institutions that have been designed by individuals and that could be changed" (SRS 43). To accomplish this, what is first needed is a "new spirit," the virtue of solidarity. In this spirit of solidarity, both Western and Eastern systems could be made to serve the well-being of people through the establishment of some form of ethically steered, mixed economy, welfare capitalism that still respects the spirit of economic initiative that tends to be stifled by the bureaucratization accompanying Eastern state collectivism (SRS 14, 22). This system has been termed "capitalism with a human face."[40]

SRS' teaching on sinful social structures seeks to go beyond the idea that strictly personal conversion is the route to social justice. Structural sins, including colonialism, and imperialism, "create an unjust distribution of wealth, power, and recognition, and thus push a section of the population to the margin of society where their well being or even their life is in danger."[41] Although John Paul argues that these structural sins are rooted in personal sin, he demonstrates some sensitivity "to the unconscious, non-voluntary dimension of social sin—to the blindness produced in persons by the dominant culture, blindness that prevents them from recognizing the evil dimension of their social reality."[42] This is rooted in John Paul's recognition that ideology can blind people, preventing them from recognizing how economic and political institutions aren't working very well, even in their own country (SRS 37). SRS continues these criticisms of the positivistic, deterministic, economistic social theories of both capitalism and communism. These theories discount personal agency, and thus reform of the institutions of both East and West can and should come from greater participation in industrial production and social planning (SRS 44-46)

As mentioned above, the motivation for this struggle for a more just society comes from greater solidarity among nations and classes. However, Baum argues that in SRS John Paul backs away from the preferential solidarity with the labor movement and/or the poor that he expressed in LE—one that recognized the potential need for conflict.[43] In SRS, the emphasis seems to be on solidarity "among all members of society in the hope that then the powerful will take better care of the weak."[44] Although there is praise in SRS for solidarity among the poor, a solidarity which is furthered by "public demonstrations" against inefficiency and corruption by public authorities, Baum rightly concludes that what is being challenged however, "are simply abuses of the social order, not the structures themselves."[45]

Economic Justice for All

In 1986, the United States Catholic Bishops published a pastoral letter on the American economy entitled *Economic Justice for All.* Following the process that led up to their previous pastoral letter on nuclear war, *God's Promise of Peace: God's Challenge and Our Response* (1983), the bishops engaged in a long consultative research process and made preliminary drafts available for public analysis. In response to such critiques, more radical elements were excised from the final draft. As a compromise document it was criticized by both the left and right.[46]

The letter takes explicit aim at how the American economy distributes economic justice in comparison to the democratic vision of the Founding Fathers, calling for "a new experiment in democracy." Not assailing American capitalism per se, it does call for a more equitable distribution of wealth. Therefore, the document offers particular political solutions in mind, rather than an explicit critique of economic theory.

The bishops, in the heritage of Catholic social teaching, target human dignity and communitarian ideals as criteria for judging the ethics of the American economic system. As they state in their opening paragraph,

> Our faith calls us to measure this economy, not by what it produces but also by how it touches human life and whether it protects or undermines the dignity of the human person. Economic decisions have human consequences and moral content; they help or hurt people, strengthen or weaken family life, advance or diminish the quality of justice in our land (EJA 1).

The communitarian aspect of economic life is stressed just as strongly:

> In our teaching, the human person is not only sacred but social. How we organize our society in economics and politics, in law and policy—directly affects human dignity and the capacity of individuals to grow in community. The obligation to "love our neighbor" has an individual dimension, but it also requires a broader social commitment to the common good. The Christian vision of economic life looks beyond them all and asks, Does economic life enhance or threaten our life together as a community? (EJA 14). The bishops are careful in their examination of the American system not to claim technical expertise in economic matters, wanting neither to adopt any particular theory nor to "resolve disputes between different schools of economic thought" (EJA 17). Instead, relying on Scripture, Catholic social teaching and "traditional American

values" (EJA 7), they critique the American economy in light of basic moral principles derived from these sources.[47]

On the basis of human dignity and community, the bishops call into question discrepancies between economic realities, and biblical, theological and democratic values. Furthermore, they go beyond critique, advocating concrete political changes to the system in response to their ethical analysis, e.g., calling for full employment, eradication of poverty, more equitable foreign policy regarding developing countries, and reiterate church teaching on worker's rights, private property, subsidiarity and equal opportunity. It is these concrete proposals that so disquieted Catholic conservatives.[48]

In this effort, the bishops assume that the American "mixed economy" (a system incorporating not only economic freedom but also limitation of the market by fundamental human rights) has not only the resources but the moral and political will to accomplish these tasks (EJA 8).[49] However, the precarious economic situation in the late 70's in the time of stagflation (a term referring to the high inflation and high unemployment of the Nixon, Carter, Ford era and the subsequently induced recession by the Reagan administration in an attempt to cure it), "calls for examination of U.S. economic arrangements" (EJA 19).[50] In response to these conditions and the resources they find already present in the American economic system, the bishops "suggest that the time has come for a "New American Experiment"—to implement economic rights, to broaden the sharing of economic power, and to make economic decisions more accountable to the common good" (EJA 21).

The bishops concentrate on moral suasion and advocating concrete policies in order to meet this aim, calling Christians especially to "explicit reflection on the ethical content of economic choices and policies" (EJA 21). Not limiting their audience to Christians, the bishops seek a common moral vision in order that all people are served fairly in economic life, to make manifest the option for the poor in American society. If that option is not exercised morally and politically, the "whole community is wounded." For the common good then, the bishops seek to provide guidance in making serious moral economic decisions. They go on to provide moral counsel concerning rights and responsibilities in such areas as daily work, unions, corporations, families, private property, the welfare system, and foreign aid. This instruction is provided in the overall context of economic freedom, but limited by accountability to the common good and the preferential option for the poor.

Despite these strengths, the bishops depart from the route taken by the papal encyclicals, in not substantially applying moral principles to the economic theory behind the economic system they are examining, indicating a basic acceptance of American "democratic capitalism," while at the same time raising serious criticisms of it. As they themselves acknowledge, the bishops tend to leave social and economic scientific issues out of the discussion. Although they do not claim to support any economic system, they do end up upholding the American mixed economy, rejecting the ideological extremes of either an unfettered free-market system or a radical dismantling of the American capitalist framework. By refusing to apply their moral principles to the economic theory behind that system, I and others argue that the bishops also implicitly endorse the present political economic system, and all its attendant problems. As Norman Birnbaum comments, a key question a more serious social analysis could have addressed is whether the bishops' initiatives are indeed possible within existing institutional arrangements.[51] This type of analysis would serve the structural analysis Mary Hobgood rightly calls for in her critique of Catholic social teaching outlined in the next chapter.

In an similar way, Charles Curran also points out this limitation of the pastoral letter:

> Comparatively little is said about the day-to-day life of the people who are working in the various capacities in the economic institutions and structures, and little is said about the institutions themselves as the corporation or business . . . emphasis on this level shows the important role played by laity and all the people of God in the economic realm. The day-to-day life of people in the economic order does not receive enough attention as it should.[52]

In this view, the bishops discussion of the role of the state, justice, human rights, preferential option, and universal destiny of goods of creation are better addressed through a more "radical" approach, though not Marxist or socialist. Rather, I argue what is needed is an improved understanding of economic theory informed by ethical discussion on the level of the person, in terms of the economic anthropological issues I've been emphasizing. Such an analysis could have also helped the bishops head off arguments from their critics. For instance, one conservative critic, James Schall maintains that the bishops should have been guided by the principle that "economics is a moral discipline insofar as it is based on sound economic policy."[53] Such a criticism could have been met in advance had the bishops incorporated an argument about the soundness of economic policy based on whether economic science has an adequate concept of the human (as developed more fully in Chapter 3) been engaged in by the bishops. Economic anthropology is certainly within the purview of the bishops, given their section on the "The Responsibilities of Social Living" which includes biblical and natural law aspects of human dignity and living in community (63-78). But it was insufficiently engaged in EJA. Further, the extensive consultation process which did include examination of economic methodology did not make it out of the footnotes of the letter.

Centesimus Annus

John Paul II's *Centesimus Annus* marked not only the 100th anniversary of *Rerum Novarum* but also the political and economic shifts in Eastern Europe toward more democratic forms of governance and shifts toward market economies after the deconstruction of the Soviet bloc. In marking the anniversary of RN, he notes the prescience of Leo XIII's condemnation of socialism (or "true socialism" as John Paul II terms communism) even before it became a political entity.

In the line of the whole of Catholic social teaching, and especially his own two previous socioeconomic encyclicals, John Paul uses Christian anthropology (the dignity of the human person) to reflect morally and theologically upon the character of capitalism and (the now failed) socialism. The fundamental error of doctrinaire state socialism (as opposed to the "market socialism" of Great Britain, Germany, the Scandinavian countries, etc.) was that it reduced the person to being a "mere cog in the state machine"(CA 15), "completely subordinated to the functioning of the socioeconomic mechanism." This anthropological error of socialism "reduces people to a series of social relationships," eliminating the "subjectivity" of the individual and society and "hindering the progress towards the building up of an authentic human community" (CA 13).

This inadequate anthropology is rooted in atheism which, by depriving a person of their foundation, leads to a "social order without reference to the person's dignity and responsibility" (CA 14). This is also the root of socialism's class struggle, which often substitutes violent conflict for any concern for the moral order or rights of others.

The failure of "real socialism" lies in its violating the rights of workers ("those very persons it claimed to protect")[54] "to private initiative, ownership of property and to freedom in the economic sector" (CA 24). CA then moves on to an evaluation of capitalism, which John Paul varyingly terms "primitive capitalism," "new capitalism," "liberalism," the "business economy," the "market economy," and the "new economy" (CA 42). Echoing LE, he states that primitive capitalism fundamentally and erroneously reversed the priority of labor over capital, rendering the worker a mere commodity. This was supported by a liberalism that grounded an incomplete grasp of human freedom. Unbridled capitalism is unacceptable due to its denial of the universal destination of material goods, its laissez-faire attitude, and its failure to provide a just wage (CA 35). He also criticizes consumerist tendencies in modern capitalist societies as being the result of the result of an inadequate anthropology focused on "human-havings" instead of "human beings" (CA 36).

Differentiating the business economy from "unbridled" or "primitive capitalism" allows John Paul to elaborate the strengths of market arrangements, a move which contributes to the distinctive approach of CA vis-à-vis its predecessors. This business economy is grounded in freedom, and recognizes the right of persons to private ownership by encouraging them to utilize their resources in a way enabling them to foresee and efficiently satisfy the needs of others, thus increasing the wealth of society. Required are important virtues such as "diligence, industriousness, prudence in undertaking reasonable risks, reliability and fidelity in interpersonal relationships, as well as courage in carrying out decisions which are difficult and painful but necessary" (CA 32). Thus the free market seems to be the "most efficient instrument for utilizing resources and effectively responding to needs" (CA 34). However, this free market economy has to avoid the errors of unbridled or radical capitalism, which stemmed from the failure to recognize the limits of a market economy. The latter forms of capitalism lack the "wherewithal to notice attend to, or give priority to deeper human and moral values."[55] It is clear then, despite some claims, that CA is not a baptism of capitalism.

Nor is it the unveiling of a new "third way." John Paul II argues that it is not the role of the church to offer economic models. Instead the social doctrine of the church is offered "as an indispensable and ideal orientation" (CA 43), a critique grounded in an authentic Christian anthropology. Even after the failure of "real socialism," He continues Catholic social thought's critical conversation with capitalism, attending to both its strengths and its weakness while offering a "criteria and perspective challenging modern society to construct ever more just economic systems."[56]

It is thus a controversial question whether CA is a move toward the "right" in John Paul II's thought. Its praise of market mechanisms—"above all they give central place to the person's desires and preferences, which, in a contract, meet the desires and preferences of another person" (CA 40)—is unprecedented in papal social teaching. Its trenchant critique of Marxism clearly does not continue any "dialogue" with it. Finally there is little if any emphasis in CA on issues of economic democracy, other than to affirm that the church supports efforts by workers for greater participation. Although the pope reiterates the view of LE that there is a positive role for conflict, he immediately quotes from *Quadragesimo Anno* to the effect that if only we could get beyond class struggle, we can come to an "honest discussion of differences founded on a desire for justice'" (QA 113) and therefore only stresses that "conflicts of interest between different social groups inevitably arise" (CA 14), not the need for solidarity with the poor or oppressed.

On the other hand, David Hollenbach argues that CA is not a move toward a more conservative social theory. He notes the pope's statement that we need a capitalism circumscribed by a strong juridical framework. But this does not seem to endorse the liberal capitalism that John Paul criticized in CA for relying on personal virtues and the state for reform; rather Hollenbach says that this framework in the pope's view "must shape the market in a *systemic and structural way*."[57] This interpretation of CA stems from John Paul's reiteration of the traditional teaching going back to Aquinas that holds the non-capitalist view that the right to private property is not absolute. Against neoconservatives who have claimed CA for their own, Hollenbach concludes that "it would be a serious mistake to think that the Pope has blessed the form of capitalism existing in the United States today."[58]

Summary of Overview

In the post-World War II period up until John Paul II, moved increasingly away from somewhat abstract explicit Christian anthropological claims vis-à-vis liberal capitalism or socialism, and to more local, more uncertain, areas of analysis and activity. For example, *Mater et Magistra* recognized the importance of socialization; *Gaudium et Spes* stressed the historicity of human transcendence and dignity; *Populorum Progressio* favored of integral development in globalization; *Octogesima Adveniens* addressed these same problems in terms of local political activity; and *Economic Justice for All* highlighted political activity in light of American ideals. This movement away from prescribing particularly permanent Christian principles, "handed down from on high" as it were, in favor of supporting social ordering linked to overcoming oppressive local economic conditions underlies Marie-Dominique Chenu's claim that Catholic social doctrine ends after OA.[59] While these stresses of John XXIII, Vatican II, and especially the emphasis in OA and *Economic Justice for All* on finding local, less universal solutions have been essential, especially in moving church teaching away from hierarchical, deductivist modes of analysis to more existential, inductive ones, important resources have been developed since then which have contributed to the development of a Christian economic anthropology.[60] For example, the social encyclicals of Pope John Paul II have made an explicit return to the economic from the political by returning to emphasizing the social over the political in critiquing mainstream and socialist economic systems.

In *Laborem Exercens* we find an extensive working out of the implications of a Christian economic anthropology in the interest of critiquing unjust theories, ideologies and structures, and toward providing concrete structural remedies in line with this anthropology and resultant critiques. As previously discussed, John Paul II proposes a definition of the human as worker, a Christian economic anthropology that enables him to critique anthropological foundations of liberal capitalism and socialism—a criticism that strikes at the roots of false economic theory and praxis. In practice capitalism violates the priority of labor (the primacy of humans as subjects over subjects of their own labor, capital) by seeking to maximize profits by paying as low a wage as possible. This was justified by economists whose economistic doctrines (especially *homo economicus* as an abstraction of the whole person) commodified labor so that its price (wages) was determined by the laws of supply and demand. Despite its Marxist roots, this error was repeated in Soviet collectivism. Thus though John Paul II agrees with the early humanist Marx on alienation of labor, Marx's scientific socialism is just as economistic as capitalism in its view of humans as economic units who followed scientifically grounded laws, on the same deterministic basis as the self-interest principle ensconced in liberal capitalism.

SRS continues this criticism of liberal capitalism and Marxist collectivism, speaking now more specifically about how both rely exclusively on enlightened self-interest and an economistic view of human beings whose economic behavior is determined by supposedly scientific laws. The context of SRS is the divide between North and South, as first and second world countries export their ideologies to the third-world in exchange for financial and technological assistance. To overcome these problems, a new spirit of solidarity is called for that serves the well-being of all people toward constructing new concrete mechanisms and institutions, ones that still respect the spirit of economic initiative, yet are ethically steered. John Paul II's emphasis is on personal agency, especially in calling for greater participation in industrial production and social planning, thereby retrieving important elements of Marx's thought. While CA concentrates on just economic structures, placing more emphasis than ever on the value of the market and the defects of capitalism, its teaching is rooted in the personalistic, anti-economistic economic anthropology of LE and SRS.

Conclusion

One argument I am making is that a more extensive dialogue between Christian social ethics and alternative economic models to mainstream and Marxist ones, such as social economics, can be extremely valuable. To sum up the fruitful possibilities of this dialogue, it would be helpful to identify some linkages among alternative economic theories such as "social economics," Catholic social teaching, and the importance of an adequate economic anthropology, or put differently, the "metaphysics of the human being as worker and consumer."[61] In connection with the analysis discussed in the preceding section, David Hollenbach contends that "the mistake of both liberal-democratic and Marxist thought has been the identification of a limited domain of human existence with the radical foundation of human rights." Liberalism erroneously limits human nature to individual human freedom while Marxism's error has been its particular interpretation of class conflict and the means for achieving social change. Hollenbach rightly adds:

> The Roman Catholic tradition recognizes that a critique of these two limited definitions of human dignity is not enough. Unless the relations between the transcendental worth of the person and the particular material, interpersonal, social and political structures of human existence can be specified, human dignity will become an empty notion.[62]

Further, the Catholic tradition needs to further develop a critique of liberal and Marxist economic anthropologies and promote an alternative economic anthropology that can ground the possibility of a new economic paradigm. This is needed because a great number of the particular material, interpersonal, social and political structures of human existence adverted to by Hollenbach rest on either liberal and (at least until recent developments) collectivist economic paradigms, with their attendant problems. Thus not only is there a need for critique of interpersonal, social and political structures, *and* economic systems; there is also a need for a renewed underlying economic anthropology. This is because, as the social economist David George argues (while recognizing the "highly problematic" nature of the precise causal relationship between theory and practice), "the habit of social economists to critique simultaneously both economists and the economic system is largely explained by the belief that ideas matter and that the economic institutions actually observed are in large measure the result of economic visions that preceded them."[63] These economic visions are related by George to beliefs and behaviors of economic agents that mainstream economics tends to obscure with its preemptive assumption that agents are maximizers.

In contrast to self-maximization, whether it be of the liberal or Marxist variety, the Catholic social economist Edward J. O'Boyle proposes a personalism that recognizes the sociality of human nature and the role of beliefs and behaviors of economic agents. In Boyle's (and CST's) terms, this "*homo socio-economicus*" is both self- and other-regarding. S/he is a "want-satisfying and need-fulfilling, utility-maximizing and utility-sacrificing, privacy-protecting and company-seeking, commodity acquiring and gift-giving" being vs. the "half-person" of the self-interested individualistic "economic man" of mainstream economics which does not differentiate between wants and needs and who "rationally" approaches its work and consumption toward maximizing its "utility" gained therefrom.[64]

Demonstrating the practical implications of a more realistic view of human economic agency, O'Boyle cogently points out that there are at least three areas in which an alternative economic anthropology as proposed by CST can enlighten discussions of the concerns of economic ethics. These are unmet physical needs, and the two central roles of economic agents: consumption and work. Mainstream economics does not view unmet need as a criterion for gauging economic functioning or success in itself, while Christian economic anthropology, personalism and humanism do. As Leo XIII points out in *Rerum Novarum,* unmet physical need "attacks the foundations of human dignity," and must be addressed by non-market forces such as the state using the principle of subsidiarity as enunciated by Pius XI and later elaborated upon by John XXIII.

Also, because a person is both individual and social, the communitarian economic ethic of CST yields a view in which consumers look "outward at times to determine and serve his/her own self interest and at times to determine and meet the needs and satisfy the wants of others, especially family members, neighbors and peers."[65] This goes beyond the purely profit-seeking maximization theory criticized especially by Paul VI. Instead, as O'Boyle points out, work also satisfies two dimensions not accounted for in this framework: needs for self-expression and for belonging. This was strongly incorporated in John Paul II's stress on the subjective dimension of work in *Laborem Exercens*. A quote from O'Boyle concludes this chapter by pointing out the necessity for an alternative economic anthropology, and thus the contribution of Catholic social thought:

> It is neither hyperbole nor clever rhetoric to assert that an authentic and long-lasting social economics cannot be constructed on the shoulders of *homo economicus* because, metaphysically speaking, *homo economicus* is seriously flawed. Until a proper replacement is found, social economists will struggle to understand and explain how the social economy functions effectively and what to do when it does not.[66]

NOTES

1. These texts can be found in *Catholic Social Thought: The Documentary Heritage*, ed. David J. O'Brien and Thomas A. Shannon (Maryknoll, NY: Orbis Books, 1992). All numbers in parentheses refer to the article numbers in the texts.

2. Giuseppe Gaburro, "Christian Anthropology as a Foundation for a New Economics," in *On the Condition of Labor and the Social Question One Hundred Years Later: Commemorating the 100th Anniversary of Rerum Novarum and the Fiftieth Anniversary of the Association for Social Economics*, ed. Thomas O. Nitsch, et al. (Lewisport, NY: The Edwin Mellen Press, 1994), 46.

3. David Hollenbach, *Claims in Conflict: Retrieving and Renewing the Catholic Human Rights Tradition* (New York: Paulist Press, 1983).

4. Paul Misner, "The Predecessors of *Rerum Novarum* Within Catholicism," *Review of Social Economy* 49 (1991): 444-64.

5. Misner, *Social Catholicism in Europe*, 132-36. Misner notes how Harmel in his later years advocated a more active role by the working class in the political process (227-32).

6. RN itself inspired Heinrich Pesch (1854-1926) to take up economics and advocate the philosophy underlying the guild system in a system of economics he called corporatism. This idea was taken up by Pius XI in QA (co-written by Jesuit disciples of Pesch), which came as close as Catholic social teaching has done to

advocating a specific economic system. While more contemporary documents such as John XXIII's *Mater et Magistra* consistently downplay corporative systems as a "third way," this document still mentions workers associations that contain a hint of this approach. John's alternative method of realigning capitalism, that of worker ownership, participation and control of firms, is echoed in subsequent encyclicals, especially John Paul II's *Laborem Exercens*, and can be seen as a modern reworking of some of the principles behind corporatism, although removed from the medieval setting of the guild system and the parliamentary functions of classical corporatist theory. Corporatism has receded in Catholic social teachings as an alternative political-economic system; yet as a system motivated by spiritual and anthropological concerns and still influential as an alternative form of microeconomic organization (limited to within a firm, or between a network of firms such as producer cooperatives such as the Mondragon cooperative system in Spain), it still functions as a model of economic relationships for continuing development of alternatives to liberal capitalism and socialism.

7. Misner, "The Predecessors of *Rerum Novarum*," 447.

8. The question is, how to do this? Leo explores three options: through employer charity or paternalism; through state intervention in redistributive schemes such as the just wage, guaranteed income or other remedies to capitalist exploitation; or through some sort of community of goods arrangement administered by a collectivist state. A fourth option, corporatism, more of a philosophy than an economic theory, was recommended by Pius XI in QA. A fifth, that of some role for a moderate socialism including worker-controlled cooperatives entered into voluntarily without state coercion, is proposed by John XXIII, Paul VI, John Paul II, and modern Catholic social economists, among others. Lonergan's economic thought, discussed in Chapter Four, pursues an original sixth option: revising economic theory itself in light of the importance of how profits over above the normal profits needed for corporations to stay in business, which he calls the "social dividend," is circulated in the economy.

9. Mary Hobgood points out how the organic conception of society adopted by Leo XIII and present in some form throughout all subsequent social encyclicals undermines the popes' critiques of capitalism by stressing stability and support for the status quo (*Catholic Social Teaching and Economic Theory* [Philadelphia: Temple University Press, 1991], 98-104). Her illuminating examination of this element in Catholic social teaching, though flawed in my view by her reduction of economic theory to her orthodox, radical and organic types, will be discussed extensively in the next chapter.

10. Aquinas' views on private property are stated in *Summa Theologiae*, II Iiae, q. 66, aa. 1 and 2. Charles Curran argues that the American Catholic social ethicist John A. Ryan is more in line with Aquinas than Leo in this issue. Instead of viewing private property as a divinely inspired right, Ryan relegated private

property to a third class of rights guaranteed by natural law, behind that of human dignity and rights such as right to marry. So, Ryan argued that if socialism better benefited the common good, it could take the place of private property ("The Changing Anthropological Bases of Christian Social Ethics," in *Readings in Moral Theology No. 5: Official Catholic Social Teaching*, ed. Charles E Curran and Richard A. McCormick [New York: Paulist Press, 1986], 207-8; John A. Ryan, *Distributive Justice: The Right and Wrong of Our Present Distribution of Wealth* [New York: MacMillan, 1916], 56-60). Leo's misinterpretation of Aquinas is ironic in view of Leo XIII's proposal in *Aeterni Patris* (1879) that retrieval of authentic interpretations of Aquinas be a source of the Catholic church's philosophical stance toward the modern world. Gerald McCool terms *Aeterni Patris* (1879) the "Magna Charta" of the 20th century neo-Thomistic retrieval of scholastic and Thomistic thought (Gerald A. McCool, S.J., "The Tradition of Saint Thomas in North America: At 50 Years," *The Modern Schoolman* 65 [March 1988]: 186).

11. Donal Dorr, *Option for the Poor: A Hundred Years of Catholic Social Teaching*. Rev. ed. (Maryknoll, NY: Orbis Books, 1992), 33.

12. Dorr, *Option for the Poor*, 33.

13. Dorr, *Option for the Poor*, 77.

14. Connected to the different emphasis in economic anthropology in QA is what Dorr describes as a different spirituality in QA than Leo's "spirituality of stability"(*Option for the Poor*, 77).

15. Hollenbach, *Claims in Conflict*, 54.

16. Rather, Pius XI agrees with Leo that "the division of goods which is effected by private ownership is ordained by nature itself" (QA 56).

17. Hollenbach, *Claims in Conflict*, 54.

18. "The sordid love of wealth, which is the shame and great sin of our age, will be opposed in actual fact by the gentle yet effective law of Christian moderation which commands man to seek first the Kingdom of God and His justice, with the assurance that, by virtue of God's kindness and unfailing promise, temporal goods also, in so far as he has need of them, shall be given him besides" (QA 136).

19. Dorr is correct in maintaining that while John did bring the Catholic Church into a more open relationship with modern society, it came at the cost of an acceptance of the Western status quo (*Option for the Poor*, 129). John stopped short of viewing capitalism as a positive good, but MM did serve to "baptize" Western welfare capitalism to a great extent, including its export to other countries.

20. On the other hand, John's emphasis on "socialization" led some conservatives to identify this increased socialization with capitalism, causing William F. Buckley to exclaim, "*Mater si, Magistra non*!" (cited in Dorr, *Option*

for the Poor, 132).

21. However, Dorr points out that John warned against Church's traditional defense of private initiative and private property was being used in ideological way and that this warning went against the "determined resistance of senior Churchmen within the Vatican itself" (Dorr, *Option for the Poor*, 138).

22. In another slant on providing a "third way" between capitalism and liberalism, John XIII, while endorsing many of the benefits of post-World War II welfare capitalism, advocated many programs of what can be called moderate socialism (Dorr, 138), including cooperative ownership and management, collectivization, and increased role for state intervention in such areas as agriculture, social security, price regulation and support (MM 123-146). Thus Hollenbach contends that the foundational norm of human dignity led John "to understand social-economic rights within a single integrated theoretical framework" emphasizing that "the protection and coordination of human rights are increasingly a task that calls for coordination within society as a whole." This warrants increased state involvement, although the state cannot be the sole guarantor of human rights (*Claims in Conflict*, 68).

23. Subsidiarity can be defined as the notion that individual or corporate action should be undertaken at the appropriate level of organization. For example, if a union is able to negotiate fair wages, the state should not overstep its boundaries and take away the union's role. As Pope Pius XI writes, according to the principle of subsidiarity "it is an injustice . . . to transfer to the larger and higher collectivity functions which can be performed and provided for by lesser and more subordinate bodies." Conversely, if "lower" collective bodies are unable to accomplish socially just policies on their own, it would be incumbent upon "higher" collective bodies such as the state to intervene (QA 79).

24. This opening to authentic human development in the name of humanism is echoed in Jacques Maritain, *Integral Humanism* (New York: Charles Scribner's Sons, 1938), who is cited by Paul VI in PP 42.

25. O'Brien and Thomas Shannon, *Catholic Social Thought*, 164.

26. Hollenbach analyzes GS from the vantage point of its acknowledgment of the historically conditioned nature of the demands of human dignity—"that the full implications of the dignity of the person cannot be known or affirmed apart from the concrete conditions of an historical epoch" (Hollenbach, 70). The precise form in which the rights belonging to this personal integrity actually take in the concrete can only be determined "in the context of an historical analysis of the patterns and institutions of social life" (*Claims in Conflict*, 73).

27. For example, the acknowledgment of human finitude in GS can also be examined as the move in official Catholic social teaching from H. Richard Niebuhr's "Christ Above Culture" stance toward church involvement in society toward a "Christ the Transformer of Culture" position, in that it recognized the

reality of sin, or the historic conditioned nature of the prospect of achieving justice. Cf. H.R. Niebuhr, *Christ and Culture* (New York: Harper & Row, 1951). An illustration of this is the contrast between GS' statement that "Man exalts himself as the absolute measure of all things or debases himself to point of despair" (79) and John's overly optimistic view of the possibility of humans' dispassionate use of reason. However, Hollenbach's emphasis on praxis within the limited conditions of human transcendence (vs. the overemphasis on human reason in "The Christ Above Culture" model), runs the risk of ignoring the role that critical economic theory can play in changing or viewing differently the concrete conditions of an epoch. For another typological analysis of this issue, cf. "The Relationship Between Theory and Praxis in Contemporary Christian Theologies," in Matthew L. Lamb, *Solidarity With Victims: Toward a Theology of Social Transformation* (New York: Crossroad, 1982), Chapter 3. Lamb describes a "critical praxis" in which "self-transformative and self-disclosive structures of freedom" described by Hollenbach and *Gaudium et Spes*, are related to the "noetic praxis of natural and human sciences...." (Lamb, *Solidarity With Victims*, 85).

28. According to Dorr, Paul took the notion of authentic or integral development from the Dominican scholar and activist Père Lebret who died before the encyclical appeared (Dorr, *Option for the Poor*, 180).

29. Dorr, *Option for the Poor*, 198-99.

30. Dorr, *Option for the Poor*, 182-83; PP 47.

31. However, as pointed out by Dorr, Paul did not appreciate the havoc colonial powers wreak not only on "the political and economic structures of colonized peoples but also on social, cultural and religious frameworks which gave order and meaning to their lives," while over-estimating the "extent to which Western science, technology, and culture have been of lasting benefit to most of the south," (Dorr, *Option for the Poor*, 186).

32. In contrast to what some advocates of democratic capitalism seem to imply, Paul clearly does not assume that poverty and underdevelopment arise from purely natural causes, or from the laziness of people living in poorer parts of the world (PP 57-60).

33. Paul VI reiterates the papal doctrine regarding private property, but stresses that it is not an absolute and unconditioned right. For example, he argues the landed estates (*latifundia*) shouldn't transfer wealth abroad, if it is gotten from resources and activity of their country (MM 24).

34. Gregory Baum, "John Paul's Encyclical on Labor," *Readings in Moral Theology No. 5: Official Catholic Social Teaching*, ed. Charles E Curran and Richard A. McCormick (New York: Paulist Press, 1986), 233.

35. Baum, "John Paul's Encyclical on Labor," 133.

36. Gregory Baum, *The Priority of Labor: A Commentary on "Laborem*

Exercens," Encyclical Letter of Pope John Paul II (New York: Paulist Press, 1982), 8.

37. Baum, *Priority of Labor*, 38-9.

38. Baum, *Priority of Labor*, 4.

39. Baum, "John Paul's Encyclical on Labor," 235. Dorr points out that "solidarity" seems to play a role for John Paul II analogous to that of class struggle in Marxist writings (*Option for the Poor*, 331). The concept of solidarity as including a strong role for opposition (as in Poland) is developed in John Paul II's earlier writings. Baum argues that on the other hand, John Paul does not move far enough toward the conflictual model as Dorr claims. Hollenbach agrees with Baum, arguing that in the pope's exegesis of the creation account from which he partly derives his model of human as worker, he does not pay enough attention to the contingencies resulting from the Genesis depiction of the Fall. See David Hollenbach, S.J., "Human Work and the Story of Creation: Theology and Ethics in Laborem Exercens," in *Co-Creation and Capitalism: John Paul II's "Laborem Exercens"*, ed. John Houck and Oliver Williams (Washington, D.C.: University Press of America, 1983), 59-77

40. Gregory Baum, "Liberal Capitalism," in *The Logic of Solidarity: Commentaries on Pope John Paul II's Encyclical "On Social Concern,"* ed. Gregory Baum and Robert Ellsberg (Maryknoll, NY: Orbis Books, 1989), 87-8.

41. Gregory Baum, "Structures of Sin," in *The Logic of Solidarity: Commentaries on Pope John Paul II's Encyclical "On Social Concern,"* ed. Gregory Baum and Robert Ellsberg (Maryknoll, NY: Orbis Books, 1989), 112.

42. Baum, "Structures of Sin," 113.

43. See also Dorr, *Option for the Poor*, 331.

44. Baum, "Structures of Sin," 121. Dorr finds a certain "blandness" and unreality in this approach, arguing that what is needed is a "social analysis which would take more seriously the causes of the class structure in society and which could then go on to examine ways in which tensions between the different classes can be overcome or lessened" (Dorr, *Option for the Poor*, 332).

45. Dorr, *Option for the Poor*, 122.

46. As Royal W. Rhodes and George E. McCarthy summarize in *Eclipse of Justice: Ethics and Economics and the Lost Traditions of American Catholicism* (Maryknoll NY: Orbis Books, 1992), 42-71 and 105-11, the letter was criticized by both conservatives and progressives, by conservatives for the bishops' endorsement of a more expansive role for government than they liked, and progressives for their endorsing liberal values within the American economy and for not incorporating a structural critique of that economy. The bishops' reliance on moral principles, both communitarian and liberal, led them to advocate greater cooperation and social equity requiring government involvement if necessary, but also away from a radical critique of the American economy.

47. Curran analyzes how EJA relates moral reflection to the state of the American economy in terms of James Gustafson's schema of four levels or stages of moral deliberation (fundamental or basic perspective, person as subject and agent, principles and norms governing human existence, and concrete judgments) as developed in Gustafson's *Christ and the Moral* Life. The value of this analysis is that it shows that how it is at the level of person as subject and agent in which the bishops fall short in their economic analysis, a position which Norman Birnbaum takes also, as discussed below. Cf. Charles Curran, "Relating Religious-Ethical Inquiry to Economic Inquiry," in *The Catholic Challenge to the American Economy: Reflections on the U.S. Bishops' Pastoral Letter on Catholic Social Thinking and the U.S. Economy*, ed. Thomas M. Gannon, S.J., with the final text of the pastoral letter. (NY: MacMillan Publishing Company, 1987), 42-54.

48. A conspicuous example of criticism from Catholic economic conservatives is by a group calling themselves The Lay Commission on Catholic Social Teaching and the U.S. Economy, *Toward the Future: Catholic Social Thought and the U.S. Economy: A Lay Letter* (Notre Dame, IN: Quodlibetal Publications, 1984), which preempted publication of *Economic Justice for All* with an alternative "pastoral letter" more conducive to American liberal capitalism than the American bishops' letter ended up being.

49. Norman Birnbaum argues that the bishops, although writing in an era of slow growth, of reduced confidence in government, and of foreign imbalances in trade, etc., take the robust economic health of the 1950's as their model, and as a result, "tend to think in terms that were appropriate three decades ago when a social contract was possible (since a higher proportion of workers were in unionized industry), when our domination of world market was evident, and when full employment and rising standard of living rendered problem of poverty apparently soluble with existing social technology ("The Bishops in the Iron Cage: The Dilemmas of Advanced Society," in *The Catholic Challenge to the American Economy: Reflections on the U.S. Bishops' Pastoral Letter on Catholic Social Thinking and the U.S. Economy*, ed. Thomas M. Gannon, S.J., with the final text of the pastoral letter. [NY: MacMillan Publishing Company, 1987], 55).

50. One statistic they quote points to the accumulation of wealth in American society. According to 1983 Federal Reserve Board, 28 percent of the total net wealth was held by the richest 2 percent of the population, with the top 10 percent holding 57 percent of the net wealth. The top 2 percent of families owned 54 percent of total net financial assets, with the top ten percent holding 86 percent of these assets. Despite the 1990's economic "boom," more recent figures indicate that this gap has gotten worse: the top 1% of Americans own as much wealth as the bottom 95% percent and the total wealth of the top 60% of Americans is 500 times the total wealth of the bottom 40% while the bottom 40% of households own one-fifth of 1% (or 0.2%) of the nation's wealth (Edward N. Wolff, "Recent

Trends in Wealth Ownership, 1983-1998," April 2000, Table 2, Jerome Levy Economics Institute, <http://www.levy.org/docs/wrkpap/papers/300.html> (22 April 2005).

51. Birnbaum, "The Bishops in the Iron Cage." This is put in a different way by Larry Rasmussen, who claims, "the bishops' account does not include a presentation of the institutional dynamics that generate the very results they lament" (Larry Rasmussen, "The Morality of Power and the Power of Morality," in *Prophetic Visions and Economic Realities: Protestants, Jews, and Catholics Confront the Bishops' Letter on the Economy,* ed. Charles Strain [Grand Rapids, MI: W.B. Eerdmans, 1989], 136); quoted in McCarthy and Rhodes, *Eclipse of Justice*, 105. According to Rasmussen and other critics from the left, such as Royal/McCarthy and Hobgood, what is needed is a structural (radical) critique of the American economy.

52. Curran, "Relating Religious-Ethical Inquiry to Economic Inquiry," 63-66.

53. Quoted in McCarthy and Rhodes, *Eclipse of Justice*, 15.

54. Patrick McCormick, "Centesimus Annus," in *The New Dictionary of Catholic Social Thought*, ed. Judith Dwyer (Collegeville, MN: The Liturgical Press, 1994), 136.

55. McCormick, "Centesimus Annus," 138.

56. McCormick, "Centesimus Annus," 139.

57. David Hollenbach, "The Pope and Capitalism," *America* 164 (June 1, 1991): 591. Emphasis added.

58. Hollenbach, "The Pope and Capitalism," 591.

59. See Marie-Dominique Chenu, *La 'doctrine sociale' de l'Église comme idéologie*, Paris: Cerfm, 1979), cited in Dorr, *Option for the Poor,* 88-9.

60. Cf. Charles Curran, "The Changing Anthropological Bases of Christian Social Ethics," 202-3.

61. Edward O'Boyle, "*Homo Socio-economicus*: Foundational to Social Economics and the Social Economy," *Review of Social Economy* 52 (1994): 287.

62. Hollenbach, *Claims in Conflict*, 91.

63. David George, "Social Economics in the Years Ahead: An Economist's Perspective," *Review of Social Economy* 51 (1993): 478.

64. Edward O'Boyle, "Challenges Facing Social Economists in the Twenty-first Century: A Catholic's Perspective," *Review of Social Economy* 51 (1993): 429.

65. Edward J. O'Boyle, "*Homo Socio-Economicus,* 292.

66. O'Boyle, *Homo Socio-Economicus*, 288.

CHAPTER 2

CREATIVITY IN CHRISTIAN ECONOMIC ETHICS: (MIS)APPLYING LIBERAL AND LIBERATIONIST ECONOMIC THEORY

As seen in the previous chapter, Catholic Social Teaching (CST) has been critiqued and criticized from the right to the left ends of the ideological continuum. Part of every reviewer's project has necessarily been one of interpretation, especially if one is trying to locate a particular encyclical, pope, or trend in terms of one's own preferred hermeneutical lens, in this case one's favored economic theory. And if one is doing anything more than mere commentary (i.e., beyond interpreting), one is invariably pointing out how CST has gone right or gone wrong, how missteps might have occurred and how one would recommend CST to proceed in the future. Due to the nature of CST as providing a type of socioeconomic theory, the critiques will often be in light of a different socioeconomic theoretical approach that will at the same time highlight what one considers CST's contributions to be and points out deficiencies of its approach.

In *Method and Theology*, Bernard Lonergan analyzes these steps in terms of what he calls functional specialization where analysis from "below up" (not proceeding explicitly from a foundational viewpoint) attempts to 1) gather the data (in this case what have the popes said); 2) interpret it (what do they mean); 3) note what was going forward (how have individual encyclicals and popes and CST as a whole developed) and 4) develop some framework to analyze whether what has developed is truly authentic development. Lonergan labels these four steps research, interpretation, history and dialectic. In the case of CST then, dialectic thus serves the function of pointing out possible biases in CST's and its interpreters' approaches; wrongheaded conclusions; faulty historical, anthropological, philosophical, economic analysis, etc. As Lonergan writes in *Method in Theology*,

> Dialectic . . . deals with conflicts. The conflicts may be overt or latent. They may lie in religious sources, in the religious tradition, in the pronouncements of authorities, or in the writings of theologians. They may regard contrary orientations of research, contrary interpretations,

> contrary histories, contrary styles of evaluation, contrary horizons, contrary doctrines, contrary systems, contrary policy.[1]

While he does note that differences in outlooks can also be the result of insufficient data and from viewing material and movements from merely different perspectives (for example the impact of CST on Latin America vs. Europe), beyond these are fundamental conflicts stemming from an explicit or implicit cognitional theory, an ethical stance, a religious outlook. A prime and very educational example of this is the conflict of interpretation between two representative commentators on CST who differ from each other on these more fundamental aspects, in this case those deriving from their respective economic theoretical interpretive frameworks.

Now that we have to a great extent done some research into, interpreted ecclesial statements, and examined some history of CST, the next step is to engage in dialectical analysis of CST's positions from representatives from the right and left and in the process argue that CST itself offers its own dialectical critique of their positions. To do this I have chosen to review interpretations and critiques of CST from two theologians: a neoconservative, Michael Novak; and a liberationist, Mary Hobgood. Both analyze CST from a perspective arising out of a particular political-economic paradigm, neo-classical and neo-Marxian respectively, and call for CST to align itself more explicitly with their preferred paradigm. My point though is not to provide just a set of critiques however enlightening to the task of dialectics that may be.

Since we have already seen how CST itself is a dialectical critique of capitalism and socialism, I end up arguing that no matter how useful Novak's and Hobgood's critiques are, they in turn need to be put in dialogue with CST's critiques of the source of their positions. So a main goal is to also "critique the critiques" in light of what I view to be important contributions CST makes to the dialogue between ethics and economics, while recognizing in turn the value of their critiques of CST. While both Novak and Hobgood claim to be within the horizons of CST, I argue that on important, fundamental points, they are not. I will extend this in the concluding chapters where I bring Lonergan's economic thought, which I believe to both be within CST's fundamental horizons and to extend them, to bear on the strengths and weaknesses of CST, mainstream liberal economics and neo-Marxist liberationist thought.

From the perspective of their respective paradigms, both Novak and Hobgood argue in some sense that in its nostalgia for pre-modern economic arrangements, CST fails to address particular economic realities and correspondingly both call in almost diametrically opposed ways for a more enlightened and liberating attitude of CST toward the modern economic realm. In the name of "productive justice" Novak urges liberating corporations and individuals so that they can more efficiently provide the goods to raise the standard of living of all, including the poor. On the other hand, Hobgood argues that while CST includes liberationist critiques of economic society that exhibit a strong fundamental option for the poor and oppressed, it also incorporates organic, hierarchical elements that align with capitalism's denying proper participation in the economic realm to some, especially the poor.

This chapter presents Novak's and Hobgood's views, to identify more clearly elements of political economics present in the social encyclicals to the end of providing legitimate critiques of CST's interpretation and integration of elements neoclassical and Marxian economics. Flaws in Novak's and Hobgood's approaches will also be addressed. The conclusion of this chapter argues that while these two perspectives contribute to an enhanced understanding of Christian use of economic theory, the nature of the flaws in Novak's and Hobgood's positions underscore my arguments that CST should either develop or incorporate an alternative economic paradigm and economic theory more complementary to its moral and anthropologically claims, as I argue Lonergan's does.

Michael Novak: To Be Liberal and Catholic

In the late 1970's Michael Novak renounced his previous democratic-socialist views to undertake an extended defense of democratic capitalism, and has since emerged as one of the most prominent U.S. Catholic neoconservatives. His overall thesis has been that Christian social ethics has erred in its bias against capitalism in favor of a socialism that only seems more consonant with gospel values. He grounds his defense of democratic capitalism in the historical developments of the last two centuries; neo-classical economic theory; theories of Anglo-American political liberalism; and, on religious grounds, a Reinhold Niebuhrian Christian realism. His exegesis of Catholic social teaching seeks to claim official support for his theories of the importance of individualistic (vs. collectivist) creativity, enterprise, initiative, responsibility and justice, and to correct what he views as anti-capitalism misinterpretation of CST. In the end, he says he is not claiming that CST should is at the service of liberal society, but it is "liberal society that best serves Catholic social thought" in that it "best uplifts the poor, institutionalizes dignity of the human person, makes possible growth and manifold activities of human associations of every sort, conspires to establish a more voluntary and open and communitarian form of life than any society of past, present or foreseeable future" (38).

The Theory of Democratic Capitalism

Novak defines democratic capitalism as a "tripartite" political-economic-cultural order of checks and balances among three otherwise autonomous realms: the economic, the political and the moral-cultural. Democratic capitalism, like the Christian Trinity, is "three entities" in one, or:

> three systems in one: a predominantly market economy; a polity respectful of the rights of the individual to life, liberty, and the pursuit of happiness; and a system of cultural institutions moved by ideals of liberty and justice for all. In short, three dynamic and converging systems functioning as one: a democratic polity, an economy based on markets and incentives, and a moral-cultural system which is pluralistic and, in the largest sense, liberal.[2]

Against the conventional view that "the link between a democratic political system and a market system is merely an accident of history," Novak asserts a much stronger connection, arguing that "political democracy is compatible in practice only with a market system. In turn, both systems nourish and are best nourished by a pluralistic liberal culture."[3] Novak argues that this is borne out historically. Not only did modern democracy and the market economy appear on the scene approximately at the same time (1776 saw both the American *Declaration of Independence* and the publication of Adam Smith's Wealth of Nations), but also there has continued a strong link between democracy and capitalism both in theory and practice:

> While bastard forms of capitalism do seem able to endure without democracy, the natural logic of capitalism leads to democracy. For economic liberties without political liberties are inherently unstable. Citizens economically free soon demand political freedoms. Thus dictatorships or monarchies which permit some freedoms to the market have a tendency to evolve into political democracies, as has happened in recent years in Greece, Portugal, Spain, and other nations. On the other

side, the state which does not recognize limits to its power in the economic sphere inevitably destroys liberties in the political sphere.[4]

Novak states further that economic growth is needed for the sustenance of democratic polity. Although no "free and fair" system guarantees "equal outcomes," the legitimacy of democracies relies on "the belief of all individuals that they can better their condition."

Along with the interdependence of the logics of democracy and the market economy, special moral-cultural presuppositions are needed:

> Without certain moral and cultural presuppositions about the nature of individuals and their communities, about liberty and sin, about the changeability of history, about work and savings, about self-restraint and mutual cooperation, neither democracy nor capitalism can be made to work. Under some moral-cultural conditions, they are simply unachievable.[5]

In this tri-partite scheme each realm pursues its own ends while serving to check excesses of the others.[6] For example, while the economic order is based upon a free-market system, excesses such as concentrations of economic power evidenced in harmful monopolies are checked by antitrust legislation of the state. The system of free initiative of economic agents embodied in the market checks governmental encroachment in the economy. Finally, moral-cultural influences constrain harmful actions by free economic agents or by the state and, on the other hand, help to provide the cultural economic ethic of responsibility needed to invigorate and maintain the democratic capitalist system.

Defending Economic Liberalism

Since at least the French Revolution, there has been an anti-liberal tradition in the churches and, particularly in the 19th century, a "virtually unanimous disapprobation of capitalist economics" (12). However, Novak maintains this newly emerging social system of political economy embodied elements both congenial to and feared by Catholic social thinkers of the 19th century. Therefore, it was not easy for them to detach what they may have agreed with (such as private property and free markets) from what they disagreed with (liberal philosophy). Thus they ended up attacking capitalism and bourgeois liberalism *en bloc* rather than by making necessary distinctions.

A primary objective then of CST has been to offer an alternative ideal of social justice.[7] However, for Novak it is again liberalism, this time in its stress on fallible human institutions vs. utopian ideals, which he says also offers a complementary ideal of workable social justice, though I would say competing in some major ways. In both CST and Niebuhrian Christian realism, society's inability to approach the ideal of social justice is due to limitations of human intellect and even more so to our sinfulness. To remedy this, Novak argues that we need a theory of how fallible institutions can nevertheless work for the attainment of social justice. Novak's interpretation of socialism as denoting the possibility of "perfect" institutions pushes him to maintain that since "the perfect is the enemy of the good," socialism and liberation theology don't and indeed can't offer viable models of social justice. Liberalism, on the other hand, with its more "realistic" view of the impossibility of infallible laws and institutions in the presence of fallible humans offers, in its "practical wisdom," a vision of the "imperfect best."[8]

In our present situation, Novak claims it is much easier to "calmly assess" what the real achievements of the liberal era have been such as the capitalist economy and the democratic polity, while distancing these practical achievements from questionable bits of analysis, theory and philosophy set forth by the 19th century political economists who helped bring the present form of democratic capitalism into existence.[9] This is necessary because "activists are not always the best expositors of realities they helped bring into being" (13). This criticism of the admittedly inadequate aspects of capitalist theories along with the presence of certain unfortunate results that capitalism "brought in its train," has served to obscure the good that this economic system did or might yet still do.

Instead of recognizing the merits of both political and economic liberalism, Catholic social teaching in the 19th century and to some extent even now shows a "serious temptation for a kind of nostalgia for the simpler, more agrarian world,"—the organic community found in pre-industrial rural village life (24).[10] In contrast to economic liberalism which centers on individual aggrandizement to achieve the common good, this view looks to communal efforts.[11] This communal approach is exhibited in CST's fondness for rural cooperatives, credit unions and corporatist economic arrangements. However, Novak asserts a critical link between democratic capitalism (a mixture of political and economic liberalism) and the communitarian ideal of CST.

Novak acknowledges that the Catholic sense of organic community seems to have more in common with socialism than with liberalism. While

CST has been a defender of a limited concept of private property, it still has largely opposed the main tenets of liberal thought: its individualism, its philosophical laissez-faire economics, and its value-free economics. However, in light of his analysis of the major social encyclicals, Novak wishes to argue that CST "has slowly but steadily come to embrace the basic institutions of liberal society in economic, political, moral-cultural systems."[12] It is on this understanding of democratic capitalism that Novak bases his critique of official Catholic social teaching.[13] He does this through a passionate reinterpretation of the very liberalism that 18th century Catholicism inveighed against in its opposition to political and economic liberalism.[14] However, Novak claims to discern a steady papal reevaluation and integration of the tenets of liberalism in the 100-year history of the social encyclical tradition, with CST and liberal institutions being "drawn toward a 'marriage made in heaven'" (xxiv). It will be my contention though that Novak reduces CST to liberal economic theory, castrating it of its consistent criticism of that theory and its destructive praxis, a facet that Mary Hobgood on the other hand highlights in her just as systematic critique of CST.

Mary Hobgood: Catholic and To Liberate

Mary Hobgood takes a more methodological approach than Novak does in her treatment of the role of economic theory. Her more analytical, typological approach eventually leads as does Novak to a dialectical, normative evaluation of CST in light of a preferred economic paradigm. Nevertheless, as enlightening as it is, I will show it is her typological categorization scheme which leads her for different reasons to some of the same pitfalls as Novak—finding a "canon within a canon"[15] within CST that ends up missing and even eliminating much of the constructive approach CST has to offer in healing economic society, the important points of which I outlined in the previous chapter.

The lynchpin of Hobgood's critique of the social encyclical tradition is her view that authentic social analysis requires persons and groups to commit themselves to a particular social theory in order to interpret economic relations in a society. This is because overarching "competing" social theories are essentially incompatible, although they may have some features in common. Hobgood locates three such competing overarching social theories or economic paradigms in Catholic social teaching - the organic, orthodox and liberationist models. Her delineation of what each paradigm is and how each is at work in the writings of the popes greatly illuminates the approach the encyclicals take to economic reality. In the process, she shows how reliance on competing economic paradigms results in inconsistencies in each of the pope's analysis.

For instance, where Novak celebrates the inroads of economic liberalism into CST, Hobgood finds these inconsistent with CST's critique of capitalism from its organic and liberationist perspectives. Her aim is to promote a better coordination of critique and praxis in Catholic social ethics. Instead of glossing over such inconsistencies, as Novak does to a great extent, Hobgood argues that for CST to be effective, it needs to adopt explicitly the liberationist model to promote church reflection and action in favor of social and economic justice.

The Organic Model

Along with Scripture and natural law, Catholic social teaching has used organic social theory. This body of theory, inherited from feudal society, lent itself especially to early critiques of capitalism. Organic social theory sees society as continuous with nature (thus the name organic) and values a hierarchically organized society undergirded "with paternal benevolence, social cooperation and commitment to the common good."[16] This stress on social relationships as "restricted by the requirements of organic harmony" conflicts with the ideology of liberal capitalism that stresses self-interest and the self-regulated market, and results in the unjust social realities of industrial capitalism.

Interestingly, however, Hobgood maintains that while the organic model in its critique of economic liberalism (along with the church's tradition of local grass-roots organizing for the poor) contains elements that can be aligned with the liberationist model, she also argues that the organic model has made more morally acceptable capitalism's generation of socioeconomic hierarchies in both the economy and the family (6).

While the organic model was more prominent in earlier Catholic social teaching of Popes Leo XIII and Pius XI, more recent encyclicals reflect mainly the orthodox and liberationist models, except for the reemergence of "traditionalism" with John Paul II, especially in *Sollicitudo Rei Socialis*. According to Hobgood, the concurrent use of the orthodox and liberationist models in the more recent social encyclicals reflects a debate in the wider field of religious social ethics and economic theory between two primary explanations of socioeconomic reality: the neoclassical (her "orthodox") and neo-Marxian (her "liberationist").

The Orthodox Model

Hobgood argues that in the "orthodox" or capitalist model (initiated by Adam Smith, continued in neoclassical economics, and assimilated unconsciously in modern market economies), persons are seen as functioning autonomously in their economic lives, and as primarily interested in increasing their own economic consumption and in maximizing their profits. People enter the market, which arises "naturally" from human exchange, by offering their resources and skills out of this desire for profit and not out of a need to sustain themselves.[17] Hobgood cogently presents how in the orthodox model, self-interest works through the market guiding resources to their most efficient use, in a manner argued by orthodox theorists to be reasonably just. Failures of the market in more traditional societies are due to people's inabilities to make the choices necessary for economic advancement, caused by particular cultural values or regional political instability. Also, where the market is in place, poverty or unemployment are seen to be problems due to temporary disequilibrium or malfunctioning that will eventually iron themselves out. Any problems that are not solved by a freely operating market in equilibrium are due to forces outside the economic system such as ignorance or prejudice, personal qualities of the poor themselves, or disturbances of free exchange from labor unions or the government.

As exemplified by Novak's tripartite schema, in the orthodox model the economic sphere is seen to function separately from political or cultural organizations. The autonomous political and cultural spheres serve to correct any abuses or excesses of the market. Thus those especially concerned with equity in the capitalism system, such as political liberals, think that the government can solve problems such as racism, sexism and unemployment through job creation, affirmative action, and increased availability of education.

According to Hobgood, the Catholic social justice tradition has reflected the capitalist model of social analysis when it has advocated the superiority of capitalism, e.g., its support of development of third-world markets and capitalist penetration in depressed areas. Their ideas of change involve agencies that are already in power such as governments, international agencies and corporate elites. Thus when utilizing the capitalist view, no matter how concerned about human welfare,[18] Catholic social teaching often assumes existing structures of capital and labor. On the other hand, in the liberationist model these structures lead inevitability to a society structured by class and promote a perception of the naturalness of a gender-based division of labor.

The Liberationist Model

Hobgood finds that CST's analyses of poverty and prescriptions for social change have also reflected assumptions that may be aligned with the liberationist social model. Hobgood's conception of liberationist social theory is rooted in radical economics, especially that of Karl Marx. It has found expression in critical forms of neo-Marxism, antiracist and socialist feminist analysis. In contrast to capitalism, liberationist social theory holds with the organic model, that natural economic activity is production for satisfying human needs, not production for profit. However, organic social theory does not address as well as liberationist theory does that the orthodox model obscures the fact that "political, cultural and market institutions do not function autonomously, but form one interlocking structure in service of private capital accumulation," though in "fairness" this is also true in some socialist governments, a prime example being the Soviet Union.[19]

For instance, through militarization, the state can sustain aggregate demand when decreasing wages in the capitalist system cannot, thus keeping corporations profitable while keeping the world "safe for capitalism." Despite the post-WWII economic boom, the capitalist segmented market has succeeded in keeping women and minorities at the bottom, instituting an underclass of structurally unemployed persons in poverty and on welfare, thereby keeping overall wages and costs down. This outcast welfare class, segregated from the mainstream by gender and race, functions to make even the worst jobs in the secondary labor market seem more attractive. Contrary to capitalist theory then, the present market system is not "natural," instead it has been created and sustained to serve the interests of a few. "Problems such as poverty, unemployment, and the arms race are not autonomous problems but are essential organizing mechanisms for the economic system itself. Private profit cannot be made without exploitation."[20] Hobgood argues that whenever Catholic social teaching incorporates the liberationist interpretation of society, it recognizes the interlocking nature of government and business in the exercise of social power in capitalist societies. For example, Leo XIII lamented vast concentrations of wealth and Pius XI "saw a direct relationship between economic power and political control as well as significant opposition between interests of capitalists who do and don't own capital."[21] John XXIII, recognizing the interlocking nature of economic and government and economic interests, noted that "vast military expenditure by state always accompanied capitalist expansion."[22] Likewise, Paul VI in PP and John Paul II in LE analyzed poverty and proposed methods of social change that can be aligned with the liberationist model, despite extensively drawing upon the capitalist social model.

In the next section, I will concentrate on a central problem faced by both Novak and Hobgood—how to reconcile seemingly opposite positions in the whole of the social encyclicals. Paul Lakeland argues that this is also a central problem for CST itself—that it so easily can be claimed by both the left and right. However, my contention is that reconciling opposites as Novak and Hobgood do by seeking to do reduce or even eliminate the tension between liberal and liberationist perspectives in CST (by preferring one completely over the other) is at best done uneasily and in the end unfruitfully. In my concluding section, against Lakeland, Novak and Hobgood, I will provide arguments how this conflagration of opposites is in reality a tremendous strength of CST.

Economic Theory Through the Tradition

The best way to benefit from Novak and Hobgood's differing approaches to the dialectic between capitalism and socialism in the social encyclicals and to note the possibility of a higher viewpoint is to place Novak's and Hobgood's analysis side-by-side in their evaluation of selected encyclicals. This journey begins with what they both would describe as Pope Leo XIII's only seemingly even-handed criticisms of both capitalism and socialism in *Rerum Novarum* (RN), carried on by Pius XI in *Quadragesimo Anno* (QA).

Rerum Novarum and *Quadragesimo Anno*

Novak argues that Leo's XIII's ambivalence toward both socialism and capitalism—which sets the tone for the subsequent tradition even beyond Pius XI—was in fact asymmetrical: Leo asserts that capitalism was correct in principle but wrong in certain elements of practice; socialism was wrong in *both* moral principle and practice. Leo wished only to reform capitalism by setting moral limits on property and by correcting imbalances of his time that gave the wealthy too much power over labor and the poor who were weak and defenseless. Leo's main theoretical criticism of capitalism was its reliance on individualism and laissez-faire political economy.

Pius XI in QA exhibits for Novak much more anger and ideological passion than RN's "irenic and balanced" (110) approach to the social problem. In Pius XI's "ferocious attack" against liberalism, capitalism as unlimited free enterprise had caused the depression and in its control over governments was contributing to political tensions between nations. However, QA did defend somewhat the moral integrity of capitalism as a system when it said that capitalism was "surely not vicious of its very nature."[23] Despite these critiques, Novak ends up praising RN and QA for inspiring reform from within liberal capitalism.

Hobgood agrees with Novak that socialism is criticized more heavily in RN but for different reasons. Instead of its organicism fueling a critique of modern economic theory as Novak maintains, she argues that it is *because* RN draws mostly on the organic economic theory it inherited from the medieval and feudal social and economic framework that it aligns itself with some major assumptions of orthodox economic theory over against socialism and liberationist economic theory. While the organic social theory she delineates does have at base communitarian values that allow it to criticize the "economic man" of orthodox economic theory, its emphasis on hierarchical social arrangements predisposed it to those aspects of orthodox theory that rely on the obligation of privilege to remedy social ills.[24] For example, the wealthy were not required in medieval distributive justice to put their social position in jeopardy by giving out of scarcity (as the gospels and early Church Fathers taught), but only in giving out of surplus. The poor's role was to suffer poverty and accept this surplus when and if given. In this way social order is maintained, and private property is thus sanctioned.

According to Hobgood, this is exactly how orthodox economic theory views economic relations. Economic power becomes congealed in a certain class (so that it is utilized more productively in investing capital and creating goods and unemployment), following Adam Smith's "invisible hand." In the orthodox [like the organic] view, the rich then had the incentive [duty] to invest their resources [give out of their surplus to the poor]; this would eliminate gross inequalities in income distribution, lessening the need for any social conflict in either model.

This affiliation of orthodox and organic theory in the early social encyclicals (despite the fact that organic theory is used throughout the social encyclicals to critique capitalism) was strengthened as both were seen as opposed to the socialist and egalitarian ideas that were feared as a threat to the church's institutional privilege. Hobgood agrees then with Novak, that this threat was perceived as much worse than the threat of liberalism, even though liberalism was by that point undermining organic social theory. Thus, the church "needed to establish itself as an ally with the bourgeois class in order to absorb the socialist threat and promote the social stability so vital to them both."[25] In Hobgood's view, Leo should have declared that the economic arrangements of capitalism create a necessary tension between capital and labor instead of settling for the possibility of equilibrium in a stratified society.[26] Thus the church's inheritance of organic social theory as well as its fear of losing its institutional influence in an increasing liberal society caused it to allow and even further the claims of orthodox economic theory. These inconsistencies make RN's solutions incapable of actually being put into effect.

Again agreeing with Novak, Hobgood points out that *Quadragesimo Anno* echoed and even deepened Leo's structural analysis of capitalism, yet did not intend to reject capitalism. For example, Pius simultaneously rejected the orthodox wage contract and the socialist view that a just wage should be determined according to the value created by labor.[27] Pius still maintained with Leo that justice was attainable within the current system and that there was no necessary tension between capital and labor created by this framework. While Pius XI's conception of acceptable union activity was somewhat broader than Leo's, his emphasis on the harmony of interests between capital and labor in Hobgood's view seems to "render unions powerless" (116).[28] Pius also followed Leo's contradictory analysis insofar as both popes call for state intervention while at the same time pointing out how the wealthy, in Pius' words have power over the "life-blood [of] the entire economic body" and are able to undertake a "fierce battle to acquire control of the state" and indeed international power (117). The result is that the state becomes a slave of the wealthy.

Thus Hobgood argues that Pius, even more than Leo, recognized the interlocking of capitalism and governmental power in the capitalist system, along the lines of analysis of the liberationist model. Alas, like Leo, Pius still argued that with the help of the church, this conflict inaugurated by capital can be humanized through state intervention on behalf of the weak and through the restructuring of the economy along corporative lines, stopping short of condemning the capitalist system. Hobgood concludes her analysis of QA: like Leo, "Pius did not render a historically possible agenda for addressing what Pius called 'a despotic economic domination' or 'the fatal internal strife that rends the human family'" (119; quoting from QA 39, 105).

Thus while Novak severely criticizes Pius XII for its "vicious" attack on capitalism, Hobgood argues that QA did not go far enough, at least in proposing viable alternatives. However, the hierarchically-based social theory offered by both popes undermined their structural analysis and their proposed remedies. This helps explain why, as Novak also claims, socialism and capitalism are not evenhandedly condemned in CST. However, for Hobgood, it was not some concession to the virtues of liberalism that led Leo and Pius to do this. It was because the hierarchical basis of organic theory was complementary with the socioeconomic hierarchies created by capitalism in the market and the family (as long as they were not too pronounced), while Leo XIII and Pius XI saw socialism as morc contradictory with organic social thcory on thcsc counts.

John XXIII and Paul VI

For Novak, John XXIII's social encyclicals, *Mater et Magistra* (MM) and *Pacem in Terris* (PT) brought the liberal human rights tradition into official Catholic social teaching. Novak appropriates John XXIII commonly acknowledged openness to liberal economic society in three ways. First, Novak especially appreciates John XXIII's "beautiful notion of the common good" as: "the sum total of those conditions of social living, whereby men are enabled more fully and radically to achieve their own perfection" (128).[30] Second, MM celebrated a "joy" for liberal institutions, based upon three fundamentals: the importance of work, private property, and the right of free association. Third, Novak maintain John's treatment of these three fundamentals showed that the Catholic understanding of the human person and human social nature revealed itself as the "true" liberal understanding in that John taught that everyone should be able to engage in productive activity and that the public should avoid restricting freedom of private citizens. In more economic terms, enhancing Pius XI's introduction the notion of "social justice" into CST, John XIII introduces the concept of what Novak terms "productive justice." This type of justice is attained when political liberty, personal responsibility and productive activity interact to establish a social economic order that attends to the needs of all, including the newly developing third-world.

While John XXIII has also been rightly interpreted as extending co-operation with Marxism, Novak stresses instead that John's cooperation with liberalism is a much significant turn in CST. John's "genius" was to place his view that "individual men are necessarily the foundation, cause and end of all social institutions," that Novak claims to be also a cardinal precept of liberalism, within a social and transcendent framework (130; quoting from MM 219). While John steered clear of explicitly accepting liberalism as a philosophical position, Novak claims that John "borrowed concept after concept from liberal institutional life" (133).[32] For Novak, as Pius XI's ideological passion contradicted Leo's irenicism, Paul VI's dictum in *Populorum Progressio* (PP) that "the world is sick" contrasts with John XXIII's optimism.

While the fundamental principles established by John did not shift during Paul's pontificate, Paul did waver between pessimism toward a world dominated by capitalism and what Novak views as a "utopian" hope for a world that yet still does benefit from capitalism. However, Paul VI, anticipating such criticism, declares that those who consider that hopes for institutions like the U.N. for cooperation instead of war, are not being realistic enough in that they don't recognize the "dynamism of a world which desires to live more fraternally (78). I would argue that Paul VI's ideals for world community are pursued through by neoconservatives like Novak through a "utopian" view that markets can achieve peace, fraternity, and even some measure of equality, rather than primarily through diplomacy (other than trade agreements to expand markets) and international political collaboration like the UN. Lonergan's analysis reveals a deep understanding of how capitalism if not sufficiently democratic instead leads to the militant capitalism we are engaging in today.

For instance, Novak points out that Paul praises development ("the new word for peace") but does not praise the nations who set this development in motion. Although explicitly hostile toward economic liberalism, Paul makes several "implicit allusions to humane achievements within liberal societies" (135): free commerce, the introduction of industry as necessary for growth progress and development, research and development, discovery, risk taking, entrepreneurial enterprise, liberal generosity involved in business, and the sense of responsibility.[33]

Paul's solution to this dialectic—that we should not abolish the competitive market system but humanize it by keeping it within just and moral limits—is for Novak an appeal to practices already being applied within liberal societies. Moreover, Paul's idealized understanding of socialistic alternatives not only fails to advert to generally corrupt characteristics of all types of governments; in effect, the only sins it does acknowledge are of economic institutions. Novak prefers a system where the moral-cultural, economic and political are equal, not least because the needed economic progress called for by Paul cannot occur if economies are not free from political domination.

Hobgood also sees development in CST with John XIII, but not surprisingly in a different direction than Novak; even more so with Paul VI. She argues that in extending the analysis of CST to all the world's poor, including the third-world, John XXIII and Paul VI both continue to mix orthodox theory with increasing amounts of structural analysis, eventually to the point of aligning some of their policy prescriptions with the liberationist paradigm. She agrees with Novak, while both still point to development as a solution for the imbalances between the rich and poor nations, their structural analyses again "called into serious question its efficacy as a remedy" (132). Again we see how someone from the left and someone from the right can argue that CST is adopting, however imperfectly, their position, with some unfortunate residue of argument from the other side.

Still Hobgood agrees with Novak that John's analysis of capitalism was less critical than his predecessors, though not because of some seismic shift in CST to economic liberalism but because of improved postwar economic conditions. In Hobgood's schema, John follows the economic orthodox analysis in his affirmation of private property and the wage system in his belief "in the application of western modes of technology to economic and political activity" (132). He also stresses the orthodox tenet that pride of place in economic development should go to the private initiative of individuals: the right to own property and exercise private initiative concerning its use was necessary to prevent "political tyranny" and to best serve the basic needs of body and spirit and to "promote the efficient generation of material surplus through the capitalist market" (133). Indeed the postwar boom had finally made possible Leo and Pius XII's vision of universal ownership of land. John maintained Leo XIII and Pius XI's stress on both the "efficacy of the state as responsible agent of the commonweal" (a tenet of liberal orthodoxy) and the "traditional understanding of the Church as agent of social change" (134).

Nevertheless, Hobgood highlights much more than Novak does the elements in John XIII analysis that were at odds with orthodox theory. For instance, John argues that the right to private property is not absolute but includes with it the responsibility to use it justly for the benefit of society. On this basis, John writes "that the right of human beings to adequate sustenance is prior to all other economic rights, including private ownership" (135). This inclusion of economic rights points to a new order of human rights beyond liberal individual rights to include rights "traditionally identified with socialism, such as rights to a job, food, shelter, clothing, and medical care regardless of sex, race or class" (136).[34] I think this ranks with Novak's contention of "productive justice" as a new notion in CST, and acts as a counterweight to it. John also strengthened the growing papal argument that the dignity of human nature and modern developments require that "all citizens should participate in the shaping of socioeconomic life" (137). This includes workers being partners not only in ownership, but also in control and management of enterprises. Also, while praising the benefits of modern development, John also warned that it led to domination, profound imbalances and inequalities among citizens, creating class differences and economic cultural and political imperialism.[35]

However, Hobgood finds that most of John's teaching belongs to either the orthodox or organic economic theoretical modes (especially his belief "in the possibility of an ordered, hierarchical society in which every social class knows its proper duty, and in which all can be motivated by a common will inspired by the Church" and in a "justice proportional to one's social location" [140]). Still, Hobgood agrees with Dorr's observation noted in the previous chapter, that while John affirmed much of the status quo of liberal capitalism, he also inaugurated moves that led to a new order of thinking about economic justice, moves that "'broke the long alliance between Roman Catholicism and socially conservative forces (142).'"[36] It is not hard to see that this interpretation is almost diametrically opposed to Novak's and raises the question as to who is right and wrong, or if both are right and wrong in different ways.

Hobgood finds that like his predecessors, Pope Paul VI's teachings on political economy contain orthodox assumptions in conflict with radical structural analysis. Paul was influenced on one hand by the failure of development policies in the third-world, which made him tend toward radical theory; on the other hand by Vatican alarm about possible revolutionary momentum in the Southern Hemisphere which prompts him to reiterate orthodox and organic perspectives on industrialization and social agency.

So on the one hand, Hobgood notes that *Populorum Progressio* and *Octogesima Adveniens* relate how "whole populations [are] destitute of necessities" due to abuses of ownership or of power (PP 30; OA 2). Modern economies, informed by economic liberalism would, left to themselves, exacerbate this separation of wealth. However, Paul either blamed these miseries on necessities of industrialization, or held that they can be remedied by politically liberal emendations to orthodox capitalism. Thus, Paul appealed to unions not to demand more than was economically feasible and not to involve themselves in political activity; rather, elites such as national or international public authorities were to be responsible for social change (149). While Paul praised Marxism as an analytical tool, he also cautioned believers not to ignore the "intimate" link between Marxism as a legitimate tool of analysis and Marxism as a theory of class struggle that denied transcendent reality (150. quoting from OA 34). Also in OA, Paul backed away from his earlier position in PP that revolutionary uprisings may be legitimate. Finally, Paul assumed a hierarchical, organic role for the institutional church which interpreted the gospels and the signs of the times to teach Christians their duties regarding the poor and the dangers of Marxism and liberalism, relying on the laity only to implement this teaching in the social order.

Still, Hobgood points out that Paul does make several claims in line with the radical paradigm, but in odds with his own orthodox analysis. His most important structural analysis concerned how poverty in the third-world was due to the legacy of colonialism, especially the single product economy. Particularly, Paul criticized Western development programs for following a neocolonialist agenda for maintaining or acquiring complete dominance of foreign economies under a cloak of financial or technical assistance. There was a wide disparity of power, Paul maintained, between rich and poor countries, and this disparity made the orthodox idea of "free" trade between equal partners ludicrous in the international situation. Because Paul regarded economic power as dependent upon political power, he saw the need to shift from the focus on economics in CST to that of political power.

In response to these inequalities and the massive suffering they cause, Paul called for "bold transformations, comprehensive structural changes, and innovations that go deep, transformations that go beyond either the scope of organic or liberal orthodox theories of societal transformation" (152). Since the Church could no longer direct what these political activities should entail, Paul left it up to local communities to analyze specific situations and determine methods of change. This may even legitimate some degree of cooperation with Marxists, among other possible options.

Another important way Hobgood finds that Paul moved toward the left was in his use of the "utopian imagination." Paul called not for an impossible ideal but a visionary yet historically possible society; the utopian imagination was to assist in this task by "perceiving in the present the disregarded possibility within it and directing itself toward a fresh future."[38] The means to achieve this vision were to include funding on the level then used for armaments and technology, and daring and creative innovations that would include modern forms of democracy broadened so that people can be "'the author[s] of [their] own advancement' and 'artisans of their destiny'" (152).[39]

Hobgood concludes her analysis of PP and OA by noting that because of the several contradictions between orthodox and radical theory these documents reflect, an evaluation of Paul VI is difficult. An example of these contradictions is that Paul diminishes the problems caused by capitalism by terming them abuses. Abuses are presumably correctable, yet Paul also indicates that capitalism had failed at its very root. Another contradiction is that Paul argued that public authorities could reform and regulate markets, but accused governments of being cloaks for further domination. Finally, he puts the emphasis on change in the political arena, but discourages revolutionary agendas in threatening existing political power.

In Hobgood's view, the use of these incompatible perspectives ends up rendering Paul's teaching confusing and limiting its effectiveness. Still, Hobgood maintains that Paul VI continues John XXIII's shift away from premodern and modern orthodox theoretical assumptions. Novak argues almost the exact opposite, that there can be discerned a steady movement *toward* modern economic liberalism as manifested in orthodox economics through Leo XII and John XIII (with slight detours with Pius XI and Paul VI), culminating with Pope John Paul II's highlighting the opportunities for personal economic initiative found within democratic market arrangements in *Centesimus Annus* (CA), a perspective which Novak considers "one of the enduring contributions of his papacy to Catholic social thought."[40] This is where Novak and Hobgood most depart company.

John Paul II

Despite Novak's perception of wavering and misunderstanding on the popes' part, the social encyclicals of Pope John Paul II, especially *Centesimus Annus*, are for Novak, the culmination of this 100-year evolution of Catholic social teaching toward embracing the principles and practice of liberal society. The theological link between John Paul II and liberalism is the pope's emphasis on "Creation Theology."

Against the closeness some commentators see between Pope John Paul II's and Marx in certain areas, Novak contrasts the pope's personalist version of solidarity with the organic "connectedness" of Marxism. This solidarity is concerned with the primacy of the individual human subject.

It is on this basis that John Paul II constructs his critical theology of economics. In placing human work as the key to the social question, Novak argues that from *Laborem Exercens* (LE) to *Centesimus Annus* (CA), John Paul II shifts from liberation to creation as motif of his theology of economics, a move which Novak claims is a "remarkably 'American' way of approaching the nature and destiny of man, role of capital and labor, private property and community" (150).

Not surprisingly, Novak disagrees with John Paul II's derogatory description of capitalism in LE,[41] arguing that the pope's strict differentiation between labor as the real efficient subject in the production process (LE 56) and capital as a collection of things (of the means of production) "excludes persons whose investments in discovery and transformation of natural resources and in means of production, go beyond self-centered indulgence in material luxuries" (154).

Still Novak is faced with the apparent difficulties in offering John Paul as a proponent of liberalism, heightened by the fact that both the right and the left have claimed the pope's social encyclicals for their own positions (as highlighted well by Hobgood below).[42] Novak's explanation for this seemingly paradoxical situation is that in LE, the church argues on the one hand against individualism, but on the other for other "liberal" values adopted by the church since Vatican II such as religious liberty and freedom of conscience. But Novak maintains that without a strong form of individual responsibility, "how can one defend liberty of conscience?" (160). The church in Novak's view needs to better acknowledge the points of agreement between the individualism it disavows and the personal liberty it embraces.

Novak concludes that while Pope John Paul II disdains capitalism as well as collectivism, democratic capitalism is in fact most compatible with the pope's "creation theology" developed in LE and CA. For example, the pope emphasized the strict connection between the human persons as subject of labor and their rights to the fruit of their labor, including rights of ownership (LE 131) and highlighted the danger of nationalization in which a "new class of government administrator comes into power" (LE 14). As means to the end of reducing the alienation involved in human work and granting workers their rights to the fruit of their labor, Novak claims that John Paul II recommended several techniques not only entirely compatible with democratic capitalist practice, but already beyond the experimental stage in many liberal societies such as employee ownership plans, although Novak ignores the point that many advocates of these plans, including John Paul II in LE, do so because they argue that capitalism does not fully address the needs of the common good.

Finally, Novak rests his case on his contention that democratic capitalism actually does improve the lot of the poor, in contrast with liberation theology, which while rhetorically announcing an option for the poor, does not in any way conceive of an economic system "creative enough to actually raise up economic standing of the poor." Instead liberation theology "offers the poor a stone" (163). Mary Hobgood argues the exact opposite, that it is democratic capitalism that most ignores the plight of the poor, and that CST should explicitly adopt the liberationist perspective to remedy that error; that is why she takes John Paul II so much to task, precisely because she finds his analysis to be the most lacking in including the liberationist perspective, despite positive appreciations of John Paul II by commentators congenial to Hobgood's approach such as Gregory Baum and Donal Dorr.

Thus, Hobgood's analysis of LE and SRS "deconstructs" Baum's interpretation of John Paul II's "shift to the left" since in her view his social encyclicals contain diminishing elements alignable with the liberationist or radical paradigm. The pope's most important argument—that economic justice can be realized only if capital serves labor—does not emerge out of radical theory because for John Paul II ownership of property is morally neutral and is not understood in a way that could constitute grounds for social conflict as in radical and liberationist theory. Stating her case more strongly, Hobgood asserts: "Despite his use of some radical categories, John Paul II basically rejected the perspective of the radical paradigm," so that he ends up favoring the organic social model and selected orthodox assumptions as a basis for social justice. Also, Hobgood finds that the pope deviates from John XXIII who sought to read the signs of the times, and from Paul VI, who argued that social organization was a product of local discernment.

Rather, John Paul's deductive methodology proceeds from abstract philosophical principles. His "first principles" include personalism, common use of goods, priority of labor over capital, and use over ownership, which can be applied in turn to concrete historical situations. The pope's stress on the power of ideas or principles to change reality[43] (features of the organic model), along with his bias toward private ownership (belonging to the orthodox model) end up "overpowering any movement toward a dialogue with radical analysis," despite Baum's claim, elaborated in the previous chapter, that LE initiated "'a critical and creative dialogue with Marxism'" (175).[44] Hobgood relates these two factors in her analysis of how LE explicitly rejects a structural analysis of economics. John Paul II's stress on the mutual interdependence of capital and labor, and his claim that economic process does not entail any mutual incompatibly and conflict between the two is a direct rejection of the radical model, which posits an a priori elimination of private ownership of the means of production. Instead, the Pope lumps private ownership of goods and private ownership of the means of production into one "reified" category of ownership (177).

The pope's lack of structural critique is also related to his idealistic moral methodology, as when the pope maintains that "economic injustice in capitalism is a result of immoral choices by individual capitalists who accepted false economic premises" (175).[45] The pope's analysis thus does not question any inner dynamism of capitalism, stressing instead the sins of early capitalists and the individual "voluntaristic" choices made by laborers; if these choices had been made differently, our current situation could have been avoided.

What about the pope's central insight that capital must serve labor? Isn't that a radical perspective? Hobgood says yes, that the pope is in a "radical mode" when he advocates co-ownership and planned economy based on his definition of capital as heritage of human labor (179). But Hobgood argues that the pope shows a disposition for private ownership when he juxtaposes this radical priority of labor over capital with the assertion that the actual structure of ownership is morally arbitrary. Instead of calling for radical structural change the pope relies mostly on hoping for the benevolent use of property by private owners (as in the organic model), which presupposes hierarchy and takes cooperation for granted. This is a departure from radical theory which holds that political democracy can only come ultimately from economic democracy. The pope moves away from true economic democracy when he says that the key problem of social ethics is that of "just remuneration." Instead of focusing on the production process, which is at the root of economic democracy, the key problem for the pope remains in the distributive end, and he thereby embraces a view in harmony with liberal orthodox analysis' concern with equity within capitalism and the system of private ownership. Though she agrees here with Novak, she obviously disagrees that this is a positive movement.[46]

Summing up, Hobgood notes that the pope does incorporate structural analysis of the roots of economic injustice when he talks about the indirect employer exercising determining influence on all socioeconomic relationships (185-6). This radical emphasis is also shown in previously-discussed elements such as the priority of labor over capital (LE 12), capital as stored labor (LE 12, 13), capital organized against workers as a main source of economic injustice (LE 13), some movement beyond a just wage to "co-responsibility in determining the use of capital and its profits as a central demand of labor" (LE 14) the need for centralized economic planning and decentralized economic ownership as one way of making the economic process accountable to individuals (LE 12, 14, 15, 18), and the workers' struggle as more than just an idea, but praxis (LE 16).

Nonetheless, Hobgood maintains that in LE the orthodox and organic models predominate. The pope's idealistic methodology, the naturalness of social hierarchies, his insistence that change can only come about through moral suasion, the exclusion of productive process from the key problems of social ethics, his insistence on non-conflictual change without consideration of the morality of existing power relationships and his explicit support of a gender-based division of labor, "situate the document comfortably within the liberal orthodox mainstream" (186). This marks a retreat from the more radical concerns found in some of his predecessors. Compared to John Paul II, John XXIII and Paul VI included more liberationist concerns for structural analyses of economic and class systems, support for mobilizing grassroots efforts, a utopian imagination to determine direction of social change, growing openness to solidarity with Marxist movements, and recognition of need for reform within the church.

Hobgood argues that *Sollicitudo Rei Socialis* makes Pope John Paul II's retreat from the more liberationist perspectives of Paul VI (especially in PP, the encyclical SRS was written to commemorate) even more explicit. Instead of appropriating or even acknowledging the liberationist dimensions of Paul VI's analysis of capitalism and social change, John Paul "makes a noticeable departure from traditional or mainstream Catholic social teaching by ignoring structural criticisms concerning causes of poverty, and by disregarding radical prescriptions of what might be done about poverty." Hobgood believes that the pope's position is not only flawed, but represents a serious departure from the wider Catholic social justice position. This is because the pope's reliance on individual conversion and charity requires that those who produced the inequalities end them and ignores the vast differentials in power between the haves and the have-nots. Instead, some conflict is necessary. SRS' refusal to acknowledge fundamental conflict, in contrast to LE's call for solidarity of workers that dealt with changing government, economic, and labor structures, represents for Hobgood the pope's retreat to liberal capitalist assumptions of relative distributions of social power and optimism regarding reform within the present system (181).

In Hobgood's view, John Paul II's individualistic understanding of traditional normative values violates a mandate central to Catholic tradition since Pius XI who opposed abandoning to charity alone the task of addressing economic structures that cause the open violation of justice. Devoid of any analysis that can be aligned with the radical paradigm, Hobgood maintains LE represents a significant departure not only from the teaching of Paul VI that it claimed to articulate more fully but from the wider Catholic social justice tradition (181).

Critique of Novak and Hobgood

There is certainly much merit in both Novak and Hobgood's analyses. Novak's contributions include the growing recognition, given the relatively stagnant world economy of the 1980s, that religious economic ethics needs to be concerned with creation of wealth as well as distribution. For example, Novak's is right to stress Pope John XXIII's conception of "productive justice" alongside commutative, social and distributive justice. Novak deserves credit for not being as libertarian in his outlook as some of his fellow conservatives regarding various forms of public assistance; his theory of democratic capitalism does rely on (limited) safety nets and a somewhat active role for government.[47] To overcome the unfortunate aspects of some forms of welfare programs, Novak demonstrates the need for emphasis on private and public virtues of promoting social justice, that don't rely on necessarily impersonal, distant, dehumanizing, and one might grant, "addictive" bureaucratic forms of public assistance programs.[48] Moreover, Novak's writings on the importance of the limitations on socialism did anticipate the momentous 1989 revolutions in Eastern Europe against state socialist regimes. In the light of the events of 1989, Novak seems to be correct that religious economic ethics need to be concerned with the realities of practical, imperfect institutional arrangements, as opposed to trying to create institutions that "overarch" workings of the now dominant market economy.[49]

As with Novak, Hobgood's analysis contributes much to the understanding of the use of economics in CST. Her breakdown of positions taken by papal encyclicals according to her three paradigms helps to both identify their influence on papal economics and point out some important inconsistencies in CST regarding theory, practice and institutions. Hopefully her explicit linking of CST and economic theory will help

Catholic socioeconomic ethics become more effective, toward acknowledging that social ethics must become more sophisticated regarding the contribution of economic thought to religious social theory, while remaining critical of what is ultimately appropriated. While the changed situation in political economics (with the failure of the Soviet economy and the 1989 Eastern European revolutions, plus the shifting official Vatican position toward liberation theology), means less future influence upon CST of the neo-Marxian/liberationist paradigm, the existence of an established radical and prophetic perspective that Hobgood delineates within the tradition of CST suggests that market capitalism will never become the dominant paradigm for CST either.

Nevertheless, Novak's reading of the papal encyclicals has faced intense criticism, which are in my view overwhelmingly valid. It is helpful to separate these critiques into two categories, the moral/theological/philosophical, and the economic. The emphasis in this chapter will be on the former, while I will analyze the latter once we have investigated Lonergan's economics as a better dialogue partner for CST. Despite part of the argument of this book that these categories can, do and should overlap, despite Novak's neoliberal positing a divide between the moral-cultural and the economic. Still for reasons of efficiency and order, I will separate the critiques into these two categories. In my conclusion I will emphasize how the economic and moral overlap, which is an important aspect I argue need more emphasis in existing treatments of Christian economic ethics and in economics.

My critique of Hobgood in relation to her critique of CST will also be separated into two parts, the first to be dealt with here and the second in my Conclusion where I review her *Catholic Social Teaching and Economic Theory* in the light of the relationship between neo-Marxian and Lonergan's economics. In this chapter I will be concerned with what I believe is her mistaken categorization of economic theory in general and more importantly within CST.

Like Mixing Oil and Water: Novak's Liberal Interpretation of CST

The two critiques I wish to emphasize here are Novak's use of political-economic liberalism as his dialogue partner for Christian economic ethics, and his economic anthropology. While this end up being a complex set of critiques, it can be summed up in once sentence: in his attempt to overcome what he deems Catholic social teaching's overly critical view of capitalism, Novak instead undermines Catholic social teaching by overemphasizing the perceived strengths of political liberalism and underemphasizing the uneasy moral status of economic liberalism. He does this especially by substituting his pessimistic and individualistic views of human nature for the more hopeful and social economic anthropology of Catholic social teaching.

First, Novak attempts, if not to identify CST with his vision of liberalism, 1) to stress the basic complementarity of these two social theories; and then 2) to indicate where Catholic social thought should be corrected in accordance with the insights that liberalism provides. This is especially true when Novak practically identifies the goal of a his vision of a revised CST to coincide with the uniquely American "tripartitc" form of political economy, despite his acknowledgment that CST "has already set in place such basic liberal benchmarks as the dignity of the human person, interdependence of all people, economic development of nations, institutions of human rights, communitarian personality, and the vocation of people to become co-creators,"[50] independent of liberal influence and even contrary to that influence.

Neoconservatives such as Novak (as well as political liberals such as David Hollenbach), demonstrate "genetic," or complementary, relationships between the views of the human in society in liberalism and CST, including those regarding human rights, the dignity of persons, the importance of voluntary communities, stewardship, entrepreneurship and so on.[51] The problem lies in how the moral-cultural realm interacts with the economic realm in the separation of realms advocated by Novak and other neoconservatives, a concept that goes back to 19th century positivism and neoclassical economics that advocated that economics and morality and religion should be kept separate. However, this approach neglects insights of CST critical of this separation. CST's position is related to economic liberalism both genetically and dialectically, meaning that Novak's claim that liberalism and CST hold complementary views of the self in society is insufficient. If the two are related dialectically as well as genetically, a belief in the essential viewpoints of CST will require that, liberalism, especially economic liberalism, "convert" to better approximate the views set forth in the social encyclicals.[52] This requires a change not only in economic science, but also in Novak's tripartite system that places economics and morality in essentially distinct realms. By not realizing this, Novak distorts both the insights offered by CST and their effective application.

For example, in his criticism of the American bishops' pastoral *Economic Justice for All*,[53] Novak maintains that his fellow members of the lay commission agree with the bishops' stress, in the tradition of CST, on the dignity and uniqueness of human life, the social nature of individuals, and the principle of subsidiarity. However, George McCarthy and Royal Rhodes are correct in pointing out that the Lay Commission's letter did this by "making human dignity synonymous with and reducible to individual rights, social justice reducible to political pluralism, and the principle of subsidiarity reducible to centralized decisions within the market economy."[54] This reduction of the social ethical prescriptions of CST to American democratic capitalism distorts the central tenets of CST. In fact, in his own works, Novak does not usually turn to CST to affirm his arguments in favor of his form of democratic capitalism. For instance, he takes his concept of creativity from Adam Smith, not from John Paul II's ideal of self-realization in the marketplace (45). As a result of Novak taking his social theory from economic liberalism, "At every stage of analysis, the meaning and interpretation of such categories of human dignity, cooperation, freedom, and the common good and community develop further apart in the two statements [the lay letter and bishops' letter]."[55]

One of the most serious questions raised by Novak's attempt to demonstrate an ever-increasing affinity between the values of CST and their embodiment in liberal institutions is, whether a "theory which has to explain away or dismiss such significant portions of CST still claim [may] validity [as a Catholic social ethic]."[56] In Novak's hermeneutic of the papal encyclicals, which privileges capitalism, he advocates a sort of "canon within a canon," arguing that popes Pius XI and Paul VI deviate from the central tradition (more favorable to liberalism) represented by Popes Leo XIII, John XXIII, and John Paul II. Even the latter popes do not fall into Novak's real canon of liberal economics; they fall under Novak's criticism too for their mistaken interpretations of economic and political liberalism, especially American liberalism.[57] As outlined in the previous chapter and reiterated in the conclusion of this one, a less biased reading of CST indicates how it criticizes both capitalism and socialism and even transcends them both. As discussed in my concluding chapter, this is exacerbated by Novak's similar gloss over the inadequacies of orthodox capitalist theory; on top of his selective use of CST to support liberal economic society, the canon he finds within the overall canon is itself deeply flawed.

My second major criticism of Novak's views regards specifically the differences between views of economic anthropology embedded in Catholic social theory and that of economic liberalism he espouses which is linked so tightly to neo-classical economics. The antagonism between these two rival anthropologies was discussed extensively in the preceding chapter as the hallmark of CST's potential contribution to a renewed economics. These divergences can be expressed in three categories: 1) self-interest; 2) individuals as primarily social beings; and 3) human dignity or self-realization. Beyond the philosophical aspects of economic anthropology there also exists a fourth theological category to be briefly touched upon here, namely the question of how sin and redemption are addressed in the Christian economic anthropologies of CST and Novak's religious legitimization of democratic capitalism.

For example, in the Novak, et al., lay letter, human dignity is described in "terms of self-reliance and self-responsibility as the individual strives to attain its own well-being." This form of dignity results from the individual having inalienable human rights as well as liberty of conscience, and is "best expressed in the individual's drive for innovation, production and private property in the competitive market economy." According to Novak, poverty ultimately stems from a lack of spiritual awareness of one's own dignity, an awareness that cannot be imposed upon people, but must be generated from within.

Thus human dignity is not something one is given, from being made in the image of God, but it is something an individual must generate for him or herself within a competitive market economy. The bishops, on the other hand, define "human dignity as the full expression of individual potential within a community of friends having civil, political and economic rights." Within this definition, economic liberalism's concepts of possessive individualism, production, private property and competition "neither hold a privileged place nor are viewed without some skepticism and suspicion," as a too narrow and limited understanding of humanity's true and individual dignity.[58] This narrow understanding of human agency in the marketplace is reflected in Novak's acceptance of the economic hardships resulting from "natural" inequalities.

For Novak, this differential invites greater creativity and incentives for individuals to better themselves and thus their standard of living. However, Novak does not fully differentiate the benefits of material incentives for successful individuals from the moral pursuit of economic activity for the good of society. As McCarthy and Rhodes state, "In Novak they are joined together so that moral self development becomes an appendage to social stability development and economic efficiency." If inequality is necessary to achieve a better society, it must provide material wealth for the whole, as well as a reward for better skill or talents of individuals. Novak instead reduces self-development to materialism and even to "the violence of market competition," which only serves to rationalize the economic inequalities of class society.[59] In terms of Lonergan's structural analysis of the human good I discuss in the next chapter, Novak conflates here Lonergan's second level, the good of order which is in this case is how the economy does work, with the third, which asks whether that economic order is truly valuable. Novak does this by equating the value of an economic system with its ability to satisfy individual desires. Instead, through personal development, these desires must be subordinated to the good of order that, through multiple interlocking schemes of cooperation, supplies these goods to the majority of the population, and to the third level which judges whether these schemes are reflective of cultural decline or progress, for example in the amount of inequality they generate.

What is lacking in Novak's analysis is a more sophisticated understanding of individual self-development. However, "Novak assumes the connection between inequality and self development as given, along with a connection between self-development and the market . . . The major [question] is whether the chief motivation of individual behavior is need for material success and security . . . ."[60] Even John Stuart Mill, Novak's "quintessential liberal"[61] realized that "men shaped by the market were not good enough to make themselves better," since "it makes everybody an aggressive scrambler for his own material benefit."[62] McCarthy and Rhodes, contra Novak and following Mill, argue that "ideals of self realization are constrained if not repressed by the structures of the marketplace. Money can neither be the goal nor measure of success in the spiritual, cultural and social quest for self-realization." Mill and the bishops view creativity as an intellectual, spiritual and political category best realizable within a society that emphasizes values of participatory democracy. Novak, on the other hand, views creativity primarily as wealth creation through development of entrepreneurial skills. Similar to what Robert Bellah and his colleagues claim in *Habits of the Heart* and *The Good Society*, McCarthy and Rhodes argue that, "A broader, economic rationality of ethical and political decisions as they affect the social whole and the common good, is not possible using this form of reasoning."[63]

Criticisms of Novak are not confined to the left. David Schindler, editor of *Communio*, a conservative Catholic journal[64] argues that the dynamic for love that lies at the heart of human relationality sets forth a prior and informing context for the exercise of human creativity. Creativity is thus more participatory than Novak's and other neoconservative's stress on individual self-creativity. Schindler reiterates the need for a suitable anthropology (he terms it ontology) for economics, one which adequately characterizes human sinfulness. Although neoconservatives do stress the importance of the fact of sin and its importance in conceiving a spirituality appropriate for our culture, when self-interest tends to invert a kind of virtue in the hands of neoconservatives, it "produces a mutual selfishness which produces material wealth but by virtue of its intrinsic dynamic creates a spiritual poverty which is exactly coincident with the production of material wealth."[65] Instead of Novak's false dilemma between self-interest and altruism, Schindler proposes a Christian trinitarian perspective, where the giving of self is always simultaneous with receiving from the other. This giving is primarily for the other. For Schindler, Novak perceives no place or need for conversion from sin; there is no "cross" in the spiritual possibilities of capitalism. Novak's understanding of the foundational meanings of personhood, self-interest, and relationality entail a conception of sin that is merely moral, failing to confront the religious ontological meaning that constitutes sin in its primitive structure.[66] Schindler finds Novak "uncritically liberal" in this regard.[67]

Schindler's criticism of liberal society granting primacy in public institutions to the economic dimension also extends to Marxist societies. Individuals in these societies weigh private decisions in manner consistent with such a primacy.[68]

Hobgood and Neo-Marxian Economics

The most important criticism regarding Hobgood's framework is that she lumps all non-radical economists together as those maintaining the economic status quo, as opposed to the transformationist bent of her liberationist model. While she acknowledges there are economic positions that can still be considered "radical," yet non-Marxist, there are also influential economists such as Amartya Sen whose writings consistently challenge mainstream economics. She is right, in that Sen, Lonergan and others who pursue alternative paradigms to orthodox economic theory are not writing from a neo-Marxist positions that Hobgood would identify as radical. But certainly they can be argued to be writing from a different and as I am arguing even in some ways preferable sense of radical—where "radical" is viewed as going to the root of the problem of much of economic theory, as I believe a recovery of an adequate economic anthropology seeks to accomplish. Other non-radical economists have self-consciously identified themselves as pursuing alternative paradigms to neo-Marxism and neo-classical economics without falling back to the organic model, Hobgood's only alternative to the liberationist and orthodox model. The vast majority of economists cited by Hobgood in her section on the radical model are neo-Marxists or else write out of the radical perspective. All others are included in the orthodox model, a group including economists ranging from libertarian Milton Friedman to liberal (in the American sense) Lester Thurow, which is a very wide spectrum indeed. While this typology helps to illuminate important but hidden commonalities, it also obscures much greater difference.

Just as Novak denies the legitimacy of all non-liberal economic analysis offered by CST, in the words of Daniel Rush Finn, Hobgood's advocacy of the radical model also fails "to investigate several important conceptual divergences between CST and the radical model on such issues as state, private property, and productivity of entrepreneurial activity."[69] This leads her to make the same problematic judgment as Novak, that CST offers no original insights (apart from organic social theory) to political economics, and thus should explicitly align itself with their specific preferred economic paradigm. However, her position that CST only combines various models in a somewhat jumbled manner ignores the possibility that CST as a whole comprises in itself (however imperfectly and susceptible to divergent interpretations) a critique of various forms of political economy. Hobgood's "failure to articulate the internal logic of CST on its own terms undercuts her ultimate claim that it is internally inconsistent.[70]

Finally, Hobgood's thesis is that the three paradigms ineffectively compete for the position of fundamental analysis of political economy in the encyclicals. She maintains that because of the inconsistencies arising from this admixture, only one should be explicitly adopted. She prefers the liberationist one because (among other things) it is "more compatible with the normative social justice claims of the Roman Catholic church, particularly its preferential option for the poor," and because of its preferability to the orthodox anthropological assumptions concerning "economic man."[71] However, her position that CST only combines various models in a somewhat jumbled manner, ignores the possibility that CST as a whole comprises in itself (however imperfectly and susceptible to divergent interpretations) a critique of various forms of political economy. As Daniel Rush Finn writes, Hobgood's "failure to articulate the internal logic of CST on its own terms undercuts her ultimate claim that it is internally inconsistent."[72] The next section of this chapter presents two perspectives on the internal consistency of CST, further undercutting Hobgood's and Novak's narrow positions, and further opening the way for alternative perspectives that integrate "normative social justice claims," while also criticizing orthodox theory's "economic man."

The Originality of Catholic Social Teaching

This aspect of the "internal logic" of Catholic Social Thought noted by Finn alludes to the possibility that, despite Novak's and Hobgood's attempts to interpret CST through the lens of either the neo-classical or radical economic paradigm, Catholic Social Thought is able "to stand on its own" using elements from both neo-classical and Marxist (and other) paradigms of economic thought along with its other sources for its commentary on socioeconomic reality. Gregory Baum and John Coleman argue exactly this point.

Gregory Baum argues for the originality of Catholic Social Teaching, which uses, yet transforms, insights from liberal capitalism and Marxist collectivism. In Baum's view, CST regards both world views as deficient, insofar as they are "based in divergent ways on purely economic concepts of the human being."[73] Leo XIII's view of society is in accord with Hobgood's organic model, described by Baum as:

> an organic community, a body politic, involving cooperation, interdependence and hierarchy, that is in need of constant reform and revitalization through ethical conversion: that is through the submission of all members of the community, leaders and people, owners and workers, to the norms of justice."[74]

In this model, government stands above the economic conflict, promotes the common good and protects the weak. Leo found a middle ground in his proposals, defending private property against the claims of socialism and the unionization of labor against that of liberal capitalism. Against this stress on organic unity, post-Vatican II CST has "adopted, transformed and integrated" more radical, modern ideas. According to Baum, these ideas, while not breaking the tradition inaugurated in papal encyclicals by Leo XIII, worked instead to "generate a dialectic within that tradition and thus [to] creatively advanc[e] it" by lifting Leo's organic conceptions "out of the problematic intellectual framework in which they were first conceived, and protect[ing] them from their reductionist implications and problematic consequences." These problematic consequences were described by Hobgood in her discussions of the limitations of organic economic theory. However, Baum argues that the introduction of three radical ideas into CST,[75] especially by Pope John Paul II, allows the church to argue for societal transformation using an original social theory. These three primary ideas are the notion of democracy, the preferential option for the poor, and the "cultural meaning of labor."

CST long remained silent on the topic of liberal democracy due to its early repudiation of liberal society in general, which it viewed as "atomistic individuals joining in a social contract that would guarantee their safety, protect their property and maximize their freedom." However, Baum claims that a concept of democracy different from the liberal concept has emerged in the theological anthropology of John Paul II. This concept "offers a theoretical basis for civil liberties while remaining faithful to the communitarian understanding of society entertained in the Catholic tradition."[76] The anthropology embedded in John Paul II's notion of democracy affirms that human beings have responsibility for their social existence. In contrast to elements of earlier CST that hierarchically delegated social responsibility, John Paul II emphasizes that all people share in responsibility for decision making. In the economic order, LE teaches that workers are subjects of production, a subjectivity that extends to co-responsibility for decisions in the work process. In the political order, SRS teaches that people are also subjects or responsible agents of their collective existence, taking a share in making policy.[77] These concepts differ from liberal social theory because they maximize personal participation instead of personal freedom.[78] Baum argues that, while Catholic theory, "with its emphasis on participation creates social relations, enhances the sense of community and generates social solidarity," liberal theory "promotes individualism and tends to undermine all non-contractual solidarities in society."[79] Baum argues further that this notion of democracy is a radical one because it extends to all institutions, including industrial enterprises, for example.

CST also has integrated another radical notion, the preferential option for the poor. This is characterized by Baum as "a commitment to look upon society from the perspective of the poor, the weak and the marginalized and to give public support to the joint struggle aimed at their emancipation.[80] John Paul II views labor as the historical agent of social change in modern society, as embodying the preferential option for the poor, thus he calls for solidarity of workers and with workers.[81] Contrary to the organic model of society adopted in earlier encyclicals with its emphasis on harmony between the classes, Baum claims that LE adopts a conflictive view of modern society, recognizing that certain sectors of the weak and poor are deprived of justice due them, and should become organized as social movement for the reconstruction of society for the common good.

This emphasis on the common good is different from the Marxist preferential option for the proletariat (itself composed of alienated and exploited workers), because CST promotes justice not only for the sake of improving material conditions but also for the sake of the "ethical and spiritual well-being of the whole society."[82] Indeed, as Lonergan's economic analysis confirms, the ethical and spiritual well-being of individuals is essential to economic well-being as they render intelligent, reasonable, and responsible decisions on how to guide the economy. Further, sinful structures not only produce suffering and misery but also damage the humanity not only of the victims but also of those who benefit materially from these structures, thus weakening the "spiritual substance" of society as a whole. It also differs from the option for the proletariat because as Baum notes, poverty is not defined purely economically. Besides those who are exploited and people deprived of material means, it includes other marginalized groups such as the unemployed, discriminated, physically disabled, elderly, etc.

Thus, just as "the Catholic concept of democracy borrowed elements from the liberal tradition, and transformed them substantively into a social theory in continuity with the communitarian tradition supported by Catholic social teaching," Baum finds that Catholic concept of the preferential option for the poor "has borrowed elements from the Marxist tradition and transformed them substantively into a social theory that recognizes the primacy of the common good and the non-economic aspects of poverty, and thus remains in continuity with Catholic social teaching."[83] As I pointed out in the preceding chapter, Baum argues that thinking of Catholic social teaching as a "third way" between liberal capitalism and Marxist collectivism is superficial, because CST transforms deficient elements based on purely economic concepts of the human being into a more anthropologically correct view, making an "original contribution to social theory and the contemporary debate on the future of society."[84] A third manner in which CST borrows and transforms ideas, maintaining emphases on morals and a fuller economic anthropology, is the view of labor inherent in more recent social encyclicals. While congruent with the Marxist insight that human relationships beings are largely created by systems of work and exchange, it avoids the Marxist mistake of viewing the called-for reorganization of society on a mechanistic, or self-interested basis.

Instead John Paul II, in Baum's view, preserves the primacy of the spiritual in that all things affecting the status of labor must respect the subjectivity, freedom, virtue and creativity of labor, along with the material benefits of the objective fruits of that subjectivity in labor.[85] As with increased participation and the option for the poor, and against in important aspects from the liberal and Marxist traditions, CST preserves the ethical dimension, and perceives it from a new perspective. While sinful structures must be changed, and societies become more just, this social reform must still include a conversion of morals on all levels of society. This does not mean that if only people become more generous and more selfless, social injustice would end, as Leo taught, for this way of teaching ends up serving to maintain the status quo while sinful structures are not addressed. Rather, as Baum states, "in the new perspective of contemporary Catholic social teaching, ethical metanoia is demanded to serve and strengthen the political struggle for the transformation of structures" (61).

John Coleman agrees with Baum, in stating that, "While social Catholicism endorsed neither liberalism nor socialism, it gradually accepted elements or emphases in each, passing them through its own discernment model. In doing so it became a complex, separate modern ideology for social life. . . . Although it shares elements with other traditions, social Catholicism is not [and should not be?] reducible to any of them."[86] Coleman makes four observations concerning papal social ideology. First, he agrees with Novak that CTS' "economic thought, while rightly stressing the need for just distribution, pays too little attention to the necessity of increased productivity as a social good. No one can distribute a wealth that does not exist." Second, more in agreement with Hobgood, Coleman finds that CST "too easily assumes the possibility of social harmony."

This is rooted in CST's reliance on organic modes for society that presumes homogenous values, not recognizing the "full reality of pluralism, especially the political implications of living in societies with especially deeply diverging views on fundamental social values." Third, the tradition has failed "to propose workable alternative institutions and ideals to the regnant liberal and socialist institutions. . . In the absence of alternative models for institutional implementation, social Catholicism will embrace the status quo."[87] Coleman calls for alternative model-thinking which can find some sort of institutional life which avoids the flaws in liberalism and socialism. My view is that the philosophical distancing of CST from liberalism and socialism creates space whereby CST can dialogue with alternative economic thinking with alternative economic models that would lead to alternative social and political institutions. Fourth, Coleman criticizes the distinction between social and the political in CST.

This trivializes political involvement and has led the church to avoid political involvement to protect the institutional interests of the church (i.e., Leo XIII's stance on limiting workers' right to strike, and the Vatican's reproach toward liberation theology). Instead the church has concentrated moralistically on the social question. However, in so doing, I believe the church has been basically correct, except where it has unduly cautioned against political involvement. On the whole, the social question depends on better answering the economic question, along with political involvement. And this involves moral and ethical stances vis-à-vis social systems and the economic principles that underlie them.

Coleman ends up endorsing the leitmotif of "neither capitalism nor socialism" running from Leo XIII to John Paul II, quoting the sociologist David Martin:

> Religion has to find a way of detaching itself from liberalism without contributing to the defeat of freedom and tolerance and of distinguishing itself from socialism without being thrown directly into the arms of socialism's enemies or denigrating the impulse to the equalization of human opportunities.[88]

Conclusion

While both Hobgood and Novak illumine facets of the relationship between Catholic social teaching and economic theory and the historical elements involved, their exclusive positions regarding their preferred economic paradigms tend to obscure any value of CST as an original social theory, especially regarding the economic anthropological critiques and correctives directed by CST regarding neoclassical and Marxian theory.

The views of Gregory Baum and John Coleman regarding the original insights of CST regarding economic theory were presented to buttress this contention, a contention that leads to my argument that 1) there needs to be an alternative paradigm(s) to the neo-classical and Marxian paradigms, one that integrates normative questions and provides a more adequate economic anthropology; and 2) CST can both contribute to and learn from such (a) paradigm(s). The next two chapters turn to Bernard Lonergan's economic thought to investigate its suitability as alternative to liberal capitalism and Marxism as a new economic paradigm more congruent with the more inclusive view of economic agency incorporated in Catholic social teaching.

NOTES

1. Bernard Lonergan, *Method in Theology* (New York: Herder and Herder, 1972), 235.

2. Michael Novak, *The Spirit of Democratic Capitalism* (American Enterprise Institute/Simon and Schuster, 1980), 14.

3. Novak, *Spirit of Democratic Capitalism*, 14.

4. Novak, *Spirit of Democratic Capitalism*, 14.

5. Novak, *Spirit of Democratic Capitalism*, 16.

6. This "tri-partite" model was first proposed by the sociologist Daniel Bell, *The Cultural Contradictions of Capitalism* (New York: Basic Books, 1976). However, contrary to Novak's well-ordered trinity of distinct realms, Bell emphasized the discordance among these realms leading to instability in society. For a more extensive analysis of the reliance of Novak on Bell and the differences between the two, cf. Gary Dorrien, *The Democratic Socialist Vision* (Totowa, NJ: Rowman and Littlefield, 1986), 79. Novak charges that Bell misses the spiritual aspects of capitalism (Gary Dorrien, *Soul in Society: The Making and Renewal of Social Christianity* [Minneapolis: Fortress Press, 1995], 196).

7. Indeed, Pius XII in *Quadragesimo Anno* did a great deal to introduce the concept of social justice into Catholic and Christian social ethics.

8. A verdict that I believe is consistent with Niebuhr's view of human nature and possibility of redemption, but nevertheless would have Reinhold Niebuhr "rolling in his grave" due to Niebuhr's consistent critiques of capitalism.

9. Novak cites the "individualism" of Jeremy Bentham, the "abstractness" of David Ricardo, and the "sentimentality" of John Stuart Mill along with "particular portions of their economic analysis" that do not do justice to the "liberating praxis" of economic liberalism (Novak, *Spirit of Democratic Capitalism*, 13). This is a pretty selective use of his liberal champions.

10. For example, in solidarism's and corporatism's attempt to reintroduce the guild system into modern economic life. This is illustrated in J.R.R. Tolkien's

Lord of the Rings where the simple, pre-industrial life is threatened by the "industrial" forces of evil which seek to wreck havoc on the moral, spiritual and physical landscape.

11. Novak does not offer an explicit definition of economic liberalism, referring the reader to Joseph Schumpeter's discussion of the various types of liberalism in the *History of Economic Analysis*. Schumpeter defines economic liberalism as "the theory that the best way of promoting economic development and general welfare is to remove fetters from the private-enterprise economy and to leave it alone." Schumpeter correspondingly offers a definition of political liberalism: "the sponsorship of parliamentary government, freedom to vote and extension of the right to vote, freedom of the press, divorce of secular from spiritual government, trial by jury, and so on . . . ." Joseph A. Schumpeter, *History of Economic Analysis*, ed. Elizabeth Moody Schumpeter (New York: Oxford University Press, 1954), 394. 'Neoliberals' or 'neoconservatives' such as Novak combine these two liberalisms by seeking a limited role for the state based upon classical economic theory. Neoliberalism/neoconservativism accepts inevitable and sometimes productive restrictions upon the market but seeks to minimize them and reassert the efficacy and even ethical nature of the market sphere.

12. Michael Novak, *The Catholic Ethic and the Spirit of Capitalism* (New York: Free Press, 1993), 37.

13. Done most prominently in *Catholic Ethic and the Spirit of Capitalism*, and *Freedom with Justice: Catholic Social Thought and Liberal Institutions* (San Francisco: Harper & Row, 1984). This book was reissued with a new introduction and concluding chapter as *Catholic Social Thought and Liberal Institutions: Freedom with Justice* (New Brunswick NJ: Transaction Publishers, 1989). Page citations in parentheses in this section will be to this revision.

14. For the Catholic opposition to economic liberalism, see Paul Misner, *Social Catholicism in Europe: From the Onslaught of Industrialization to the First World War* (New York: Crossroad, 1991).

15. For example, Luther's denigration of the Epistle of James in the New Testament because it tended to undermine his doctrine of justification of faith (James 2: 20: "You foolish man, do you want evidence that faith without deeds is useless" [NIV]).

16. Hobgood, *Catholic Social Teaching and Economic Theory: Paradigms in Conflict* (Philadelphia: Temple University Press, 1991), 4. All subsequent pages references in parentheses in this section will be to this book. Her article, "Conflicting Paradigms in Social Analysis," in *The Logic of Solidarity: Commentaries on Pope John Paul II's Encyclical "On Social Concern,"* ed. Gregory Baum and Robert Ellsberg (Maryknoll, NY: Orbis Books, 1989), 167-185, treats the same material in a more summary fashion.

17. The presence of resources to fulfill adequate needs such as food, etc. is

assumed by capitalism.

18. Thought she distinguishes liberal orthodox economists and social theorists (e.g., John Maynard Keynes) from conservative thinkers (Milton Friedman), Hobgood includes in the orthodox model those from both ends of this conservative-liberal spectrum. For example, neoconservatives such as Novak, and liberals such as John Kenneth Galbraith and Lester Thurow belong to this model. This is because, as opposed to radical theorists (e.g., Samuel Bowles and Herbert Gintis) who argue that the market is a facade for what really goes on in social relations, liberal-conservative theory focuses on the market; the person as owner, buyer, seller; and value-free analysis. Thus, most liberal orthodox strategies involve strengthening aspects of welfare capitalism as it currently exists, such as job training, affirmative action, increased education, election of ethically sensitive people to corporate boards, price controls, etc. This seems to me a somewhat simplistic distinction between liberal and orthodox. For example, there are economists such as Amartya Sen who, while not a radical economist, argue that economics is a value-laden enterprise and that economics should incorporate a broader view of the human person than the utilitarian "economic man" of orthodox economics.

19. Hobgood, "Conflicting Paradigms in Economic Analysis," 171. This is why John Milbank argues that organic social theory cannot be mixed with liberal economics as especially John Paul II tries to do. However he does not concur with Hobgood's neo-Marxism, advocating instead a Christian, democratic socialism ("On Complex Space" in *The Word Made Strange: Theology, Language, and Culture* [Cambridge, MA: Blackwell Publishers, 1997]).

20. Milbank, "Conflicting Paradigms," 173.

21. Milbank, "Conflicting Paradigms," 173.

22. Milbank, "Conflicting Paradigms," 174.

23. QA 101.

24. The organic view compared society with the human body, with the organism of the whole body taking priority over individual limbs (69 n.5).

25. Hobgood offers several examples of ways that the church sought to maintain order in society by allying with the old nobility throughout Europe against various socialist movements, (105-106). In Hobgood's view, this fear of socialism caused Leo XIII and Pius XI to misinterpret Aquinas' view of private property, as noted in the previous chapter.

26. Hobgood finds this manifested also in Leo's call for worker's associations to enable labor to offset somewhat the excessive power of capital, while at the same time limiting the power of worker's associations in favor of keeping order. Also, despite maintaining that the wealthy often control political power to the detriment of the poor, Leo relied on the state to exercise a "fatherly solicitude" toward the weak and unprotected poor. Both examples illustrate the importance

of maintaining "equilibrium" in capitalist society of both orthodox and organic theory (Hobgood, *Catholic Social Teaching and Economic Theory*, 108-11).

27. As shown below in Ch. 4, Lonergan's economics proposes a third way of viewing the wage contract.

28. Hobgood argues the reason why Pius placed fewer restrictions on unions than Leo was because Pius did not see a strong role for unions anyway in the corporative scheme he was proposing as a solution to the social problem.

30. Novak is quoting MM 65.

32. I disagree with Novak's claim that while John XXIII does acknowledge the presence of evil in the world, it should be attributed to the pope's "liberal realism" (133). The pope's limited acknowledgment was rightly broadened by *Gaudium et Spes* and Paul VI to attack the structural injustices of capitalism which were viewed by the council and John's successor as transformable, a stance with which Novak takes issue.

33. In my conclusion, I argue that while Lonergan's economics can help us understand why despite Novak's protestations, CST and especially Paul VI are able to promote these elements while still criticizing the liberal capitalism that Novak promotes.

34. Another problem with the liberationist paradigm, most especially in its connection with Marxist thought, is its dialectical relationship with existing political and economic structures that Hobgood associates with liberal orthodox political economic theory, no matter how "enlightened" they may be in incorporating freedoms of religion, assembly, democratic participation, etc. Liberationist reliance on Marx's *aufhebung* or radical overturning of existing political and economic structures leaves unresolved the relation of these freedoms to the radical changes Hobgood desires. By tolerating such strong polarities between the economic rights that she argues more properly belong to socialism and political rights that help make up economic liberalism, she tends to diminish her arguments.

35. According to Hobgood, this caused John XIII to modify the aspect of the principle of subsidiarity proposed by Pius XI and Pius XII (and later Novak as he interprets the principle) that sought to "deny the right of civil authorities to interfere in the operations of organizations closer to the grass roots" (137). John used this principle instead to "emphasize the need for public authority to intervene when power was too great to be left in private hands without damage to the common good, especially the poor" (138). Thus, in John's interpretation, the principle of subsidiarity justified the state collectivizing property if required by the common good.

36. Hobgood quotes from Donal Dorr, *Option for the Poor: A Hundred Years of Catholic Social Teaching*. Rev. ed. (Maryknoll, NY: Orbis Books, 1992), 107.

38. OA 37. Jacques Maritain elaborates the social implications of a "New

Christendom" as a "concrete historical ideal" in *Integral Humanism* (New York: Charles Scribner's Sons, 1938).

39. PP 34. An example of an organization that seeks to promote integral development is the United States Campaign for Human Development.

40. Novak, *The Catholic Ethic and the Spirit of Capitalism*, 85.

41. That capitalism inverts the priority of labor over capital (LE 60).

42. For example, Novak cites Gregory Baum's argument that with LE the church has shifted to the left. Cf. Baum, "John Paul II's Encyclical on Labor," *Readings in Moral Theology No. 5: Official Catholic Social Teaching,* ed. Charles E Curran and Richard A. McCormick (New York: Paulist Press, 1986), 3.

43. Similarly, Paul Lakeland takes the pope to task for adopting too narrowly the "teaching model" of effecting social change *(Theology and Critical Theory* [Nashville: Abingdon Press, 1990], 76).

44. Gregory Baum, *The Priority of Labor: A Commentary on "Laborem Exercens," Encyclical Letter of Pope John Paul II* (New York: Paulist Press, 1982), 3.

45. A common neo-Marxist, liberationist critique of economic theory is that "economics is class," pure and simple (as I have heard in personal conversations with and from conference presentations from liberationist theologians). Therefore any development of an economic theory which seeks to provide true economic premises to be followed responsibly by economic agents is by definition "idealistic moral methodology." I challenge this assumption in my discussion of Lonergan's economic thought in the next two chapters.

46. This lack of structural analysis in LE in favor of moral idealism and preference for elements of orthodox analysis has ramifications for both John Paul's discussion of human work and his discussion of appropriate agents of social change, aspects that at first glance seem to reflect a Marxist understanding. As in Marx, work in LE is seen to have a positive role in that work properly should allow people to experience joy in their creativity, solidarity with others, and expression of human dignity. However, Hobgood says LE upholds the purely positive nature of all work, even jobs that are full of drudgery. By describing all work as full of both suffering and the joy of creativity, the encyclical ignores the segmentation of work that creates social class. By ignoring the class segregation of work and by affirming all of work without differentiation, it implicitly endorses this existing segmentation. Thus it remains in harmony with orthodox economic theory that treats all persons as equally free to participate in economic activity (Hobgood, *Catholic Social Teaching and Economic Theory*, 181).

According to Hobgood, the pope's discussion of social agency also looks at first like a radical perspective. The pope declares that there has been a general struggle going on between workers in all societies and owners of the means of production and he calls for ever new movements of solidarity of workers. But as with its discussion of work, LE's failure to make a structural analysis of class constrains this effort in that the workers' struggles the pope supports are for alleviation of poverty and hunger, not for changes in basic power structures, including that of basic class structures.

47. Hobgood, *Catholic Social Teaching and Economic Theory*, 11-12.

48. Cf. E.J. Dionne, "Capitalism With Soul: Novak on the Catholic Ethic. Review of Michael Novak, *The Catholic Ethic and the Spirit of Capitalism*," *Commonweal* 21 (May 21, 1993): 11.

49. Cf. J. A. Varacalli, "Review of Michael Novak, *Freedom With Justice: Catholic Social Thought and Liberal Institutions*," *Religious Studies and Theology* 6 (Jan.-May 1986): 52.

50. Herbert T. Mayer, "Review of Michael Novak, *Freedom With Justice: Catholic Social Thought and Liberal Institutions*," *Currents in Theology and Mission* 13 (June 1986): 177.

51. Novak overstates the case though when he claims that many of the values and institutions lauded in CST are not original, but derivative from other traditions including the liberal tradition. For example, Matthew Lamb cogently argues that *Dignitatis Humanae* ("Declaration of Religious Freedom)," of Vatican II, co-authored by John Courtney Murray, S.J., did not draw its claims of religious freedom from liberal notions, derived from Hobbes, Hume and Locke, but "on the social nature of man and in the very nature of religion" (*Dignitatis Humanae*, 10; quoted in Matthew Lamb, "Modernism and Americanism Revisited Dialectically: A Challenge for Evangelization," *Communio* 21 [Winter 1994]: 630-662).

52. For genetic vs. dialectical differences see Bernard Lonergan, *Insight: A Study of Human Understanding*, vol. 3 of *Collected Works of Bernard Lonergan*, ed. Frederick E. Crowe and Robert M. Doran (Toronto: University of Toronto Press, 1992) 242-67, 426-55, 484-507, and *Method in Theology*, (New York: Seabury Press: 1972), 236-37.

53. The Lay Commission on Catholic Social Teaching and the U.S. Economy, *Toward the Future: Catholic Social Thought and the U.S. Economy: A Lay Letter* (Notre Dame, IN: Quodlibetal Publications, 1984).

54. George E. McCarthy and Royal W. Rhodes, *Eclipse of Justice: Ethics and Economics and the Lost Traditions of American Catholicism* (Maryknoll, NY: Orbis Books, 1992), 44.

55. McCarthy and Rhodes, *Eclipse of Justice*, 46-47.

56. Craig Nessan, "Review of Michael Novak, *Freedom With Justice: Catholic Social Thought and Liberal Institutions*," *Dialog* 25 (Spring 1988): 156.

57. McCarthy and Rhodes argue further that both Novak and *Economic Justice for All*'s synthesis of CST and the "American experiment" does not

recognize the conflict between moral principles of CST and the structures of American society (*Eclipse of Justice*, 44).

58. McCarthy and Rhodes, *Eclipse of Justice*, 46.

59. McCarthy and Rhodes, *Eclipse of Justice*, 76.

60. McCarthy and Rhodes, *Eclipse of Justice*, 77.

61. Novak, *Freedom With Justice*, 81-107.

62. McCarthy and Rhodes, *Eclipse of Justice*, 80.

63. McCarthy and Rhodes, *Eclipse of Justice*, 84.

64. May we someday anticipate an "Instructions to Neoconservatives" letter from the Vatican, expressing theological concerns with Novak and others' writings, analogous to the "Instruction on Certain Aspects of the 'Theology of Liberation'" (Sacred Congregation for the Doctrine of the Faith, 1984)?

65. David L. Schindler, "The Church's 'Worldly' Mission," *Communio* 18 (Fall 1991): 387.

66. David L. Schindler, "Christology and the Church's 'Worldly' Mission: Response to Michael Novak," *Communio* 19 (Spring 1992): 174.

67. Schindler, "Christology," 178.

68. Schindler, "Christology," 173.

69. Daniel Rush Finn, "Review of Mary E. Hobgood, *Catholic Social Teaching and Economic Theory*," *Horizons* 20 (Spring 1993): 185.

70. Finn, "Review of Hobgood," 186.

71. Hobgood, *Catholic Social Teaching and Economic Theory*, 247.

72. Finn, "Review of Hobgood," 186.

73. Gregory Baum, "The Originality of Catholic Social Teaching," in *Rerum Novarum: A Hundred Years of Catholic Social Teaching*, edited by John Coleman and Gregory Baum (London: SCM Press; Philadelphia: Trinity Press International, 1991), 61.

74. Baum, "Originality of Catholic Social Teaching," 55.

75. However, these "radical" ideas are not isomorphic to Hobgood's radical paradigm. For example the notion of democracy falls more closely to the liberal paradigm adopted by Novak.

76. Baum, "Originality of Catholic Social Teaching," 56.

77. Baum, "Originality of Catholic Social Teaching," 56.

78. Although Novak argues that freely entered contractual and non-contractual association serves to increase participation in political, economic and social processes. See John A. Ryan, *A Living Wage: Its Ethical and Economic Aspects* (New York: Macmillan, 1906), 43-65; Hollenbach, *Claims in Conflict: Retrieving and Renewing the Catholic Human Rights Dimension* (New York: Paulist Press, 1991); and Michael Schuck, *That They May Be One: The Social Teaching of the Papal Encyclicals, 1740-1989* (Washington, DC: Georgetown

University Press, 1991), 178-180, for how Catholic social teaching regards human dignity as the foundation of justice, over against the rights allocated by liberal theory or the state.

79. Baum, "The Originality of Catholic Social Teaching," 57.

80. Baum, "Originality of Catholic Social Teaching," 58.

81. *Laborem Exercens* 8.

82. Baum, "Originality of Catholic Social Teaching," 59. Hobgood criticizes CST as avoiding struggle against others (i.e., LE 8, 20) because this stance works toward derailing radical social change in favor of the oppressed, which may end up upsetting societal structures (Hobgood, *Catholic Social Teaching and Economic Theory*, 183-84).

83. Baum, "Originality of Catholic Social Teaching," 59.

84. Baum, "Originality of Catholic Social Teaching," 62.

85. This has been a knock against socialism that it wants mainly to increase size of the pie and share of the pie going to workers.

86. John A. Coleman, S.J., "Neither Liberal nor Socialist," in *One Hundred Years of Catholic Social Thought: Celebration and Challenge*, ed. John A. Coleman, S.J. (Maryknoll: Orbis Books, 1991), 36.

87. Coleman, "Neither Liberal nor Socialist," 39.

88. Coleman, "Neither Liberal nor Socialist," 40; quoting David Martin, *The Dilemmas of Contemporary Religion* (Oxford: Basil Blackwell, 1978), 73.

CHAPTER 3

HEALING IN LONERGAN'S ECONOMIC THOUGHT: TOWARD AN ADEQUATE ECONOMIC METHOD

The main issue in my examination in the first half of this book of the different approaches of Novak, Hobgood, and Catholic social teaching has been economic anthropology and its importance in constructing adequate economic paradigms. The purpose of the second half is to investigate how the thought of Bernard Lonergan, an important Christian thinker and polymath[1] can contribute to economic methodology, economic anthropology, and the task of constructing an alternative macroeconomic paradigm. It will also probe the significance of an alternative understanding of the economy that avoids the "value-free" assertions of positivistic mainstream and Marxian economics, and that expresses a more humanistic and Christian view of the person.

One of the earliest titles of *Macroeconomic Dynamics: An Essay in Circulation Analysis* (ECA) was "Towards a Pure Theory of Social Economics.[2] Though later changed, this suggests an obvious connection between his economic thought and alternative economic theories to capitalism and socialism such as Heinrich Pesch's "solidarism" that was inspired by *Rerum Novarum* and in turn inspired *Quadragesimo Anno.* The discarded title was probably not an attempt by Lonergan to place his own thought in direct relationship to any particular variant of social economics as exhibited in Pesch and *Quadragesimo Anno* extant when Lonergan was writing ECA from 1930-1944. Rather, it shows that Lonergan shares a view common among economists that were not devotees of the marginalist, orthodox school: that economics necessarily must include an explicit consideration of the moral aspect of economic theory. In classical economic thought, this latter conviction goes back at least to Adam Smith, is continued through Alfred Marshall, only to be eclipsed in the "marginalist revolution" beginning with Marshall and others in the 1870's that abstracted individual economic agency from its social context and by Marxist economics who viewed economic agency as determined by its social context—eliminating moral freedom from economic decision-making. Against the marginalist mainstream and the Marxist alternative, for Lonergan and many other economists of this period, any adequate economics must be a "social economics," guided by observant, intelligent, reasonable and responsible moral agents. As discussed in Ch. 1, that has also been the dominant approach of magisterial Catholic social teaching beginning with *Rerum Novarum*'s response to the "social problem."[3]

Lonergan himself took a course in economic ethics at Heythrop College with Lewis Watt where undoubtedly *Rerum Novarum* with its discussion of such issues as the justifications for the just wage was a principal text.[4] Lonergan's economic thought is certainly conversant with the tone of the social economic approach to economic morality in the work of Heinrich Pesch,[5] whose thought was instrumental in the writing of *Quadragesimo Anno.* So while Lonergan sought to provide an economic analysis that went beyond papal economics, he was influenced by the views of the person inherent in Catholic social economics as embodied in the works of Watt, Pesch, Leo XIII and Pius XI, and second, by the concern among these writers to find a new type of political economy alternative to that of capitalism and socialism. This is evidenced in the title of one of Lonergan's two economic manuscripts, begun in the 1930's, *Towards a New Political Economy.*

Connection of ECA to Lonergan's Later Writings

Lonergan's economic methodology and anthropology are found implicitly and to some extent explicitly in his books, and scattered throughout various of his essays and articles, most of which touch only tangentially upon critiques of mainstream and Marxian economics.[6] However, *Insight* and *Method in Theology* follow a three-fold scheme of progress, decline, and redemption (what Lonergan earlier in his career termed "renaissance"), which Lonergan developed in the 1930s at the same time he was writing ECA.[7] This schema was aimed at providing a philosophy/theology of history to correct Marxist and liberal views of history. The intimate relationship between Lonergan's writings on economics and his later published writings on philosophy and history are highlighted in the title he gave to the course he taught on economics at Boston College in the twilight of his life, "Macroeconomics and the Dialectic of History." Aside from these considerations, Lonergan provides enough material to construct a Lonerganian economic methodology critical of, yet in dialogue, with mainstream and Marxist economic methodology.

While there is some attention to methodology in the economics manuscript, ECA itself deals most directly with elaborating a macroeconomic theory. So the task of constructing an explicit economic methodology must rely on investigating his later works. The question arises, then: what is the relationship between ECA and Lonergan's later philosophical, theological and social thought as presented extensively in *Insight* and *Method in Theology* and in his published and unpublished articles? The answer centers on issues of scientific method, found especially in *Insight*[8] and questions of human moral agency and community, found mainly in *Method in Theology*.[9] An integration of Lonergan's positions on these matters into an explicit economic methodology and anthropology can critically dialogue with positions taken in mainstream and Marxian methodology and anthropology, and contribute to methodological debates in economics and Christian social ethics that I addressed extensively in discussing and critiquing Novak and Hobgood in the previous chapter.

Interestingly, there are remarks that appear to allude to the value of ECA's analysis throughout Lonergan's later writings. For example, in *Insight* Lonergan writes, "An economy can falter, though resources and capital equipment abound, though skill cries for its opportunity and desire for skill's product, though labor asks for work and industry is eager to employ it; then one can prime the pumps and make X occur; but because the schemes are not functioning properly, X fails to recur" (235). In a similar vein, in *Method in Theology* Lonergan complains of the inadequacy of "iron laws" of economics in the same context that he speaks of moving away from the scientific ideal revolving around necessity (280, 315). The most conspicuous instance where he relates the epistemological and methodical issues of his more famous works to ECA occurs in his article "Healing and Creating."[10] In this essay, Lonergan wonders whether economists will ever learn to apply indeterminacy to human action as physicists have learned to apply it to atoms (from the Heisenberg principle), much less free will. This is a clear criticism of the mechanist views of human nature of mainstream economists. By eliciting an explicit economic methodology alongside Lonergan's macroeconomic theory, I wish to show that his methodology, economic anthropology, social thought and economic theory combine to provide more than a new macroeconomics. He is also presenting an alternative economic paradigm to mainstream and Marxian economics.

The differences between Lonergan's approach and that of mainstream and Marxist economic methodology center mainly on Lonergan's emphasis on the role of human intelligence, the corresponding intelligibility of economic process, and moral economic agency in the pursuit of the good of economic order. The point here is that economies are not mechanisms which merely take inputs and spew outputs to be distributed by the impersonal market, as mainstream economics would have it. Rather, Lonergan holds that the development of the economy is not only intelligible, but intelligent. As he puts it, because economic systems are "increasingly intelligent, increasingly the fruit of insights and decisions, the analogy of merely natural process becomes less and less relevant."[11]

The importance of explanatory structure in the social sciences and in economics in particular is underlined by William Matthews, who argues that, "a clarification of its [economic process] nature is one of the really great intellectual challenges of the end of the present century. In whatever area of experience we are involved, without understanding we are blocked, we cannot go on, nor project our way forward."[12] In the next chapter, I will investigate Lonergan's specific use of analytic methods appropriate to economics as a human and social science in an attempt to provide the sort of understanding and explanatory power needed for making intelligent, reasonable and responsible individual and socio-political decisions. Such decisions, in turn, can promote economic functioning and help provide an adequate standard of living for the entire community, instead of the current situation where those in the top income classes are taking a larger and larger proportion of a seemingly smaller and smaller pie.[13] Lonergan's conception of the structure of the economic human good instead stresses cooperation relying upon human value-choices, self-transcendence, conversion, and "terminal" values, beyond mechanist conceptions of the achievement of the human good.

Various commentators authors have placed Lonergan's epistemology, views on scientific method, and his social criticism in the context of Lonergan's philosophy/ theology of history. Their approach tends to follow Lonergan's own location of these issues in relation to the rest of his thought. Other works on Lonergan's thought have treated his views on these issues on the scale of being a "meta-methodology"[14] or "an organon for our time."[15] By contrast, I select or abstract particular aspects of Lonergan's thought on these matters in order to compare Lonergan's economic methodology with that of orthodox economics and to some extent that of Marxist and social economics. My limited attempt here to link Lonergan's gnoseological and methodological writings to his social thought comes closest to authors that have linked these writings to the structure of the human good, social progress, and political theology,[16] but again my more narrow approach focuses on the human good as economic.

"Generalized Empirical Method"

Any notion of the human good is necessarily a vague notion. As Terry Tekippe points out, it is "one of those very basic notions for which it is difficult, if not impossible, to find something more fundamental in terms of which to define them; and any definition given must be analogical, because the good is an analogical reality." The classic definition of the good is that it is what all things desire (*bonum est quod omnia appetunt*).[17] However, the human good can be described with precision greater that which meets universal desires. Lonergan identifies a three-level hierarchical structure of the human good: that of appetite, the good of order, and that of judgment and cultural values. The human good is a complex set of recurring schemes, a product of material resources, human drives and feelings, intelligence, values, deliberation and action. As a product of material resources, human drives, and human intelligence and distorted by human bias, it is subject to decline as well as progress. To investigate the effect of human intelligence, values, and bias upon the human good, Lonergan develops a generalized empirical method, or a critical realism, which requires that human scientists pay attention to the data of consciousness *as well as* the data of sense. Lonergan's method points the way for the human sciences to empirically, critically, dialectically, and normatively promote the human good and help to reverse social decline.[18]

For Lonergan then, the possibility of achieving the human good is in large part dependent upon the contribution of critical human science.[19] His positions on the possibility of a critical human science are directly related to his views on the achievement of scientific objectivity. These views, in turn, grow out of his views on human knowing, in that he argues both scientific and practical knowing contain an invariant structure or method.[20] According to Lonergan, this normative structure allows us to reach reasonable judgments in ethics and economics.[21] Pivotal to distinguishing his position from empiricism and forms of positivism is his broadening of what is considered empirical in empirical science (or just science) to include the data of consciousness.

Lonergan on Human Knowing[22]

Since Lonergan's positions on human knowing are more like a "way," to discuss his work on cognition as a cognitional "theory" is somewhat a misinterpretation.[23] To fully grasp the object of Lonergan's cognitional writings requires that the reader self-appropriate his or her own cognitional activity and knowing. Such self-appropriation is the aim of Lonergan's seminal work on human cognition, *Insight: A Study of Human Understanding*. However, in order to discuss Lonergan's cognitional thought here, it is necessary to briefly summarize this "way" of epistemology.

Fortunately, Lonergan himself presented helpful summaries of the extensive material on cognition in *Insight*, in "Cognitional Structure," *Understanding and Being*, and *Method in Theology*.[24] Lonergan himself summarizes the aim of *Insight*: "Thoroughly understand what it is to understand, and not only will you understand the broad lines of all there is to be understood but so you will possess a fixed base, an invariant pattern, opening upon all further developments of understanding."[25] His concern in his cognitional theory is to, "in the procedures of the human mind . . . discern a transcendental method, that is, a basic pattern of operations employed in every cognitional enterprise."[26] This is aimed at "revealing human knowing as a dynamic structure."[27]

For Lonergan, human knowing is a dynamic compound structure of experience, understanding and judging. It is an activity which is "self-assembling" and "self-constituting"[28] and it is whole, in that "each part is what it is in virtue of its functional relationship to other parts; there is no part that is not determined by the exigencies of other parts," such that "so that the removal of any part would destroy the whole, and the addition of any further part would be ludicrous."[29] Therefore, according to this conception, none of the activities involved in human knowing (seeing, hearing, smelling, touching and tasting; inquiring, imagining, understanding, conceiving; and reflecting, weighing the evidence, and judging), are *in themselves* human knowing. For example, against empiricism, sense activities such as seeing, hearing, smelling, touching, tasting are not knowing, without the "accompanying glimmer of understanding."[30] Against idealism, acts of understanding (inquiring, imagining, understanding and conceiving) require prior presentations of sense, for without these, there is nothing to understand, and thus no occurrence of understanding. Further, against most views of human knowing beyond empiricism and idealism, sense combined with understanding is not sufficient for knowing either. To sense presentations (experience) and understanding, Lonergan adds the role of judging (reflecting, weighing the evidence, judging) which enables one to make judgments of at least probable fact.[31] So finally, like experience alone; understanding alone; and even understanding combined with experience; judgment alone is not knowing. Judgment without understanding is arrogance, and passing judgment independently of experience is to "bypass facts."[32] Furthermore, human knowing in Lonergan's schema occurs intentionally as conscious, intelligent, and rational, not from any "blind natural process." This human intentionality Lonergan terms the "unrestricted desire to know" and it is something possessed at least potentially by everyone.[33]

Attainment of truth is thus achieved when one's reflective understanding guides the process of knowing from data to intelligence to judging, from the experiential into a judgment whether or not "a" is so, in other words whether an insight is a correct apprehension of what is really going on. Judgment is thus the operation of intentional consciousness that responds to the further question of "Is it so?" and requires an affirmative or negative answer to whether, in fact, "a" is "b," or in other words whether the conditions for a to be b are fulfilled. If indeed a is judged to be b, the judgment that a is b is "virtually [as if] unconditioned." The conditioned judgment is virtually unconditioned because there are no further relevant questions to be asked—its conditions have been fulfilled.

Lonergan is therefore a realist philosopher in the Thomist tradition in that the truth that is acknowledged in the mind through reflective understanding corresponds to reality.[34]Critical realism is different from other types of realism (such as naive realism and neo-Thomism) in that he explains what knowing is and how it takes place: the real is what we come to know through grasping the virtually unconditioned. As Lonergan puts it, "objectivity is the fruit of authentic subjectivity"—making sure one is paying attention, cultivating and pursuing the questions arising from intentional consciousness (our underlying unrestricted desire to know), and making sure one asks all the relevant questions needed to make sure one's judgment has fulfilled conditions for concluding that an insight, a hunch, a hypothesis—a potential piece of knowledge—is indeed true.[35] Of course the operations of consciousness arise in communities of concern and inquiry wider than the particular individual.

The effort of authenticity required to come to pay attention to experience, notice patterns in it and make reasonable judgments, Lonergan names the transcendental imperatives: Be attentive, be intelligent, be reasonable. However, human authenticity requires that one act or not act responsibly in response to probable judgments of fact achieved in the cognitional process. One's actions must be consistent with one's knowing in order to be authentic. Thus an added imperative is added: Be responsible.[36] The actual verification of critical realism or "knowing knowing" is a matter of self-appropriation, which is difficult, because while one may routinely experience, understand and judge, rarely does one advert to what exactly goes on without much concentration and intent on knowing what goes on and when one is knowing. While *Insight* is a 700+ page compendium of cognitional theory, exercises designed to help the reader appropriate his or her "data of consciousness," and critiques of other positions, Lonergan does offer a more common sense defense of his positions, for:

> not even behaviorists claim that they are unaware whether or not they see or hear, taste or touch. Not even positivists preface their lectures and books with the frank avowal that never in their lives did they have the experience of understanding anything whatever. Not even relativists claim that never in their lives did they have the experience of making a rational judgment. Not even determinists claim that never in their lives did they have the experience of making a responsible choice.[37]

But what guarantees that even authentic attendance to one's subjectivity leads to objectivity? In his treatment of this more metaphysical question, Lonergan holds that first of all, the intention of human cognitional activity is intrinsically objective, that is, human knowing is self-transcending. This self-transcendence is realized when human knowing reaches an unconditioned, that is when it has answered all relevant questions and positively fulfilled conditions of a truthful statement (e.g., whether this growling, snarling animal before me is a rabid dog—something that can not be reliably determined just by "taking a look."). In other words, correct judgments of fact take us beyond being "locked up" in ourselves by fulfilling all the necessary conditions. This results in conclusions "independent" of the subject seeking to attain correct understanding. In Lonergan's words, "For a judgment that this or that is so reports, not what appears to me, not what I imagine, not what I think, not what I wish, not what I would be inclined to say, not what seems to me, but what is so." Given the human condition, overcoming "what I imagine," "what *I* think," and what I and my ego wishes to be takes some effort and dedication.

Similarly, moral self-transcendence goes beyond dramatic, individual and group bias to objective value and results in benevolence and beneficence, of honest collaboration and true love.[38] The intention of the dynamic structure of human knowing is being in its totality. The intention is unrestricted, because there is "nothing that we cannot question." It is also comprehensive, "for questioning probes every aspect of everything; its ultimate goal is the universe in its full concreteness." So the "being" intended in our infinite questions for intelligence and judgment is identical with reality, since both being and reality embrace "the concrete totality of everything."[39] Lonergan calls philosophical positions that do not regard human knowing as the compound of experience, understanding and judgment, as "counterpositions."

There are two basic counterpositions to critical realism, naive realism and idealism (termed eternal adversaries by Frederick Crowe and Robert Doran).[40] Naive realism is a position for which knowledge consists primarily in "taking a look"; the idealist position is held by those that grant the role of intelligence in knowledge, but do not grant the proper role to judgment concerning whether conditions are fulfilled to grant that reality has been reached.[41] While it is beyond the scope of this book to compare Lonergan's epistemology to that of Aristotle, Aquinas, Hume, Kant, etc., much less epistemological views involved in hermeneutics and post-modernism, Lonergan's epistemological views do have important implications when compared with positions on human knowing taken by economic methodology of mainstream economists.

A final note regarding Lonergan's cognitional theory. He maintains that the fundamental elements of his cognitional theory are invulnerable because one has to assume his basic account of human knowing in order to challenge it. So, if one claims that he has overlooked some important aspect, one reveals that there is an experiential level to human knowing. Challenging Lonergan's interpretation of the data on human knowing presupposes the existence of an intellectual level at which experience is apprehended. To argue that his account has "failed to fulfill this or that condition necessary for affirming its truth" (for example claiming that Lonergan is too optimistic about people really wanting to know reality), presupposes the critical or reflective level involved in human knowing of judgment, along with the intellectual level being judged and the experience that is conceptualized at the intellectual level."[42]

Further, such criticism also reveals the dimension of moral transcendence, because such lengthy, risky and possibly frustrating criticism would be undertaken "only as a result of a judgment of value and a decision."[43] While Lonergan would agree that the operations of and relations among of intentional consciousness are not universal but only in the sense that those who do not follow this pattern are not being authentically human—they in some measure are oblivious to significant data, being "stupid" in not noticing patterns in the data, jump to conclusions without asking questions for judgment, or act without sufficient recognition of "what is going on" in the situation. However, it is one thing to acknowledge that everybody to some extent does not follow through with their subjective exigency toward intellectual and moral transcendence—it is another thing when a human science (here economics) is not sufficiently observant, intelligent, and reasonable and thus does not lead people toward responsible decisions and actions.

Scientific Method

Science is the preeminent example and a specialization of the general process of knowing outlined above (we are for a moment suspending the questions that motivate scientists, especially economists, and elements that can frustrate the "pure desire to know" that it is the basis of authentic science). It is a pursuit of knowledge that aims to know the "nature" of a particular entity.[44] The scientific process, which Lonergan stresses is a method, not a "toolbox," begins with selection of data in accord with the heuristic anticipations which guide the scientist's inquiry. An initial insight into this data reveals a possible explanation for particular data in question. An example is Galileo's insight that there is a correlation between the instantaneous velocity of a falling body and the length of time it has been falling.

This methodical process also makes the emergence of insights more likely. The new ideas that emerge as expressions of these insights can be formulated as hypotheses and checked experimentally. In Galileo's case, he painstakingly tested his hypothesis under all possible circumstances (except in the perfect vacuum, the only circumstance in which the law of acceleration can hold perfectly). Further testing either confirms the law or enables the scientist to discard the insight, or find further data that can lead her to correct it or move on to the discovery of further laws. Thus scientific method is a self-correcting process, "which proceeds by methodical inquiry to the accumulation of more extensive and precisely specified data, more inclusive and rigorously formulated hypotheses, and to an ever closer fit between the data and the consequences of the hypotheses."[45] These resulting verified scientific theories concern the relation of things-in-themselves, going beyond relations of things-to-us.

A prime example is the periodic table, where atoms were classified historically in the history of chemistry at first in observational terms of quantity, etc., with more knowledge added on until relationships were discovered that enabled scientists not only to classify atoms, but to predict the discovery of new atoms. These predictions relied on discovering principles in the arrangement of atoms (protons, nuclei, electrons, etc.) that are relations of things-to-themselves. In this process, elements became defined by their relations to one another, not in terms, at least in their ordinary meaning, of substance, quantity, quality, etc. Objects determined by relations to each other, have no immediate relation to us, to our sensible apprehensions, yet they form the basis from which more than three hundred thousand compounds can at least in principle be composed. In this process, "Modern science employs the procedure of withdrawing from the relations of things to us, considering the relations of things to one another and attending to similarities there, in order to determine the 'nature of. . . .'"[46]

Science is a specialization of the unrestricted desire to know that is part of all authentic subjectivity. Scientific knowledge thus results from "explicit, methodical effort to arrive at knowledge for its own sake without paying any attention to the practical utility that may arise from it."[47] While this may sound extreme in that it discounts the very pertinent reality that scientists are motivated toward pursuing knowledge for particular ends (from helping the human race to promoting one's career). But to achieve really useful knowledge, scientific investigation must sublimate personal, social and even religious desires to questions of what constitutes objective fact and theory. Otherwise, the results will be manipulated consciously or subconsciously toward the results one is hoping to get. Lonergan's view is thus differentiated from instrumentalist views of scientific method.

Scientific Realism

As in the general process of knowing, scientific method relies on insight into experience (data), conceptualization of these insights (hypotheses and theories) and judging as to the truth of the theory (verification). Another example of scientific verification is given by the scientific process that seeks to know whether it is true whether or not the hypothesis (which comes from an insight into the data) that oxygen is a better explanation for what our respiratory system seeks in the air we breathe than the theory of phlogiston. As Hugo Meynell relates, "We have then to determine what the evidence would be which would induce us to deny with good reason to accept each of these theories. Next we establish what relevant evidence there is by observation or experiment, and so have adequate grounds for affirming, at least provisionally the oxygen theory and rejecting phlogiston theory."[48] The answer is only provisional since it is conceivable that evidence might come to light in the future which would lead scientists to abandon oxygen theory. Modern science is the current "best guess" into the nature of things.

Lonergan's position thus is in agreement with positivists that theories need to be verified, yet avoids the well-known difficulty with the positivist denial of the truth of normative statements; namely the positivist claim that for statements to be verified they must be strictly empirically verified is itself a normative or value judgment which cannot be strictly empirically verified itself. For Lonergan, scientific method in itself is normative, because it follows the normativity of the process of human knowing present in human questioning, reflection and objectivity. This normativity does not require to be posited by a theory that steps outside that theory to verify it, as positivism does. Instead it must be verified, or better appropriated, by the knowing person, who identifies in his or her sense and intellectual activities, that she or he actually senses (or notices data), grasps patterns in that data, and makes judgments about whether those patterns are indeed accurate.

Lonergan's transcendental method, as opposed to positivistic philosophy of science, thus relies to a great extent not only on the data of observation but also the data of consciousness, because communities of scientists rely upon questions for intelligence and reflection. Positivists, by neglecting the role of understanding and judgment (these roles it denigrates as psychologism) in our knowledge of the world are unable to provide verified theories which state how the world at least probably is. In Lonergan's approach, the world as it really is, is the "term asymptotically approached by intelligent and reasonable inquiry into the data of experiences."[49] Considering that mainstream economic theory is essentially positivist, providing a theory which claims more appropriate criteria for scientific understanding than positivism has important implications.

Method in the Human Sciences

A major question in the philosophy of science is the relationship of the natural to the human sciences.[50] Lonergan's position is that first of all, human sciences must proceed roughly the same way as in the natural sciences, following the empirical method common to all science.[51] However, their different subject matters (humans vs. for example, electrons) entail different philosophical and scientific exigencies. Since humans possess at least minimally potential self-control and free-will, explanation can still be sought in the human as well as the natural sciences, but prediction cannot be a major goal as it is in influential spheres of economic, political science and sociology.

The possibility of scientific objectivity can be extended to the human sciences, but with important caveats concerning the objects of scientific analysis: human subjects. Lonergan's view must again be distinguished from major competing interpretations. While positivism also seeks objective explanations that are publicly verifiable, "it eliminates as quite irrelevant to the scientific explanation of human behavior the accounts given by the agents themselves," because these explanations are by nature individual and subjective. For example, as Meynell points out, the orthodox Marxist view claims that unless an agent or an observer can describe the agent's behavior in terms of class conflict and the economic situation, that explanation is ideological.[52] Or if a manager reports that she actually gives bonuses to her workers to show her gratitude for their work, a mainstream economist would view this as some expression of self-interest related to increasing their productivity, etc.

In the normative conceptions of human knowing and action discussed above, the human behavior studied in the social sciences must be explained as "due to a certain mixture of attention and inattention, of intelligence and failure in intelligence, or reason or lack of reason,"[53] plus responsibility, or lack of responsibility. A crucial aspect for understanding human behavior then is the regular failure of humans to suppress unwanted insights. Lonergan terms these failures, or aberrations of understanding, biases or scotoses. The different types of bias—dramatic, individual, group, and general—will need to be discussed at length below.

Social scientists use their own experience, intelligence and reason to come to know the range of experience and inexperience, intelligence and lack of intelligence and so on, which account for human behavior of others. By ruling out any explanation in these terms positivists end up unable to account satisfactorily for their own scientific endeavor, and incapable of objective explanations, their stated goal. With this fuller sense of economic agency, Lonergan's conception of human behavior and its use in social scientific analysis also clearly runs far away from the mainstream economic anthropological concept of "economic man" in its consideration of cultural values and he exigencies of human reasoning.

Thus scientific method in the natural sciences must be distinguished from appropriate methodology in the human sciences. As Lonergan points out, this lack of distinction is at the root of misunderstandings in economics and other human sciences (even raising the question whether positivistic economics should even be considered a science):

> The empirical human sciences have developed in recent centuries, and they cannot be classed with natural sciences. However, as human

> sciences are actually carried out at the present time, to a large extent, they can be so classed. Trying to ride the bandwagon of physicists and chemists, the science of man is pursued as though man were just another electron or another atom. . . . For if scientific knowledge of man is in terms of types of knowledge that are possible for electrons, then there is no question of developing a science of man that can speak to man.[54]

What is distinctive about the human community studied by the human sciences is that it is constituted by meaningful activities, including the very process of scientific method used to study these meaningful activities. So, in economics, for example, both the cognitional activities of the members of the scientific community and "the production, exchange and financial activities of the members of the economic community" are meaningful.[55] The explanatory function of the human sciences concerns the question of whether there are patterns of relations among these activities. As in all science, theoretical explanation is sought by determining the "appropriate dynamic system of significant variables, and their correlative functional relations."[56] However, in the human sciences, since agents are intentional, the significant variables are constituted by meaningful human activities. As a product of human science, such explanatory structures must be empirical, critical, dialectical and normative. Each of these dimensions will be discussed below.

Although both seek to be empirical, the method of human sciences must be distinguished from that of the natural sciences. According to Lonergan, human science as science has its empirical principle, and as human has its "dialectical principle." These two principles have their concrete realization in the ongoing scientific community, so that critical analysis can reflect "both on the human community to which human sciences are applied and on the scientific community that develops and revises the human sciences."[57] As empirical, human sciences follow the natural sciences (and Lonergan's cognitional theory) in that "there are no true factual judgments without a foundation in relevant data." However, because the relevant data include data of consciousness as well as the sense data, human science must be critical as well as empirical. This conjunction implies neither behaviorism which confines human psychology "to the methods available in animal psychology," nor does it imply positivism, because positivism "overlooks the *a priori* contained in man's questions for intelligence, for reflection, for deliberation."

Finally, statements about factual knowledge are not to be extended to moral or value judgments, because these are normative and not factual.[58] However, does not sever the connection between "positive" theory (facts) and normative praxis (value) as maintained in modern economics since Lionel Robbins and found predominantly in David Hume's and Max Weber's famous fact/value distinction. Rather, modern science as understood by Lonergan includes both theory and practice as "distinct parts of a single reality." This is because human understanding includes both mounting to its presuppositions (theory) and descending to its applications (practice). In other words, human knowledge is the result of "fact" questions put to our experience and intelligence: "What is it?" and "Is it so?" In the moral realm, these two types of questions are asked again, but to our intelligent and reasonable assessment of possible courses of action, "What is it?" and "Is it so?" (the best possible course of action), becoming "act questions." The last stage is the actual action taken, but which can also (and is) be put forward as a question, "Will I do it or not?" and is answered through my will and by my action rather than through putting further questions to understanding.[59] While complex moral problems would require answers to complex fact and act questions and a fuller account of moral action requires integration of the roles of feeling, stages of moral development, etc., this breakdown of moral actions into fact, act, and decision questions, shows how theory and praxis are intimately related in human fact-gathering, deliberation and action.[60]

Human Biases

The dialectical principle of human science is the recognition of an anthropological principle: it is the recognition that: "the data on man are ambiguous: man's actions may be good or evil; his statements may be true or false; his development may be authentic or unauthentic."[61] Objectively, in the human community progress proceeds by scientific and common sense insights that are relevant, and if incomplete must be completed by further insights and so on. But along with progress there is decline. That is so because there are the biases that corrupt the recurrence and application of insights needed for social progress.[62] Lonergan treats four different kinds of bias, that of the dramatic bias of unconscious interests, individual bias or egoism that "endeavors to circumvent public purpose for private gain," group bias which through "shared delusions . . . considers its self-interest a contribution to the well-being of mankind," and finally the general bias of common sense which views common sense knowledge as the whole of knowledge, denying theoretical insights needed to restore human progress. Instead of the objective situation becoming more intelligible through scientific analysis and common sense, it becomes less and less so through the effect of these biases.[63]

Dramatic bias operates at the level of elementary passions. Individuals exclude unwanted insights and the further questions arising from them from their deliberation. This results in a "withdrawal from the outer drama of human living into the inner drama of fantasy" that results from misunderstanding both ourselves and others that our insights and testing them against others' insights and experiences help to provide.[64] Individual bias moves beyond dramatic bias in that it uses insights and intelligence sometimes extremely well, but at the same time it egoistically *consciously* sabotages intellectual operations in order to serve the individual's self-interest of the egoist. With a sense of irony, Lonergan gives us a picture of the egoist: "With remarkable acumen one solves one's own problems. With startling modesty, one does not venture to raise the relevant further questions, Can one's solutions be generalized? Is it compatible with the social order that exists? Is it compatible with any social order that proximately or even remotely is possible?"[65] Instead of eventually raising these further questions regarding the goodness of its project, individual bias refuses self-transcendence and deliberately follows paths that only satisfy his or her spontaneous desires.

Group bias results when egoistic individuals, seeking to overcome their isolation from others, incorporate and widen their individual bias by consolidating with others the same self-centered concerns. Instead of finding one's place in society by "contributing their specialized expertise toward the common good," toward finding the group's role in cooperating to construct and value a flourishing social and economic order, group bias works to distort proper technological, economic and political development through exercising its power against it.[66] As William Loewe explains, "each group has its own needs and interests, and these present themselves with far more vividness than can the general good of order with which they must be integrated."[67] Group bias not only affects societal configurations (illustrated in sexism, racism, militarism, classism, etc.),[68] it also distorts progress on the material level. Instead of fruitful ideas being put into use by the practical common sense of society, "only those ideas which reinforce, or at best fail to threaten, the dominant power structure are put into practice."[69]

Beyond the egoism resulting from individual bias and the power of group bias to reduce progress to mindless material expansion, there lies general bias, which completes the destructive drift of bias by entering explicitly and vocally into the public realm of detached intelligence, the world of theory and interiority. People of common sense, though fully justified in their competence in dealing with practical problems of living, may exhibit *ressentiment* toward people of differentiated consciousness, those who are able to relate not only things to themselves but things to each other, such as in the sciences and other theoretical disciplines. In the crisis of human culture caused by dramatic, individual and group bias, common sense becomes resigned to the "fact" that the destructive cycles cannot be broken and that further developments of intelligence are irrelevant to breaking the "social surd."[70] Any attempts to form questions, insights and ideas that would serve to radically transform all achievements that the culture has attained through its practical intelligence thus far are resisted because they are seen to be merely representing the interests of another interest group. In general bias, common sense itself has reached ascendancy in the culture. However, this is fatal to a culture, in that it traps cultures in what Lonergan terms "the longer cycle of decline."[71] In the longer cycle of decline, common sense is unable by itself to come up further questions, insights and ideas or else "mutilates them through compromise."[72]

General bias of practical intelligence, entranced by its own competence in the practical realm and bolstered by theories that legitimate its short sightedness, condemns and dismisses the analysis of thinkers of more detached intelligence attempting to "lay bare the irrationality of the situation" and "find creative steps" for reversing the dynamic of the long cycle of decline; as a result particular culture disintegrates, putting at risk all its achievements.[73]

Consequences of Bias

That human science is dialectical, leading to both progress and decline, has ultimate consequences for human community. If the community's biases are not begun to be overcome, the unintelligibility of the situation becomes a "social surd," an objective fact that "both mirrors and reinforces a subjective spirit of darkness."[74] Corrupt praxis does not totally neglect the theoretical realm, however; it receives support in the form of "pseudo-theory."[75] Objectivity in the social sciences becomes corrupted; it is not enough that biases stagnate social order, instead, people want their biases justified and "thus provide a market for an ideology that would justify their ways in the eyes of faltering followers and envious opponents." Finally, the powers-that-be find that "mere ideas no longer work," and invoke the "power to compel, the power of technology, of economic pressures, of political discrimination, of passionate ideology."[76]

Finally, human sciences as empirical, critical, and dialectical, are also normative. This is due to the above discussed fact that human sciences include the data of consciousness, that "major portion of the data so often ruled out of court,"[77] in which are found built-in norms of intelligence, rationality and responsibility. With the empirical data and data of consciousness, human sciences can "learn to distinguish between progress and decline, between liberty that generates progress and the bias that generates decline," and "be of estimable value in aiding man to understand himself and in guiding him in the implementation of that understanding."[78] With a human science that is empirical, dialectical, critical and normative,[79] culture—"the set of meanings and values inherent in a way of life"—can be "an independent factor that passes a detached yet effective judgment upon capital formation and technology, upon economy and polity."[80] Without such a human science, culture becomes merely a "factor within the technological, economic, political process, more and more of a tool that serve[s] palpably useful ends."[81]

Relevance of Lonergan's Considerations For Mainstream Economic Methodology

In my view, Lonergan's normative scientific method also points up the inadequacy of the positivistic methodology of orthodox economics on at least three important counts. First, because positivist mainstream economics fails to recognize the differences between natural and social sciences, it is misguided. Second, it is not only misguided, it does not attain scientific explanation on the level of natural science, despite its reliance on the method of the natural sciences. Third, its emphasis on modeling itself on natural sciences with its focus on prediction rather than explanation results in an *inhuman* science that does not provide people with precepts for living. In other words, by modeling itself positivistically on natural sciences (more exactly, its emphasis on prediction and quantifiability adopts more and more the methodology of mathematics),[82] economics as now constituted fails to be the normative, prescriptive science that it ought to be. Lonergan follows Edmund Husserl, viewing the role of the social scientist, including the economist, as more akin to a medical doctor than a "disinterested" natural scientist. He paraphrases Husserl to the point that, "If there is anything wrong with your health, there exists a whole array of scientific disciplines at your disposal to help you recover. But Husserl adds, Europe is sick, the situation in Europe is disastrous, and what do we have to help? Just quacks."[83] For the health of the human community, economic problems beg to be solved, but because of its methodological difficulties, there does not exist an economic science sufficiently concerned with explaining what went wrong and how to correct it.

In a lengthy statement worth presenting as a compact discourse on the empirical, dialectical, critical and normative foundations of economic science, and the practical consequences of positivistic conceptions, Lonergan says this concerning the subject matter of economics:

> [Economics] is an empirically, intelligently, rationally conscious subject that develops in intelligence and reasonableness, is an entity that even from viewpoint of scientific method, has to be approached in a manner essentially different from the study of atoms or plants or animals. And it's only insofar as the human sciences will be willing to expect some philosophic commitments or, on the other hand, be masters of all possible philosophic commitments that they'll be able to think on a level that is truly human in their human sciences. If the economist in his analysis of the economy, is concerned to make plain to people as individuals that certain procedures are just as intelligent as stepping on the accelerator and the brake at the same time, he's talking to them as men. And they by their use of their intelligence and reasonableness will individually or cooperatively be able to carry out his precepts and avoid grand-scale blunders. But if he thinks of economic activity as predictable events in the same manner as the 19th c. physicists did, or as statistically probable events, he's dealing with an objective manifold, and his only way of dealing with it will be through government or through propaganda, or through psychological conditioning, or though the police state, or what you please. The link between the human science and its application will not be human; it will be subhuman. It's a problem of considerable dimensions—a number of dimensions that are all pretty enormous.[84]

While Lonergan criticizes 19th century economic science for its determinist, materialist nature, he notes that it did possess the quality of seeking to "issue precepts to free men."[85] Its precept of *laissez-faire* over against the prevailing stateist-orientated mercantilism of the time and its advice to individuals to be thrifty and enterprising, resulted "in an enormous economic development."[86] While Lonergan finds that 19th century economics and its precepts were ultimately inadequate, resulting by the end of the century, an "asinine" political economics based upon marginalist economic theory, he argues that "nevertheless they serve to illustrate the difference between a human science as uttering precepts, and a human science as predictive, as imitating what a physicist or chemist does."[87] Lonergan instead envisages economic science as telling free people something that they can do for themselves and for their community, not simply predicting as in purely positive economics.[88] The flip side of this that it also informs ethicists and other people concerned with the role of values in the economy how to channel their benevolence.

The Subject in Economic Analysis: Economic Moral Agency

Up to this point, the term "human" in regard to economic agency has only been used in opposition to non-human terms like electron, etc., without filling it with much positive content. Negatively, Lonergan talks about bias as corrupting human cognition and action, and about how economic scientists have not fulfilled their responsibilities in many ways. More positively, Lonergan rightly stresses the importance of moral agency as an important anthropological principle. The mainstream economics account of "economic man," either discounts economic moral agency or leaves it to other disciplines, which has the same effect within economics as discounting it. In contrast, as will be seen in the next chapter, Lonergan's economic analysis has a strong role for moral economic agency.

Lonergan's account of economics as a social science not only recognizes the potential ability and responsibility of economic science to issue precepts, but also the abilities of economic agents to use their intelligence and responsibility to carry out these precepts. This ability to use intelligence has already been adverted to in the discussion above on human knowing. Normatively, people ask questions concerning their experience toward discovering intelligible information (What is it?). Upon asking questions for intelligence, they come to probable judgments of truth (Is it so?). In order for their actions to be consistent with their understanding and judgment, Lonergan argues one must act responsibly upon the results of these judgments. This fourth level (Is it worthwhile?) is a further level of human intentionality ignored by mainstream (and Marxian) economic anthropology.[89] "Economic man" chooses on the basis of maximizing utility, based on subjective satisfaction received from potential objects of choice, within the limits of an income constraint. Any room for agents to choose on unselfish or altruistic motives is reduced to their increasing their utility as a result of such actions. However, critics of orthodox economics like the Nobel Prize-winning economist Amartya Sen have pointed out that this conception reveals a possible contradiction because unselfish or altruistic actions may in fact reduce the subjective satisfaction of the choosing agent.[90]

On the other hand, moral conversion of agents is their actuating of their ability to choose not only the basis of satisfactions, as in "economic man," but also on the basis of values, many times transcending our self-interest. Lonergan holds that the possibility of moral conversion implies that economic agents are in reality self-creating, "open-eyed and deliberate," rather than passive responders to stimulation or stable preference functions.[91] An adequate expansion of the concept of "economic man" would have to consider the ability of economic agents to choose on the basis of values and not satisfactions. This conception would remove many of the behavioristic (as in behaviorism) conditions that mainstream economics requires for it to maintain its scientific status based upon its ability to predict the outcomes of changing variables and move it toward the type of human science Lonergan envisages.

The Structure of the Human Good

The above reflections on the difference between Lonergan's thought and mainstream economic methodology have important implications for the structure of the human good. The human good as envisioned in the methodological individualism of mainstream economics regards the well-being of society as resulting from the actions of self-seeking, utility-maximizing atomic individuals.

Important implications follow from a discovery that mainstream economics relies on an inadequate model of "economic man" as a theoretical tool for the structure of the human good. Following Lonergan's analysis, these include, first, that current economic theory provides merely analytical and pseudo-predictive power, not explanatory power which would enable economics to be a prescriptive science to guide society toward the human good. Second, the concept of economic man provides no "room" for humans to be moral agents, because the morality or ability to transcend one's own interests for the greater good is not part of economic agency as self-interested, utility-maximizer. Third, because economic agents in mainstream economic anthropology only act to maximize given sets of preferences, there is no "receiving end" for whatever prescriptive statements economics could provide if based upon a more adequate economic anthropology.

Value Neutrality and Community in Economics

Although mainstream economics claims to be value neutral, mainstream economic methodology ends up promoting definite social values and a distinct idea of a "good" socio-economic-political structure, namely that of the free market supported by values of economic freedom.[92] Lonergan's economic anthropology offers a different structure of the human good, based upon persons attaining social and economic ends through actualizing values, rather than self-interested preferences. In a comment seemingly intended to distance his conception of the structure of the human good from that of economic liberalism, Lonergan states that:

> ... there is a still further dimension to being human, and there we emerge as persons, meet another in a common concern for values, seek to abolish the organization of human beings as the bases of competing egoisms and to replace it by an organization on the basis of man's perceptions and intelligence, by reasonableness and by responsible exercises of freedom.[93]

Lonergan's Structure of the Human Good

Clearly, for Lonergan as with Catholic social teaching and social economics, the structure of the human good is at once individual and social. Lonergan goes even further than the communitarian nature of Catholic social teaching by even denying an *a priori* distinction between subject and object: "Prior to the 'we' that results from the mutual love of an 'I' and a 'thou', there is an earlier 'we' that precedes the distinction of subjects and survives its oblivion."[94] As seen in the table on the following page, each of the three levels of the human good involves 1) individuals in both their potentialities and actuations, 2) cooperating groups and 3) ends.[95] The good of order as exemplified in this diagram "consists basically in 1) the ordering of operations so that they are cooperations and ensure the recurrence of all effectively desired instances of particular good and 2) the interdependence of effective desires or decisions with the appropriate performance by cooperating individuals." As Lonergan relates, it is not "some design for utopia, some theoretical ideal, some set of ethical precepts, some code of laws, some super institution. It is the actually functioning or malfunctioning set of if-then relationships guiding operations and coordinating operations."[96] While most of the terms are self-explanatory, and many of the relationships between them are plain, some terms and Lonergan's hierarchical structure require elaboration, especially because certain terms such as liberty have different meanings in Lonergan's schema than, for example, political liberalism. Lonergan distinguishes individual and social levels of the human good (the first two vertical columns). The third column, "ends," are the goals of individuals, societies and cultures.

Figure 3.1: Structure of the Human Good[97]

Individual	Social		Ends
Potentiality	*Actuation*		
capacity, need	operation	cooperation	individual goods
plasticity, perfectibility	development, skill,	institution, role, task	good of order
liberty	orientation, conversion	personal relations	terminal values

The components of strictly individual agency consist of human potential and human actuation of this potential, and this agency occurs on three (horizontal rows) levels in Lonergan's scheme. These three levels correspond to Lonergan's three levels of experience or empirical, insight or intelligence, and judgment. They also correspond respectively to the vital, social and cultural realms of human interaction.[98] On an empirical level, individuals are capable of learning and doing, and experience need. This potential actuated on the empirical level results in operation. On the empirical level, that of vital values, the ends of agency are particular goals, and the social means to achieve these ends is cooperation. On the second level, of intelligence and social values, people possess the potentiality of developing their capacities, and thus plasticity and perfectibility can result in human development and particular skills. On the social level, through the development of institutions, people assume various roles in which their particular skills are utilized in various tasks. The end achieved on the level of individual intelligence and social mediation of that intelligence is the good of order.

An example Lonergan gives to differentiate achievement of the good of order from particular good, is that a particular good is one's breakfast in the morning and something like a newspaper to read as one eats. The good of order goes beyond particular goods as growing foods and getting them to market, and running a newspaper (and maintaining roads and indeed the economy) goes beyond mere eating and reading the results of these mammoth projects. The good of order extends to having one's breakfast and a newspaper *everyday*, and this good of order is usually only recognized as such when there is a newspaper strike or economic breakdown when these particular goods do not become regular or as easily procured. In other words, it exists on the level of social values, e.g. the common good.

The third level is that of human judgment and cultural values. As humans, we have the capacity for liberty and its actuation is that of orientation or conversion. Liberty in Lonergan's thought is not just the Lockean freedom to pursue one's happiness or satisfaction, but the ability to criticize any finite course of group or individual action. It is orientation or conversion, because judgment involves choosing on the basis of value. Individual orientation and conversion, along with social mediation of orientation and conversion in personal relations, intends the goal of terminal values.

As the anthropological considerations as functioning in Lonergan's conception of the structure of the human good show, the human good relies upon the ability of humans to achieve moral self-transcendence, opting "not for the merely apparent good, but for the true good." In this achievement the person is existing authentically, and in doing so, "he is constituting himself as an originating value, and he is bringing about terminal value, namely a good of order that is truly good and instances of the particular good that are truly good." This is contrasted to an idea of the structure of the human good such as liberal economics that relies on personal decisions being based, "not in the values at stake, but in a calculus of the pleasures and pains involved."[99] For Lonergan, the consequences of ignoring value-choices and the constitutive dimensions of culture, in favor of pursuit of satisfaction in economic and political theory and practice are dire:

> The better educated become a class closed in upon themselves with no task proportionate to their training. They become effete. The less educated and uneducated find themselves with a tradition that is beyond their means. They cannot maintain it. They lack genius to transform it into some simpler vital and intelligible whole. It degenerates. The meaning and values of human living are impoverished. The will to achieve both slackens and narrow. Where once there were joys and

sorrows, now there are just pleasures and pains. The culture has become a slum.[100]

Conclusion: The Structure of the Human Good as Economic

As discussed above, one of the roles of a critical economic science is to seek explanatory understandings of economic processes in order to enable members of a culture to pass "a detached yet effective judgment upon capital formation and technology, upon economy and polity."[101] *Macroeconomic Dynamics: An Essay in Circulation Analysis* is an attempt to provide an explanation of the human good as economic in terms of functional relations between dynamic and meaningful human activities of production, exchange and finance. Lonergan's later work, particularly *Insight*, laid out his original cognitive theory that provides the analytical tools needed to promote a critical realist explanatory model of all scientific inquiry that can overcome the pitfalls and inadequacies of positivist economic methodology. *Method in Theology* in turn proposes a framework of the human good in which self-interest, though important, works in conjunction with cooperation and self-transcendence. The economic good of order, however imperfectly realized in present predominant mixed-market economies turns out to be much more complicated and intentional than Adam Smith's "invisible hand" that magically transforms self-interest into the "common good."

Therefore, since economic relationships and the standard of living, especially the need to increase that of the poor, are such important dimensions of human living, the intelligent and responsible direction of the economy is crucial. As Michael Novak points out, the way the economy is directed is also important socio-politically, with considerable implications for human institutions such as a democratic polity. With Novak, Lonergan also seeks a democratic capitalism, but stresses '*democratic* capitalism' against Novak's 'democratic *capitalism*.' Further, Lonergan's economics as democratic increases the economic well-being while Novak's democracy as capitalistic undermines democracy. On the cultural level, intelligent, responsible and democratic functioning of the economy both derives from and contributes to culture.

Since the cognitive and productive capacities and actuation involved in economic agency not only determine how intelligently and responsibly an economy will function, the institutional context of society in turn shapes human character. This aspect counters the overemphasis of neo-Marxist or socialist economics that Mary Hobgood relies upon in that Lonergan recognizes that human and social transformation have to go hand-in-hand. Finally, Lonergan's proposal of an intelligent, reasonable direction of the economy by individuals and communities of character is fully congruent with Catholic social teaching, with the additional macroeconomic understanding needed to guide that vision. Lonergan's aim in ECA is that the precepts resulting from such an analysis "would guide individuals and their communities in their deliberations of what they will make of themselves."[102] In his view, this requires a "new science" of economics to stem the tide of increasing bureaucratic control that inevitably results from liberal democratic and socialist democratic "preoccupation with the use of scientific prediction and manipulation 'for the relief of man's estate.'"[103] The "new science" which Lonergan claims promotes a "more democratic constitution of our exchange economies"[104] is the subject of the next chapter.

NOTES

1. Lonergan wrote books and articles on religion, mathematics, philosophy, theology, methodology, economics, and social ethics.

2. Frederick Lawrence, et al., "Editors' Introduction," in Bernard Lonergan, *Macroeconomic Dynamics: An Essay in Circulation Analysis*, ed. Frederick G. Lawrence, Patrick H. Byrne, and Charles Hefling, Jr., Vol. 15 of *Collected Works of Bernard Lonergan*, ed. Frederick E. Crowe and Robert M. Doran (Toronto: University of Toronto Press, 1999), xxvii.

3. I am indebted to Paul Misner for his comments to me on this issue. See his *Social Catholicism in Europe: From the Onslaught of Industrialization to the First World War* (New York: Crossroad, 1991) for the use of the term social economics in the tradition of social Catholicism.

4. The teacher of the course, Lewis Watt, authored *Capitalism and Morality* (London: Cassell and Company, 1929) and *Catholic Social Principles: A Commentary on the Papal Encyclical "Rerum Novarum"* (New York: Benziger, 1930).

5. While Lonergan read and took notes on at least part of Pesch's *Lehrbooks*, he left no critical reflections on his notes on Pesch preserved at the Lonergan Institute at Regis College in Toronto.

6. Despite Lonergan's "intellectualist" approach, as Frederick Crowe points out, "Lonergan was oriented by a deep-lying pastoral concern" (Frederick E. Crowe, S.J., "Lonergan as Pastoral Theologian," in *Appropriating the Lonergan Idea*, ed. Michael Vertin [Washington, DC: The Catholic University of America Press, 1989], 127). Patrick Byrne makes the same point in elaborating on a

personal remark Lonergan made to him: "Late in his life, his theoretical work on economics, and arguably his work in philosophy and theology throughout his career, was undertaken so that 'the widows and the orphans won't starve'" (Patrick H. Byrne, "*Ressentiment* and the Preferential Option for the Poor," *Theological Studies* 54 [1993]:241).

7. Michael Shute, *The Origins of Lonergan's Notions of the Dialectic of History: A Study of Lonergan's Early Writings on History* (Lanham, MD.: University Press of America, 1993), [xxiii-xxviii].

8. Lonergan, *Insight: A Study of Human Understanding,* ed. Frederick E. Crowe and Robert M. Doran, Vol. 3 of *The Collected Works of Bernard Lonergan*, ed. Frederick E. Crowe and Robert M. Doran (Toronto: University of Toronto Press, 1992; first ed. 1957).

9. Lonergan, *Method in Theology* (New York: Seabury Press, 1972).

10. Bernard Lonergan, "Healing and Creating in History," in *A Third Collection*, ed. Frederick E. Crowe (New York: Paulist Press, 1985), 100-109, given originally as a lecture in May 1975.

11. Lonergan, *Insight*, 235. As David Nordquest expresses it, the future development of human societies "comes to depend less on material conditions and more on the stock of operative insights and oversights" (David A. Nordquest, "Lonergan's Cognitional Theory: Toward a Critical Human Science," *Review of Politics* 56 [Winter 1994]: 89). As will be seen in the next chapter, for Lonergan even the so-called "price mechanism" is a reflection of more fundamental series of schemes (operating through classical and statistical laws) whose functioning conditions the operation of prices in the economy.

12. William Matthews, S.J. "Explanation in the Social Sciences," in *Religion and Culture: Essays in Honor of Bernard Lonergan*, Timothy P. Fallon and Phillip Boo Riley, ed. (Albany: State University of New York Press, 1987), 245.

13. Such explanatory power seeks to provide "discernible criteria inherent in the productive process which can give guidance for responsible action" (Jane Collier, referring to Lonergan's economics, in *The Culture of Economism: An Exploration of Barriers to Faith-as-Praxis* [Frankfurt am Main: Peter Lang, 1990], 253).

14. Matthew Lamb, *History, Method and Theology: A Dialectical Comparison of Wilhelm Dilthey's Critique of Historical Reason and Bernard Lonergan's Meta-Methodology*, AAR Dissertation Series, no. 25 (Missoula, MT: Scholars Press, 1978).

15. Frederick Crowe, *The Lonergan Enterprise* (Cambridge, MA: Cowley Press, 1980). Chapter 1 of this work was published as *Method in Theology: An Organon for Our Time*, The *Pere* Marquette Theology Lecture (Milwaukee: Marquette University Press, 1980).

16. Cf. M. Shawn Copeland, "A Genetic Study of the Human Good in the

Thought of Bernard Lonergan" (Ph.D. diss., Boston College, 1991); T. A. Dunne, "Lonergan on Social Process and Community" (Th.D. dissertation, Regis College, Toronto, 1975); Matthew Lamb, *Solidarity with Victims: Toward a Theology of Social Transformation* (New York: Crossroad, 1982).

17. Terry J. Tekippe, "The Crisis of the Human Good," in *Lonergan Workshop*, Volume 7, ed. Frederick E. Lawrence (Atlanta, GA: Scholars Press, 1988), 314.

18. Robert Bellah, et al.'s views on American culture, in *Habits of the Heart: Individualism and Commitment in American Life* (New York: Harper and Row, 1985) and *The Good Society* (New York: Vintage Books, 1991), in my view share this same aim. For a comparison of Lonergan and Bellah and his co-authors, see Paul E. Hoyt-O'Connor, "Lonergan and Bellah: Social Science and Public Philosophy," *Proceedings of the American Catholic Philosophical Association* 68 (1994): 259-70.

19. David Nordquest correctly argues that "Lonergan's studies of how we come to know, of the patterns of our insights and oversights, point the way 'beyond ideology' to what Lonergan calls a critical human science" ("Lonergan's Cognitional Theory," 71).

20. As Nordquest points out, "Concrete appropriation of how we come to know is fundamental for any critical human science" ("Lonergan's Cognitional Theory," 73).

21. On the difference between normative as involving value judgments vs. normative as a kind of explanatory framework, see Lawrence, et. al. "Editors Introduction," ECA, lv-lvi.

22. For a good, critical introduction to Lonergan's epistemology, see David Tracy, *The Achievement of Bernard Lonergan* (New York: Herder and Herder, 1970), especially 123-132, "The Nature of Reflective Consciousness and of Judgment." Tracy offers not only a clear explanation of Lonergan's cognitional theory or "way of knowing" but also in this section generally locates Lonergan among other philosophers of consciousness such as Kant, Hegel, Newman and Pierce.

23. Lonergan characterized *Insight* and the exercise of self-appropriation that it consists of as "both a way and something like a theory," and fundamentally a "way" ("An Interview with Fr. Bernard Lonergan, S. J." in *A Second Collection*, ed. William Ryan and Bernard Tyrell [Philadelphia: The Westminster Press, 1974], 213).

24. Lonergan, "Cognitional Structure," in *Collection*, ed. Frederick E. Crowe and Robert M. Doran, Vol. 4 of *The Collected Works of Bernard Lonergan* (Toronto: University of Toronto Press, 1988; 1st ed. 1967); *Understanding and Being: An Introduction and Companion to "Insight,"* ed. Elizabeth A. Morelli and Mark D. Morelli, Vol. 5 of *Collected Works of Bernard Lonergan* (Toronto:

University of Toronto, 1990; 1st ed. 1980), 239. *Method in Theology*, "Chapter 1: Method."

25. Lonergan, *Insight*, 22. Emphasis in the original text.

26. Lonergan, *Method in Theology*, 4.

27. Lonergan, "Cognitional Structure," 206.

28. Lonergan, "Cognitional Structure," 209. And "thus critically reflected on to be truly known" ("Lonergan's Cognitional Theory," 72).

29. Lonergan, "Cognitional Structure,"206.

30. For example, seeing alone is "mere gaping" (Lonergan, "Cognitional Structure," 206).

31. Lonergan, "Cognitional Structure," 206f.

32. "To pass judgment on what does not understand is not human knowing, but human arrogance" (Lonergan, "Cognitional Structure," 207).

33. Lonergan, "Cognitional Structure," 207. To go somewhat more deeply into what specifically human understanding and judgment entail, understanding is the answer given by human intentionality to the question "what is it?" put to the data of sense or imagination. The answer to this question is an insight, or grasp of intelligible patterns in the data, which is put in the form of a concept. But, since insights are a "dime a dozen," frequently of untested validity, human knowing must take a further step.

34. This is not to say that Lonergan is a "neo-Thomist." While Lonergan did seek in his *Verbum* articles to correlate his critical realism with that of Aquinas, John Henry Newman's thought was more influential in Lonergan's thinking. Indeed, Lonergan had the bases of his own cognitional theory well-developed before he began to read St. Thomas extensively. See Frederick Lawrence, "Lonergan as a Political Theologian," and David M. Hammond, "The Influence of Newman's Doctrine of Assent on the Thought of Bernard Lonergan: A Genetic Study," *Method: Journal of Lonergan Studies* 7/2 (October 1989), 95-115.

35. Hugo Meynell, "Lonergan's Theory of Knowledge and the Social Sciences," *New Blackfriars* 56 (Sept. 1985): 391.

36. Lonergan, *Method in Theology*, 55.

37. Lonergan, "Cognitional Structure," 210.

38. Lonergan, *Method in Theology*, 104.

39. Lonergan, "Cognitional Structure," 213.

40. Editors footnote, 302 note k.

41. Lonergan, "Cognitional Structure," 214.

42. Nordquest, "Lonergan's Cognitional Theory," 78.

43. Lonergan, *Method in Theology*, 19.

44. Scientific pursuit of universals is contrasted by Lonergan with the practical knowledge produced by common sense, which is "simply part of the desire to live and knowledge is part of living." Common sense knowledge is not pursued

for its own sake, as an end in itself. More concretely, scientists want "as many insight as are necessary in order to arrive at set of definitions and principles that will enable him to deal universally with all possible situations of defined type, " while common sense aims at a body of knowledge that "that with the minimum of further insights that will be able to deal with any concrete situations that arise in his living" (Lonergan, *Understanding and Being*, 86).

45. Edward MacKinnon, "Cognitional Analysis and the Philosophy of Science," *Continuum* 2 (Fall 1964): 356.

46. Lonergan, *Understanding and Being*, 66.

47. Lonergan, *Understanding and Being*, 97.

48. Hugo Meynell, "Lonergan's Theory of Knowledge and the Social Sciences," *New Blackfriars* 56 (Sept. 1985): 391.

49. Hugo Meynell, "Lonergan's Theory of Knowledge," 394.

50. Various understandings of this relationship are found in *Understanding and Social Inquiry*, ed. Fred R. Dallmayr and Thomas A. McCarthy (Notre Dame, IN: University of Notre Dame Press, 1977). The problem is treated at length and given extensive historical context by Richard J. Bernstein in *Beyond Objectivism and Relativism: Science, Hermeneutics, and Praxis* (Philadelphia: University of Pennsylvania Press, 1983.

51. Lonergan's explication of the canons of empirical method is found in *Insight*, Chapter 3.

52. Meynell, 388. Lonergan's position, positivistic and Marxist positions are also joined by a fourth perspective that limits any explanation of human behavior to those given or capable of being given by the agents themselves. This is associated with ethnomethodologists such as Clifford Geertz and by Peter Winch in *The Idea of a Social Science and its Relation to Philosophy* (London: Routledge, 1963).

53. Hugo Meynell, "Lonergan's Theory of Knowledge," 382.

54. Lonergan, *Understanding and Being*, 96.

55. Matthews, "Explanation in the Social Sciences," 247.

56. Matthews, "Explanation in the Social Sciences," 247.

57. Bernard Lonergan, "Moral Theology and the Human Sciences," *Method: Journal of Lonergan Studies* 15 (1997): 6. This article was originally written circa 1974 and was found after his death in his files (cf. Frederick E. Crowe, "Lonergan's 'Moral Theology and the Human Sciences,' Editor's Introduction," *Method: Journal of Lonergan Studies* 15 (1997): 1-3).

58. Lonergan, "Moral Theology and the Human Sciences," 7f. For a cogent and wide-ranging discussion of the presence and problems of positivistic philosophical concepts in economics, methodological individualism and Milton Friedman's instrumentalism, see Homa Katouzian, *Ideology and Method in Economics* (New York: New York University Press, 1980).

59. I am helped here greatly by Kenneth Melchin's discussion of Lonergan's

approach to human moral decision-making in *Living With Other People: An Introduction to Christian Ethics Based on Bernard Lonergan* (Collegeville, MN: The Liturgical Press, 1998), 22-27.

60. For a constructive typological analysis of the relationship between theory and praxis in Christian theology, cf. Matthew Lamb, "The Relationship between Theory and Praxis in Contemporary Christian Theologies," *C.T.S.A. Proceedings* 31 (1976): 149-78. Lamb locates Lonergan, along with political and liberation theologians in his fifth model, "Critical Praxis Correlation," the other models being "The Primacy of Theory," "The Primacy of Praxis," "The Primacy of Faith-Love," and "Critical Theoretic Correlation." (This article also was revised as Chapter Three of Lamb's *Solidarity With Victims: Toward a Theology of Social Transformation* [New York: Crossroad, 1982]). Lamb finds that the "Critical Praxis Correlation" model places praxis as "not only the goal, but also the foundation of theory," which differentiates it from the "Critical Theoretic Correlation" model's emphasis on the aim or goal of theory being praxis. According to Lamb, because of the "union in difference" between theory and praxis in the former model, "The demands of theory for coherence and adequacy, for rigorous verification of truth-claims, are not minimized but intensified in this model." This is because "those demands cannot be met by appeals to axioms, principles, paradigms, activist programs, [or] faith commitments . . . ." (Lamb, "The Relationship between Theory and Praxis," 82). This last point will become more clear in the discussion of ECA in the next chapter in which it is shown how norms for economic praxis are derived by Lonergan from the intelligibility of economic process, not from moralistic principles imposed on economic process. From an economic methodological view, Lonergan's position in my view is an exemplary form of Larry Dwyer's decision-theoretic model of social inquiry, discussed in Chapter 3 above, which he characterizes as a search for *valuable* truth. Questions and values concerning the quality of human life play an explicit role in this approach.

61. As Lonergan explains it, dialectic is "a concrete unfolding of linked but opposed principles of change" (*Insight,* 242). In human understanding, the presence or absence of intellectual, moral or religious conversion gives rise to dialectically opposed viewpoints or horizons. Dunne aptly describes dialectic as "the activity of two opposing determinants of social conscience" ("Lonergan on Social Process and Community," 29).

62. Lonergan's views of progress and decline are embedded within his overall philosophy/theology of history, based upon the religious themes of creation, fall and redemption. As he notes: "In my rather theological analysis of human history my first approximation was the assumption that men always do what is intelligent and reasonable, and its implication was an ever increasing progress. The second approximation was the radical inverse insight that men are biased and so unintelligent and unreasonable in their choices and decisions

[resulting in decline]. The third approximation was the redemptive process resulting from God's gift of his grace to individuals and from the manifestation of his love in Christ Jesus" (Lonergan, "Insight Revisited," in *A Second Collection*, ed. William Ryan and Bernard Tyrell (Philadelphia: The Westminster Press, 1974), 272). Understanding history for Lonergan requires understanding how these three vectors are constantly at work.

63. Lonergan, "Moral Theology and the Human Sciences," 10.

64. Lonergan, *Insight*, 214.

65. Lonergan, *Insight*, 245. As William Loewe puts it, "The irony of egoism emerges from the fact that total commitment to the project of fulfilling one's spontaneous desires demands that at least one desire, the desire to know, must be denied" ("Dialectics of Sin: Lonergan's *Insight* and the Critical Theory of Max Horkheimer," *Anglican Theological Review* 61 [April 1979]: 229).

66. "[W]hile intelligence heads for change, group spontaneity does not regard all changes in the same cold light of the general good of order" (Lonergan, *Insight,* 248).

67. Loewe, "Dialectics of Sin," 230.

68. For an analysis of these issues using Lonergan's theoretical framework, see M. Shawn Copeland, "The Interaction of Racism, Sexism, and Classism in Women's Exploitation," in *Women, Work and Poverty* ed. Elisabeth Schuessler Fiorenza and Anne Carr (Concilium: Theology for the Eighties, vol. 194, 1987), 19-27.

69. Loewe, "Dialectics of Sin," 231.

70. Lonergan takes the notion of "surd" from mathematics where it is used to describe an unintelligible condition, e.g., the square root of a negative number. The "social surd" is then a condition in which dramatic, individual, group and common sense bias have coalesced to prevent the required understanding of a declining social situation to be uncovered and addressed. Cf. *Insight*, Index s.v. "social surd."

71. In Lonergan's functional analysis of human progress, decline in Lonergan's terms is simply the deterioration in living conditions produced by any of the types of bias, which short-circuit the human ability to progress through "a succession of insights, courses of action, changed situations, and fresh insights" (*Insight*, 249).

72. Lonergan, *Insight*, 226.

73. Lonergan, *Insight*, 253.

74. Lonergan, "Moral Theology and the Human Sciences," 10.

75. William Loewe points out how the example of Machiavelli demonstrates Lonergan's assertion that "pseudo-theory" supports and advances corrupt praxis: In making the facts of corrupt praxis the sole determinants of subsequent action, it dignifies the aberration which they concretize with the aura of an ideal, and the probability of further corruption jumps geometrically (Loewe, "Dialectics of

Sin," 233). In the specifically economic realm, Lonergan asserts that mainstream economists are like Machiavelli, albeit unconsciously, in their concern "with the factual, practical truth and not with fancies; like him they have no taste for imagined commonwealths and principalities which never were, because they look at how men in fact do live and not at such stuff as how men ought to live" (ECA, 95).

76.. Lonergan, "Moral Theology and the Human Sciences," 10.

77. Lonergan, *Insight*, 260. Lonergan gives Durkheimian sociology and behaviorist psychology as examples of human sciences that bar the data of consciousness.

78. Lonergan, *Insight*, 261.

79. To reach a critical standpoint, it has to be normative" (Lonergan, *Insight*, 261).

80. Bernard Lonergan, "The Response of the Jesuit as Priest and Apostle in the Modern World," in *Second Collection*, 183; quoted in Carla Mae Streeter, in "Glossary of Lonerganian Terminology," in *Communication and Lonergan: Common Ground for Forging the New Age*, ed. Thomas J. Farrell and Paul A. Soukup (Kansas City: Sheed & Ward, 1993), 317. As Streeter points out, Lonergan understands culture in an empirical manner in which "certain meanings and values inform a human community as it lives life as a continuous slow development or a rapid decline" (Carla Mae Streeter, "Glossary of Lonerganian Terminology," 318).

81. Lonergan, *Insight*, 262.

82. A personal anecdote may help to illustrate this problem. An economics professor in a graduate level course I was taking in "mathematics for economists," mused out loud in class one day that most of the articles in growth theory (which we were studying that day) were tautological in nature, meaning that the stress was not on attempting to explain that aspect of economic process, but only to model economic "reality" in mathematical terms. Not surprisingly, his next remark was to the effect that most of these articles were written only for other economists who had the requisite mathematical training, and with no further relevance (or understanding) to be gained. He was not complaining about this situation, only explaining the current state of the field.

83. Edmund Husserl, *Crisis in European Sciences and Transcendental Phenomenology: An Introduction to Phenomenological Philosophy*, trans. by David Carr (Evanston: Northwestern University Press, 1970), 269f.; quoted in Lonergan, *Understanding and Being*, 194. Lonergan extrapolates Husserl's opinion to his overall point here, "The human sciences have tended to assimilate themselves as much as possible to physics and chemistry and biology, and in general to the successful sciences. The more that assimilation proceeds, the less able they are a help to free men" (*Understanding and Being*, 194). Both Husserl and Lonergan thus use the analogy of medicine (prescriptive advice for living) for the knowl-

edge needed to address the deteriorating social conditions of modern life. Philip McShane elaborates on the role of the "local economist" in Bruce Anderson and Philip McShane, *Beyond Establishment Economics: No Thank-You Mankiw* (Halifax, Nova Scotia: Axial Press, 2002).

84. Lonergan, *Understanding and Being*, 363-4.

85. In fact, if one were to examine closely the positions of Novak and other more conservative economic ethicists who favor liberal economic theory, one would find that it is 19th century economic theory that they wish to recover for integration into Christian economic ethics.

86. Lonergan, *Understanding and Being*, 194.

87. Lonergan, *Understanding and Being*, 194.

88. Lonergan's conception of economic science has important implications for democracy: "Economics and other human sciences can thus be conceived as instruments of human liberty and development, or they can be conceived as instruments of the concentration of governmental power, where the individual is incapable of doing anything without government approval of what he is doing and without government financing to enable him to do it" (*Understanding and Being*, 195). In more Marxian terms, Lonergan related in a 1975 paper that the "large establishment and bureaucratic organization are a fourfold source of that conjunction of dissatisfaction and hopelessness that is named alienation and foments revolutions" [including the "Republican revolution" of the 1994 United States general elections] ("Prolegomena to the Study of the Emerging Religiousness of Our Time," in *Third Collection*, 61; quoted in *Understanding and Being*, 417, editors note c.)

89. Lonergan's emphasis on moral agency or responsibility contains a component beyond self-consistency between knowing and acting. This further component is moral conversion. Between the writing of *Insight* and *Method in Theology*, Lonergan comes to better terms with the necessity for values and feelings as motivators of action that are more powerful than the appeal for self-consistency between knowing and acting as emphasized in *Insight*. Frederick Crowe analyzes this shift in "An Exploration of Lonergan's New Notion of Value," 51-70, and "An Expansion of Lonergan's Notion of Value," in *Appropriating the Lonergan Idea.*, 344-59.

90. For example, Amartya Sen, "Rational Fools: A Critique of the Behavioral Foundations of Economic Theory," *Philosophy & Public Affairs* 6 (1977): 317-44.

91. The classic lampoon of the isolated "economic man" of neoclassical economics" is by Thorstein Veblen in *The Place of Science in Modern Civilization and Other Essays* (1915):

> The hedonistic calculator of man is that of a lightning calculator of pleasures and pains, who oscillates like a homogenous globule of desire and happiness under the impulse of

> stimuli that shift him about the area, but leave him intact. He has neither antecedent nor consequence. He is an isolated, definitive human datum in stable equilibrium except for the buffets of the impinging forces that displace him in one direction or another. Self-imposed in elemental space, he spins symmetrically about his own spiritual axis until the parallelogram of forces bears down upon him, whereupon he follows the line of the resultant. When the force of the impact is spent, he comes to rest, a self-contained globule of desire as before (*The Portable Veblen*, ed. and with an introduction by Max Lerner [New York: The Viking Press, 1948], 232-233).

92. While this distinct value-system and corresponding structure of the human good is at best implicit in mainstream economic reasoning, still a definite idea of the structure of the human good (i.e., limiting government intervention in the market) drives mainstream economic reasoning. On this basis, mainstream economics is value-centered (and based on group bias), rather than "value-free."

93. Lonergan, *Method in Theology*, 10.

94. Lonergan, *Method in Theology*, 57.

95. Lonergan, *Method in Theology*, 48.

96. Lonergan, *Method in Theology*, 49; cf. also Lonergan, *Insight*, 596.

97. Lonergan, *Method in Theology*, 48.

98. As M. Shawn Copeland relates, "Through attentiveness to the various presentations of experience, inquiry, understanding and analysis, criticism and judgment, deliberation and decision, we come to understand the structured complex of needs and desires, operations and cooperations that cause society to function" (Copeland, *A Genetic Study of the Human Good in the Thought of Bernard Lonergan*, 259). Kenneth Melchin exploits this structure to develop a Lonerganian approach to Christian ethics (*Living With Other People: An Introduction to Christian Ethics based on Bernard Lonergan* (Collegeville, MN: The Liturgical Press, 1998), while Robert Doran has incorporated Lonergan's dialectic of community, etc. into a prolegomena for a systematic theology (*Theology and the Dialectics of History* (Toronto: University of Toronto Press, 1990).

99. Lonergan, *Method in Theology*, 50. Cf. also Frederick Lawrence's discussion of how liberal economics reduces Lonergan's second and third level of the human good to the first ("The Human Good and Christian Conversation," in *Communication and Lonergan: Common Ground for Forging the New Age*, ed. Thomas J. Farrell and Paul A. Soukup (Kansas City: Sheed & Ward, 1993), 248-68.

100. Lonergan, *Method in Theology*, 99.

101. Bernard Lonergan, "The Response of the Jesuit as Priest and Apostle in the Modern World," in *Second Collection*, 183; quoted in Carla Mae Streeter, in

"Glossary of Lonerganian Terminology," in *Communication and Lonergan: Common Ground for Forging the New Age*, ed. Thomas J. Farrell and Paul A. Soukup (Kansas City: Sheed & Ward, 1993), 317.

102. Lonergan, *Insight*, 237

103. Lawrence, 101.

104. Paul Hoyt-O'Connor, *Bernard Lonergan's Macroeconomic Dynamics* (Lewiston, NY: Edwin Mellen Press, 2004), 14.

CHAPTER 4

CREATIVITY IN LONERGAN'S ECONOMIC THOUGHT: *MACROECONOMIC DYNAMICS — FOR A NEW POLITICAL ECONOMY*

The Macroeconomic Problem

As discussed in the previous chapter, a characteristic emphasis of proper economic methodology is understanding how particular processes work; for adequate understanding and responsible action it is not sufficient that something works, we must know why it works. In the context of scientific inquiry, it is therefore crucial to discover the significant variables, in Lonergan's words, "the ones that account for things being the way they are."[1] In the case of economic inquiry, economists have to be able to be specific about what adjustments to individual and/or institutional behavior may be needed to promote a healthy functioning economy.[2] Since the political process relies on such advice to formulate economic policy, without this knowledge of macroeconomic process, politicians can only "throw up their hands,"[3] or else pursue policies that make economic conditions worse and/or favor only the wealthy or pursue agendas that serve only purely political purposes.

Since Lonergan's *Macroeconomic Dynamics: An Essay in Circulation Analysis* (ECA)[4] deals with macroeconomic theory, the significant variables will be aggregates of individual economic variables. Examples of aggregate variables from mainstream economics include gross national product (GNP), the overall price level, the quantity of money available in the national economy, the rate of inflation, and the unemployment rate, etc. (4). The "economic problem" as understood by Lonergan is the task of understanding significant aggregate variables, not in order to predict changes in these aggregates, but to provide some understanding of political-economic problems such as high inflation, high employment, differentials in income distribution, and the persistence of cycles of booms, repressions and depressions. In order then to understand changes in aggregates, economic analysis first has to identify which aggregate or aggregates are significant, those which give some understanding as to how different activities relate to each other (9).

Lonergan's Economic Analysis

A primary feature of Lonergan's analysis is his claim that orthodox macroeconomic theory has what can be called an 'attention deficit' in its lack of reflection on the cyclic nature of the economic process. The Great Depression of 1929-1933 that inspired him to write ECA showed to the world that economic crises such as sustained deep depressions were not only possible—against what orthodox theory had held up until that point—but were actually integral to the workings of a self-regulating open market. Writing somewhat contemporaneously with Lonergan, one of John Maynard Keynes' important points of departure from neoclassical macroeconomic theory was his claim that there existed no automatic corrective mechanism to keep an economy at equilibrium full-employment.[5] Keynes' corrective, a mix of fiscal and monetary policy designed to regulate demand for goods and investment, yielded the "Keynesian revolution" in both theory and practice and generally is given credit for the post-World War II mixed economy and economic boom.

However, the 1970's and early 1980's saw the presence of high rates of both inflation and unemployment, termed "stagflation," a phenomenon which again was not supposed to be possible according to mainstream economic theory, and which called into question the by then predominantly neo-Keynesian economic theory and policies. While Lonergan's macroeconomic theories were occasioned by the crisis of the Great Depression, his return to his economic thought in the 1970's and 1980's was stimulated by this crisis of stagflation.[6] In both cases, his focus on economics was in response to his perception and moral concern that mainstream economics whether as neo-classical, the "Keynesian synthesis," or re-emergent monetarism was not up to the economic task.

More specifically, the lack of attention that mainstream economics has paid to the distinction between "basic" goods (corresponding to what are known in common and economic parlance as consumer goods) and "surplus" goods (corresponding to producer goods) is what obscures discovery of the crucial wavelike or cyclic nature of production in the economy that results from the mutual conditioning of the production of the one type of good upon the other.[7] This oversight then leads to the familiar business cycle in both theory and practice.

On a deeper level, this lack of reflection is rooted in orthodox theory's tendency to content itself with analyzing different types of goods in terms of "what they are to us" rather than "what they are in themselves." For example, goods tend to be differentiated in mainstream thought only as to whether they are consumer goods or producer goods. Also, economics typically recognizes only one "circuit" of exchange, between households and firms. That is, money flows to firms in exchange for goods while wages and salaries flow to households in exchange for services performed. While this simple model is capable of being extended to incorporate financial and government sectors, plus foreign trade, it fails to differentiate on one hand, between "basic" goods (and accompanying flows of money) that contribute directly to the standard of living and, on the other, "surplus" goods (and accompanying flows of money) involved in the manufacture of the tools and machines needed to produce basic goods. Surplus goods contribute "only" indirectly, many times in a very roundabout way, to the standard of living. Orthodox analysis has thus failed to note that each "stage" of production has its own price level, quantity of production, and velocities, accelerations, and decelerations of production within a given time period.[8]

Lonergan's economic analysis attempts to show that these basic and surplus "circuits" of production are crucial because they interact with each other toward either 1) economic growth and a higher and more equitable standard of living for all or else, 2) economic contraction and a lower overall standard of living. In the process of transforming descriptive categorizations of economic process to explanatory analysis, Lonergan discovers that mainstream economics' concepts and reliance on the role of prices and profits were also inadequate to these tasks. Concurrently, it also incorporates wrongheaded ideas of economic moral agency.

Circuit analysis instead seeks to understand the normative dynamics of the interaction between production, exchange and finance within each circuit, and between the two circuits. Only in this way can economic agents possess the understanding to make timely and enlightened economic decisions. Revisiting the themes from my introductory chapter, Lonergan's economics responds to the need to know "what" we are talking about in moral inquiry. As Lonergan is said to have remarked, "if you want to help the poor you should start by studying economics." As discussed in Chapters 1 and 2, this exigency is the least integrated aspect of economic ethics. Lonergan's economics is also relevant to the overall concerns of well-being, human freedom, and democracy. Lonergan terms his economics a "democratic economics" because it relies neither upon a faceless market mechanism nor upon centralized, bureaucratic governmental action.[9] Rather, *Macroeconomic Dynamics* replaces both naive reliance on the price mechanism and the need for overly technocratic, socialistic control of individual economic agents, by better equipping economic agents, including governments, to guide production, distribution and finance toward a just *and* flourishing economy.[10]

Economic Methodology and Anthropology

As addressed in the preceding chapter, Lonergan's implicit economic methodology seeks a non-deductivist approach to economic reality.[11] Instead of making unempirical and simplistic assumptions about economic anthropology (e.g., self-interested maximization of utility) and economic processes (e.g., the model of pure competition) there is an explicit attempt in ECA to build upon research, observations, insights and judgments concerning how economic processes actually work and how economic agents can react either intelligently or unintelligently and in either morally enlightened or egoistic ways.[12] Or as Lonergan wrote, "there are discernable criteria in the productive process." Whether these criteria are able to be discovered and successfully adverted to—"understood or not, affirmed or denied, observed responsibly or disregarded"—depends on whether this project is undertaken by a "community of love or a community of egoists" (5).

To arrive at the significant variables needed to provide a dynamic, realistic and explanatory understanding of modern industrial market-oriented economic process (and to point out errors other investigators have made in highlighting relatively insignificant variables), Lonergan examines three fluctuating and cyclic factors of dynamic economic process: production, exchange and finance. The first step in determining significant variables is differentiating between levels of production, then noting its cyclic nature, then implications for the activities of exchange and finance.

The Productive Process

Lonergan defines the productive process as "the totality of activities bridging the gap between the potentialities of nature, whether physical, chemical, vegetable, animal or human nature, on the other hand, the actuality of standard of living." Although actual activities vary over time and among regions, standards of living of particular economies always derive from creative combinations of these potentialities of nature. Also, in all cases, the standard of living is not attained once and for all, but is accomplished through a process of continuous succession of activities, by "rhythmic repetition of constant or mobile routines" (19-20).

The productive process of the economies of communities generates not only standards of living, but the possibility of even higher standards of living. This is accomplished by using some portion of the technology and resources available in the economy to make tools that can, in turn, make other machines. In this way, a distinction is made between consumer or basic goods and producer or surplus goods according to how each relates to the standard of living: basic goods go directly into the standard of living while surplus goods go indirectly into the standard of living.[13]

Divisions of the Productive Process

Because the provision of the standard of living is accomplished through basic production, the emergent standard of living is equivalent with the rate of the process of basic production.[14] In other words, what is currently in basic production is neither some potentiality of physical or human nature, nor is it what has been produced and sold to consumers in a previous time period. So neither a tree nor a factory belong to basic production, but the use of the tree and use of the factory do. On the other hand, surplus production relates indirectly to the standard of living. That is, a new shoemaking machine does not enter into the standard of living, only its ulterior products do (23-5).

Another way of saying this is that the rate of production in the basic stage exists in a "point-to-point" relationship to the emergent standard of living. For example the production of bread can be conceived in terms of how many bushels of wheat go into producing so many loaves of bread. On the other hand, surplus production is the production of production components or maintenance of production for either the basic or next "lower" stage of production.

That is, the first level of surplus production makes production components for the basic stage of production and the second level of surplus production makes production components and provides services for the first level of surplus production, and so on. For example, in the basic circuit, bread is produced by processing wheat to be consumed as part of one's standard of living. The production of a scythe or harvester is on the first level of surplus production. The production of tools to make scythes is on the second surplus level, the production of computers to more efficiently produce the tools to make the scythes is on the third level, and so on. It is on a higher level than a point-to-point relationship. A scythe is not consumed in the production of a certain amount of bushels of wheat, even less would be a computer used in the making of tools to produce scythes.

What is true for the production of material elements in basic and surplus production is true also for the services involved in basic and surplus production. For example, the transportation of a given amount of wheat to bakeries and a truckload of loaves to supermarkets is done only once for these given amounts. However, the transportation of a new bread-delivery truck to a bakery is not done once per given amount of bread deliveries, but the service of transporting the truck is "repeated" over and over again for each delivery the new truck makes. Also some types of basic or surplus services are not incorporated into a material object, an example of this being a cab ride (25).

Dynamic Division of the Productive Process

It may seem at this point that Lonergan is only indulging in classification for classification's sake; an objection might be that while these divisions are interesting, of what value are they to actual macroeconomic analysis? His answer is that adequate understanding of economic process is only accomplished through functional analyses of the stages of production. The division of the production process into basic and surplus stages is neither purely descriptive, technical, nor proprietary. In this way Lonergan is able to transpose descriptive and proprietary notions, such as what portion of the gains of production go to whom, or should go to whom, in terms in light of a more explanatory account. For example, the relations among different types of elements—what they are in themselves—as reflected in the Periodic Table of Elements, differs from how say copper "appears" differently to us than hydrogen. Functional analysis reveals the difference between the law of gravity as expressed as the relationship between mass of objects and the distance between them, for example the gravitational pull between an apple and the earth vs. a mere description of the apples on the tree vs. a technical report of the effect of gravity upon apples as in Newton's famous story of being hit on the head by one vs. finally, a proprietorial relation as in Augustine's infamous "explanation" in the *Confessions* that if apples are still in the tree they belong to the owner of the tree, but if they are on the ground they belong to anyone who wants one.

The distinction between functional definitions,[15] and technical and proprietary definitions is essential to be able to arrive at a normative, explanatory account of economic or any other process.[16] Lonergan, in trying to discover the relationship between production and exchange in the basic and surplus circuits, stresses the functions that rates of either basic or surplus production and rates of payment play, rather than elucidating technical explanations. Technical explanations are of little explanatory use and merely describing proprietary control over production also does not provide explanatory usefulness and even tends to obscure functional explanation. For example, both capitalist and Marxist economics stress the proprietary nature of surplus goods as the value of goods over and above the value created by labor. For Marx surplus goods are by definition something appropriated from workers by capitalists (26, 33 fn. 34).[17] In capitalism, profits are incentives, "the rightful reward" for the risk undertaken by entrepreneurs, owners of capital and banks, etc. Labor gets its share of additional profits only after it "trickles down."

In other words, a virtue of Lonergan's analysis is that it does not depend on specifically who is producing, what firms are involved, or what factor of production we are talking about (capital, labor, management).[18] Lonergan instead desires to understand how production exists as an ongoing process—within this process, "surplus" represents functionally "ever higher complementations of potentialities of nature,"[19] rather than "what is left over" or what is "appropriated" by capitalists from labor. The rights and responsibilities of labor and management (and government) are elucidated by the analysis, not supposed by it as in again both capitalism and Marxism.[20]

Circuit Accelerations

Because the surplus stage of production is only indirectly related to the standard of living, it affects the standard of living usually only at the end of a series of stages or waves of acceleration of the productive process. But when it does finally get around to impacting the standard of living through the increased production of basic products, this impact is often enormous. This acceleration is the key not only to the dynamic nature of modern economic process,[21] but has also been integral to the changes in society since the industrial revolution such as division of labor, third-world development, socialist production, and Soviet-style five-year plans.

Acceleration of the productive process, in either basic or surplus production, can take place either over the short or long-term. Short-term acceleration is considered by Lonergan to be merely the result of more efficient use of existing capital, management or labor, and is usually restricted to one or a few companies at a time. It is also restricted by the level and availability of technological development (either of goods or ideas in management).[22] Long-term acceleration or production, on the other hand, is accomplished through the acquisition of more equipment and/or more efficient equipment and is not limited to one company or even one industry. Innovations such as the advent of steam power, electricity, the assembly line, the use of computers, etc., allow more efficient production throughout the economy. This type of acceleration is long-term because "it changes the basis on which short-term acceleration works" (32). That is, long-term acceleration improves and/or increases the equipment which a short-term acceleration can use in order to achieve its maximum output. For example, a company can only do so much to boost production without a technological improvement. Probably the best example, though in many ways regrettable for the workers as even Adam Smith pointed out,[23] is how the assembly line and division of labor not only increased production but almost the very nature of production.

Because long-term acceleration of the productive process relies upon the use of improved and/or additional equipment, in order for it to be achieved, each level of production must turn to the next highest level of production. For example, long-term acceleration in the basic stage is achieved through additional equipment acquired from the lowest stage of surplus production. Correspondingly, long-term acceleration in the lowest stage of surplus production is obtained by procuring equipment [and maintenance] from the next highest stage of surplus production, and so on. As Lonergan put it, "the structure of the productive process is a series of stages, where each stage is an aggregate of rates of production, and each lower stage receives from the next higher stage the means of long-term acceleration of its rates" (33). This shows how sustained changes in the rates of one stage are conditioned by flows of products for other stages.

An example of this dynamic mutual conditioning is the fact that if demand in the basic stage of production is strong enough, there is the possibility of a long-term acceleration throughout the economic process. That is, basic production will need to turn to the lowest state of surplus production in order to effect a long-term acceleration to meet its demand. For example, over the short-term a shoe manufacturer can increase the hours worked of its employees but in the long-term will need to purchase a more efficient shoemaking machine to boost its productivity. The lowest stage of surplus production may in turn have to procure from the next higher level of surplus production the means to meet the increased demand from the basic stage (i.e., the shoemaking machine company incorporates computer control), because short-term acceleration would not be enough to meet this demand, and so on. The limit is reached in the highest level of surplus production where the only form of acceleration available to it is short-term because there ultimately in this time frame, there is no further technological improvement to be had. The overall expansion is limited by the need for each level for maintenance and replacement of more and more complex equipment (34).

Cycles of the Productive Process

An important feature of Lonergan's analysis, a feature that sets it apart from other analyses such as those of Marx and Schumpeter (and other Austrian economists such as Hayek), is that Lonergan does not hold that business cycles are inevitable.[24] While Marx and Schumpeter went a long way towards explaining business cycles in capitalism, they concluded that not only are these cycles inevitable, their occurrence and worsening would lead toward the destruction of the free-market system. Lonergan instead argues for the possibility of the occurrence of a "pure cycle," which is a matter, "simply, of the surplus stage accelerating more rapidly than the basic stage, then of the basic stage accelerating more rapidly than the surplus," rather than the "cycles of booms and slumps, with positive and then negative accelerations" usually connected with business cycle theory. As Lonergan put it "only under certain conditions [but usual] of human inadaptation" does this pure cycle result in the familiar business cycle (35). It thus would be helpful to give a first approximation of the full definition of the pure cycle.

A Glimpse of the "Pure Cycle"

A first approximation of a description of the pure cycle is that there is a wave or surge in either the basic or surplus circuit which tapers off once the flow of new equipment and new services comes to an end in that circuit. Although production tapers off in that circuit, it does not mean that the rates of production in the economy as a whole decrease. As one circuit tapers off, the other circuit moves from a stationary state to an accelerative state, which tapers off and the cycle begins again when either the surplus expansion leads to its normal aim in a basic expansion. When the basic expansion tapers off, the economy "rests" in a stationary state at which the gains of the previous expansion is maintained. Then through human intelligence and creativity, a surplus expansion begins again. Human economic agents necessarily need to adapt their spending and investing in accord to the exigencies of whatever phase of the pure cycle happens to be in; if not, the familiar business cycle results. Of course, agents must be able to understand first what cycle the economy is in.

This pure cycle as a phenomenon general to modern economic process results from long-term acceleration of the economic process. As Lonergan put it, "It is to be expected, in the first place, that either a long-term acceleration does not occur at all or it occurs in a massive fashion . . . ." (117). He gives three reasons for why the regular occurrence of at least the possibility of the pure cycle would be generalized throughout the economy. First, as discussed below, a long-term acceleration throughout the economy would be massive because capital formation relies upon results from long-term planning. Second, the supply of even a single product depends upon many activities of many enterprises; thus an increase in demand ranges over several products. This leads to even more "development in series of productive units," and the introduction of more and/or better equipment will not take place in a random way, but toward an overall expansion. Third, the emergence of both new ideas and of concrete conditions necessary for their practical implementation forms "matrices of interdependence," in which the "emergence of new ideas and of the concrete conditions necessary for their productive implementation" proceed in dependence upon each other.[25] So for Lonergan, "economic history is a succession of time periods in which alternatively the conditions for great change are being slowly accumulated and later the greater changes themselves are being brought to birth" (36).[26]

Exchange

Once the productive process has been broken down in ECA and the existence if not full explanation of cycles and waves in production have been examined, Lonergan adds analysis of economic exchange to its analysis of the productive process. This is essential to economic analysis, not only because economic exchange is integral to any economy that has progressed beyond primitive fruit and nut gathering, but because the movement of payments where some medium of exchange, money, plays some fundamental role correspond to the movement of goods, a process which especially highlights the circulatory nature of the economy. As the productive processes of circuits are mutually conditioned, so are the movement of payments throughout the circuits; this provides the framework for Lonergan's discussion and explanation of rising and falling wages and prices. As Patrick Byrne writes, "Their [payments] theoretical relevance in Lonergan's analysis pertains to the way in which they facilitate or obtrude the productive process, and ultimately transform the potentialities of nature into a standard of living."[27] This is different from the price mechanism as the primary agent in distributing the receipts of commerce and the wages from employment. As Lonergan claims: "What [ECA] reveals is a mechanism . . . distinct from the price mechanism, for it determines the channels within which the price mechanism works" (19). As Byrne explains, "an ecology of mutually conditioned rhythms of production and payments" is a more appropriate way of conceiving of what we call an economy than something guided by a price "mechanism."[28]

In this way, Lonergan's analysis can help reorientate modern economics away from the over reliance in economic theory upon automatic equilibrating market forces. As Nicholas Kaldor argues in his article, "The Irrelevance of Equilibrium Economics," Adam Smith "went wrong" when he became enamored with price/profit determination, etc.:

> The difficulty with a new start is to pinpoint the critical area where economics went astray . . . I would put it in the middle of the fourth chapter of Vol. I of The Wealth of Nations. . . . In [that] chapter, after discussing the need for a social economy, Smith suddenly gets fascinated by the distinction between money price, real price, and exchange value and from then on, hey presto, his interest gets bogged down in the question of how values and prices for products and factors are determined. Once can trace a more or less continuous development of price theory from the subsequent chapters of Smith through Ricardo, Walras, Marshal, right up to Debreu and the most sophisticated present-day Americans."[29]

Thus, corresponding to rates of aggregate production, and to differences and correlations between the basic and surplus stages of production, are monetary exchanges, or aggregates of rates of payments. Central to the operation of an monetary exchange economy is the reality that what is produced and not sold is an unfinished product, that is, it has no economic value (39-40).[30]

Rates of Payment

ECA moves on to making essential distinctions and classes of payments that "provide the link between the dynamic structure of the productive process and dynamic structure of monetary circulation" (46). This discussion of classes of payments is based upon the "dynamic structure of process," and the rates based upon these classes are needed to arrive at an analysis of circulation. These rates of payments are defined by Lonergan as:

> Basic Expenditure (E') = the expenditure of consumers purchasing the emergent standard of living. For example, a woman purchases a book.
>
> Basic Receipts (R') = the receipts of basic expenditure by the final agents of basic supply—the money paid for the book.
>
> Surplus Expenditure (E") = the expenditure of producers purchasing surplus products—the bookstore purchases a new cash register.
>
> Surplus Receipts (R") = receipt of such expenditure by final agents of surplus supply—the money received for the cash register.
>
> Basic Income (I') = the initial payments entering basic demand—the woman's paycheck or other source of income that is "set-aside" for purchases such as books.
>
> Surplus Income (I") = the initial payments entering surplus demand—the money set-aside from their receipts by the bookstore to purchases such as cash registers.
>
> Basic Outlay (O') = the aggregate of initial payments involved in basic production during a given interval—e.g., the money paid to workers, saved or invested or paid for surplus products.
>
> Surplus Outlay (O") = the aggregate of initial payments involved in surplus production during a given interval—e.g., the money paid to workers, saved or invested or paid for other surplus products (46-8).

These definitions and the circulatory relationships between them are relatively straightforward and reflect Lonergan's division of the production process into two distinct circuits. The movement of goods and money between the respective functions and the two circuits is depicted on the next page (Figure 4.1) from the helpful diagram provided in ECA.[31] It is important to remember, however, that for Lonergan such things as basic and surplus income and demand are not "places" that correspond to business enterprises or consumers. Rather, they are functions. An example

Figure 4.1: Diagram of Economic Circulation

(Bernard Lonergan, "Diagram of Rates of Flow," ECA, 55)

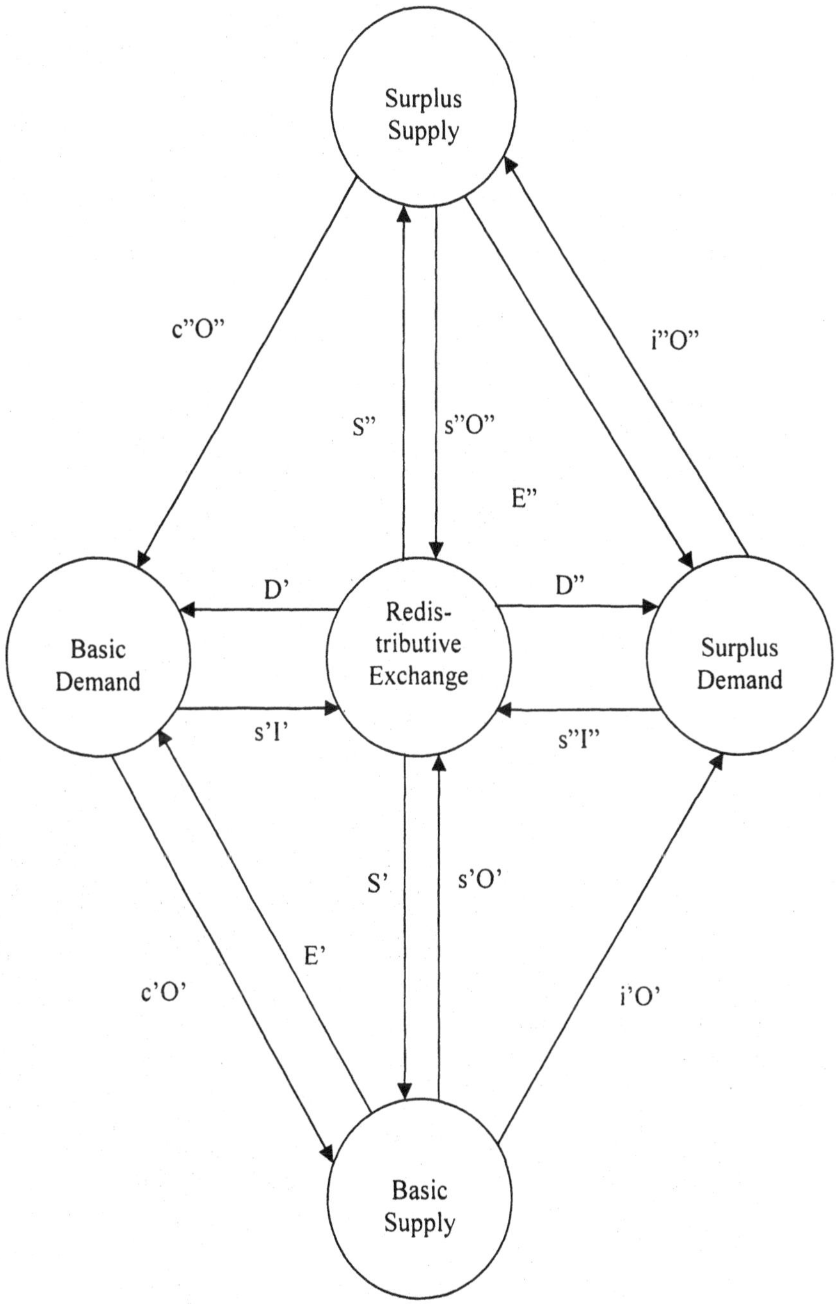

of this is that once a paycheck is received, the amount of that paycheck destined for purchase of consumer goods belongs to basic demand and the amount of that paycheck destined directly (through investment) or indirectly (through savings) for purchase of surplus goods belongs to surplus demand.

Therefore, it does not matter whether the paycheck originated from employment in the basic or surplus sector, but is dependent upon the decision of the employee to consume or save/invest. A more concrete, if not typical example would be if from my $2,000 paycheck, I spend $1000 on the immediate demands of my standard of living (food, mortgage or rent, etc.), and spend $1000 on purchasing a backyard windmill supplying energy to a local die maker in surplus production. The resulting basic and surplus demand is dependent on my decision, not upon whether I received my paycheck from working as a restaurant worker or as a steelworker.[32]

The circulatory nature of these rates of payment is shown in the "baseball" diagram on the following page. Consumers (individuals or firms) purchase goods produced in either the basic or surplus circuit (E' and E"). The producers in each circuit receive this money (R' and R"). Initial payments paid to factors of production (in the aggregate, O' and O") provide the resources (I' and I") to make expenditures for (enable demand for), expenditures in either the basic or surplus circuit.

However, because firms are dependent upon money from either receipts from prior sales or from other source, and because not all of basic and surplus income end up purchasing goods, there arises a complexity which leads Lonergan to introduce the notion of a monetary function into his analysis. In introducing this notion, he also takes an important step towards defining the circulation of money. As will be seen, the circulation of money is not merely a rotational movement of money but rather a "circular series of dependence of some flows on payments on other flows" (48).

Lonergan provides these definitions concerning the monetary function:

> Basic Demand = money held in reserve for basic expenditure, on its way to entering E'.
>
> Basic Supply = money on its way from R' to O', from receipts of firms engaged in basic production in this period to outlays in basic production in the next
>
> Surplus Demand = money held in reserve for surplus expenditures, on its way to entering E"

Surplus Supply = money on its way from R" to O", from receipts of firms engaged in surplus production in this period to outlays in surplus production in the next

Redistributive Function = money held in reserve for any number of redistributive purposes (banks, governments, stock market, etc.)

c'/c" = the proportion of income derived from basic/surplus productive process (O'/O") destined to be spent on the standard of living (48).

Thus there exists the fractions c' and c" of O' and O" respectively that move to basic demand. Correspondingly:

i'/i" = the fraction of O'/O" that moves to surplus demand and,

s'/s" = the fraction of O'/O" that moves to the redistributive function, where

c + i + s = 1, since money received is either spent on basic products, invested/saved or spent on surplus products.

The significance of these equations is that they introduce the "crossover" relationships between basic and surplus production. This is crucial in Lonergan's analysis, because it not only brings to light the fruits of Lonergan's implicit definitions of basic and surplus production, but also because it allows for the possibility for individuals and governments to rationally direct the economy.

Crossovers Between the Basic and Surplus Circuits

The crossovers are represented in Fig. 4.1 (1) by the term c"O" and in (2) by the term i'O'. They are termed crossovers because both c"O" and i'O' are "leakages" from one circuit to the other. In (1), there is the contribution of c"O", or the fraction of initial payments to workers in surplus production that go to surplus demand. Thus a fraction of wages paid out to workers in the surplus stage ends up being spent upon the standard of living, or the products of the basic stage. In (2), the crossover is i'O', or that fraction of outlays that go toward surplus demand, or toward purchasing the products of surplus production to be used in the basic stage of production.

The importance of defining these terms and understanding these relationships is that for equilibrium—which is dynamic, not static—to be established in the system, these crossovers must balance. Without this balance, either the basic stage is drained for the purpose of the surplus stage or the surplus stage is drained for the purpose of the basic stage. If the pure cycle is understood as both stages as constantly accelerating, albeit one either faster or slower than the other, depending upon what part of the pure cycle the economy is in, the drainage represented by the unbalancing crossovers means that one cycle must be decelerating instead. This development ends up in the familiar business cycle, with its cycles of booms and slumps, growth and recession, increase in the standard of living for all (for a time) and consequently miserable levels of unemployment. Lonergan's analysis highlights the importance of understanding what the crossovers are, what mechanisms cause them, and how we can adjust our exchange, production, and financial actions to try to balance them.

Coordination of Financial Operations

Before moving on to a more explicit discussion of the actual mechanisms of acceleration in the basic and surplus stages of production and their mutual conditioning, it is important to determine the necessity and possible effects of money coming into and out of the circuits from and into the redistributive function through the activity of bankers, etc., who are able to make loans to basic and surplus demand and supply.[34] Since monetary flows can be correlated with production and consumption of goods and services in the basic and surplus circuits or stages, the flow of money payments between the circuits and between the redistributive function and the circuits must be cyclical as well. For the pure cycle to operate, these money payments must be coordinated with the respective cycles.

In order to add the flow of rates of money into and out of the redistributive function to the circuits, the following notations and definitions were added to Lonergan's analysis:

S' = the amount of money added to basic supply from the redistributive function
S" = the amount of money added to surplus supply from the redistributive function
D' = the amount of money added to basic demand from the redistributive function
D" = the amount of money added to surplus demand from the redistributive function
M' = the total amount of money added to the basic circuit
M" = the total amount of money added to the surplus circuit (51-52).

Leaving the effects of government fiscal and monetary policy and foreign trade aside for the moment, the change of quantity of money per unit interval, or put more simply, the amount of money (while remembering Lonergan is always talking about rates of production, acceleration, movement of money, etc.) added to the basic circuit (M') is dependent upon five separate rates of money moving into and out of the redistributive function and between the two circuits. These are: 1) the addition of money from the redistributive function to basic supply (S'); 2) the addition of money from the redistributive function to basic demand (D'); 3) the amount of money per unit interval moving out of basic outlay into the redistributive function (s'O'); 4) the amount of money per unit interval moving out of surplus outlay into the redistributive function (s'I'); and 5) the crossover difference already defined as c"O" - i'O' (the money leaking from the surplus circuit to the basic minus the money leaking from the basic to the surplus.). Any of these rates, including the total money added to the basic circuit can be a negative number.[35] Money diverted from expenditures and outlays into the redistributive function, and money added to basic and surplus demand and supply from the redistributive function are also depicted in Fig. 4.1.

Finance: The Importance of the Redistributive Function for Circuit Acceleration

The inclusion of the role of the redistributive function in the overall analysis yields an additional process to that of the basic stage being maintained and accelerated by a series of surplus stages. Lonergan's first task, once the redistributive function is acknowledged, is to correlate the magnitude of the need for money in the basic and surplus stages with the magnitudes and frequencies of turnover in the productive processes. Understanding these correlations underlie the importance of circulation analysis: "On that basis, it will be possible to distinguish stable and unstable combinations and sequences of rates in the three main areas [production, exchange and finance] and so gain insight into the long-standing recurrence of crises in the modern expanding economy" (54).

Circuit acceleration takes place without hindrance when quantities of money move freely between the circuits and the redistributive function, especially transfers of money from the redistributive function to the circuits. More specifically, the "normal" entry and exit of money to and from the circuits in a healthy expanding economy is from the redistributive function to the supply functions as basic and surplus supply adjusts to projected increases or decreases in demand. Correspondingly, redistributive transfers to demand (D' - s'I' and D" - s"I") and the crossover differences must vary only slightly from zero in order for this normal movement of money to or from the circuits through the supply circuits to exercise a stimulating effect toward either positive or negative circuit acceleration. If redistributive transfers to demand are significant they have the possibility of being deleterious (e.g., inflationary) to proper economic functioning, from "not being directly related to demands of production."[36] If they are not balanced through equal and opposite redistributive transfers to surplus demand there will be also be problems (e.g., deficit spending). And if the crossover is not equal to zero, there will be draining of the circuits. Although, as with supply, ineffective demand can be remedied by drawing upon reserves (in the form of cash or credit) from the redistributive function, but as Lonergan says, "neither cash nor credit will avail against a sustained inequality of crossovers" (70). As will be seen in the next section there is always the corresponding threat that expansions will be prematurely curtailed as a result.

The General Theory of Circuit Acceleration

Lonergan's general theory can be very briefly summarized as: changes in the productive process, or more explicitly, in phases of the production process resulting from mutual conditioning between the basic and surplus circuits are correlated with 1) the resulting changes in rates of payments in exchange and financial transactions; and 2) necessary intelligent and responsible changes in rates, payments and financial transactions in order to avoid turning natural wavelike acceleration and deceleration phases in the productive process into either price spirals in a boom and spiraling unemployment in a slump. The difference between Lonergan's approach to mainstream economics is that the pure cycle allows these changes to occur in an intelligent and responsible fashion whereas orthodox economics maintains either that the business cycle is inevitable or can only be managed by curtailing expansion to some extent, thus "short-circuiting increases in standard of living for the whole in favor of keeping inflation low.[37] Lonergan's analysis allows for the existence of inflationary and deflationary periods in necessary rhythm with different phases of economic expansion.

Phases in Economic Expansion

It is necessary now to discuss how the economic process can expand from a stationary state and the resulting range of possible adjustments that can occur in rates of production, rates of payment and rates of transfers to and from the redistributive function. The significance of this move away from the stationary state is its possible effect on the overall standard of living in an economic system.

The simplest assumption is that movement away from a stationary state begins in the basic circuit through what Lonergan terms a *minor basic expansion*. This is a good first example of the mutual conditioning between the basic and surplus circuits. A minor basic expansion is continued and terminated when firms in the basic stage of production take up slack in production capacity either by employing more workers or putting into use unused or underfunctioning plant and equipment; this of course results in a greater abundance of consumer goods and services. In this particular case of acceleration, expansion may proceed slowly but also may "gradually spread to the whole basic process, and only be forced to end when unemployment is full and all productive capacity is in use" (76). The effect upon rates of payment is that rates of basic outlay and basic income increase in the expansion.

However, while a minor basic expansion is inherently limited, the greater the magnitude of the expansion, the greater the likelihood that it may trigger a *minor surplus expansion*. This happens as the need for maintenance of existing plant and equipment and for additional machines causes the crossover from basic outlay to surplus demand to increase in the form of payments by basic firms to surplus firms for replacements of worn parts and for particular machines, especially if new basic firms start up production in response to increased demand. Like the minor basic expansion, a minor surplus expansion consists of taking up slack in the productive process. Surplus rates of outlay and income accordingly also increase in a minor surplus expansion.

As unemployed workers are added to surplus production, aggregate (although not average) wages paid in surplus outlay increases and the crossover from surplus outlay to basic income increases (as workers spend their income on basic goods), increasing basic demand to purchase the standard of living. Since there has not yet occurred a notable increase in basic production, this new demand causes prices to rise in the basic market, with no corresponding increase in costs to basic producers. This rise in basic profits provide an additional incentive for basic expansion, which is accomplished through increased purchase of investment in surplus goods of new equipment and greater maintenance of old, and in turn additional support for the minor surplus expansion directly through the crossover and indirectly through the redistributive function as basic savings (S' - s'O') eventually find their way to surplus outlay (S" - s"O").

Prices would also seem to be required to be at least constant in the surplus circuit during the expansion, because otherwise firms would incur losses as the gap between outlays made when prices were high and receipts when sales were low would be constantly increasing. So as production goes up, prices need to stay at least constant or rise with it. Another necessary pressure is caused as demand increases for labor and limited resources, increasing costs and prices for final prices. This inflationary pressure is healthy; attempts to keep inflation at a minimum at this point could stall the expansion of production and employment.[38]

Although this expansion is termed "minimal" by Lonergan (because it does not result in any great expansion of surplus goods), it may lead to a *major surplus expansion* (76-80). This is possible because the surplus process exists on many levels; that is, the surplus process produces not only the basic processes' means of production, but also its own, in many degrees of "roundaboutness" (76). Thus if a minor surplus expansion is deep enough, it provides demand for more machinery and equipment and more efficient machinery and equipment, which are produced on the next level of surplus production, and so on. Surplus expansions can also be initiated in the surplus circuit with innovations sparking a minor and then major surplus expansion, demonstrated in ECA by Lonergan's stress on innovation and his frequent advertence to Schumpeter's important work on entrepreneurship and growth ("creative destruction") in the economy.

In this example, although minor basic expansions may trigger minor surplus expansions which may in turn cause a major surplus expansion, the "natural goal"[39] of a major surplus expansion is a *major basic expansion.* The effect of the major surplus expansion on the basic stage occurs only with a lag, the length of that lag depending upon the number of stages in surplus development and the length of time it takes "to get each of the stages running and keeping up with the other stages" (77). For example, the tremendous increase in consumer use of the Internet has derived from the increased technology made available by products from various stages in the surplus sector, such as larger servers, faster computer processors, larger distribution networks, and other technological developments that operate the Internet itself, developments which can be said to have proximately begun with the introduction of personal computers in the 1970's.

The financial sector can also be a cause of lags. This is because, as discussed above, an influx of increasing quantities of money is needed for expansions to burgeon.[40] Any acceleration in the circuits calls for increase in quantity of money in order for each circuit to expand production throughout the circuit at current prices. In fact, a major surplus expansion requires massive inflows of money along from banks and other lenders and investors to the surplus economy (S" - s"O"). These allow increase the rate of production and purchases of innovative surplus products. This need for massive new flows to surplus supply brings out the crucial significance of savings to "underpin the whole redistributional area of the economy" (70).

Phases of the Major Surplus Expansion

The major surplus expansion in Lonergan's analysis consists of three phases: the initial, the transitional, and the closing phase. In the initial phase, the surplus process is in self-development as investment flows from the redistributive function to surplus outlay, and money flows through the crossover from basic outlay to surplus income. Since surplus production provides both the basic means of producing and its own means of production, the intentional internal development of the surplus circuit in a major surplus expansion (caused by a sufficiently great minor surplus expansion) yields an enormous increment in surplus outlay and income.[41]

The transitional phase of a major surplus expansion unfolds as major surplus expansion begins to deliver its "proper fruits" in an enhanced rate of widening and deepening of basic enterprises as they take advantage of new and efficient modes of production and/or services. For a while surplus outlay and income increases as surplus sales increase not only to surplus firms that the surplus circuit serves, but also the basic firms it now begins to serve. But sooner or later, the self-development of the surplus sector begins to taper off. Tapering off of acceleration of surplus production implies lower or at least slowing demand for workers and lower aggregate wages, which lowers the income in the surplus circuit and money spent by surplus workers in the basic market. This source, in other words, "ceases to be a gusher" of windfall profits for basic suppliers (79). At the same time, the (lagging) basic sector expansion is causing an increase in demand for labor, increasing wage rates and further lowering the basic price spread. Also, unemployed workers in the surplus sector are able to transfer to basic production and receive their wages there. In Lonergan's analysis, these developments herald the closing phase of the major surplus expansion and hopefully the opening of the major basic expansion. The lagging but potentially massive major basic expansion is marked by increases in demand for labor in the basic sector, rising real wages, increased production per individual basic enterprise, increased basic enterprises, and a boost in the standard of living for the entire economy.[42]

I say hopefully because at this point the overall success of the economic system is measured by the extent to which the major basic expansion can be completed. The system's success is measured by the absence of "mishaps" (e.g. numerous plant closings), inflation, unemployment, and breaks in confidence in the economy as it "makes its way serenely into the haven of the stationary state" (80). Lonergan stresses that the goal of a new stationary state resulting from a successful major basic expansion is not the "mere backwardness" of an economy that has no potential for growth, nor of "stagnation when disastrous crash follows on an earlier apparent triumph." Instead, the stationary state in a pure cycle preserves all the gains of the preceding minor and major basic and surplus expansions. At this point the economy is content to reproduce its gains at a constant rate. This state will last as long until there is new impetus for further developments in the economic process resulting from human invention and enterprise, or until new developments are "grasped by human intelligence and eventually become practically conceived possibilities." Thus expansion in the surplus circuit is not necessarily driven by demand, but because a few people envision, "however obscurely and indistinctly," what their innovations make possible and are able to find needed financial backing. For example, the start of UNIVAC did not presuppose the subsequent demand for computers.[43]

In the pure cycle, when the basic expansion reaches its full term, that is, if economic agents have made intelligent and responsible decisions, the total income of the community will be distributed correctly (and justly). This responsibility-oriented understanding is a long way from the self-correcting market envisioned by classical economists and from the reliance on deficit spending by Keynesian neoclassical economists. It also avoids the pitfalls of the 'inevitable' business cycle such as negative accelerations, contractions of production, unemployment or inflation.[44]

"The Dangers of Misadventures and Palliatives"

The possibility of a pure cycle in Lonergan's analysis immediately brings to mind the possibility of the 'impure' cycle. Indeed, Lonergan argued that without an understanding of the exigencies of the pure cycle, a malfunctioning cycle is highly likely to occur. The history of the trade cycle with its heights and accompanying expectation of "higher" heights and/or continued prosperity, followed invariably by painful low periods attests to this. Lonergan's emphasis on correct understanding emphasizes responsible human decision making according to the exigencies of the pure cycle. This stress on responsibility is tied through this analysis to the saving/investing/consuming/producing decisions of all economic agents, whether individuals, labor unions, corporations or nations, or even international bodies.

As noted above, a major source of decline in the economy according to ECA is the failure for crossover of aggregate rates of payments between the basic and surplus circuit to balance. Small perturbations in the crossover balance, as long as they come close to balancing out, will not seriously wound the economic process. However, sustained, or as Lonergan called them, systematic excesses in the crossover balance will be severely deleterious over the long run. As will be seen, excessive crossovers are usually due to mistakes both in economic practice and theory: mistaken expectations connected with rising profits, a mistaken notion of what constitute profits themselves, and the mistaken presumption that the profit motive should be the primary motivation of business.[45] Also, economic actors besides businesses must adjust their decisions in line with the pure cycle. Individuals, groups of individuals such as labor unions, and governments must act intelligently, reasonably and responsibly for the economic good of order to function towards providing an increasing and equitable standard of living throughout the economy.

Misadaptation to the Exigencies of the Pure Cycle

For example, take an excessive crossover in favor of the surplus circuit over the basic circuit. As seen in the diagram, i'O' would be greater than c"O", period after period, permanently removing money from the basic circuit to the surplus circuit. The consequence of this is determined generally by the price mechanism, and the 'laws' of supply and demand.[46]

If money is drained out of the basic circuit, there results ineffective demand for the supply of basic goods. When this happens, prices will tend to fall, reducing profits of enterprises engaged in basic production. In order to at least maintain current profits, firms will likely cut back or downsize their rates of production and their workforce. In doing so, they reduce still further money available for basic consumption, shrinking further profits and provoking further cutbacks, and so on. This recessionary state of affairs can lead to a depression when receipts to firms become so low that those not sheltered by rents or market share go bankrupt. The depression will eventually reach an equilibrium position with low production and high unemployment.

If the recession lasts long enough, the depression takes over and threatens the financial stability of the economy. The ongoing process of sound firms becoming marginal and finally going bankrupt provides a stimulus for investors to flee the stock market, selling off their stock holdings in anticipation of still further losses. Bankers stiffen their credit policy, also finding that their accounts are dwindling as deposits lessen and withdrawals mount. As they attempt to collect collateral to close this gap, they find that its value has "declined greatly or even become worthless" (81). Banks begin to close their doors and finally the government calls a moratorium on runs on banks , as happened in the Great Depression. But, according to ECA, recovering the financial system cannot be the first step back toward a healthy economy. The economy can only be re-instituted through reestablishing snapped lines of production or building up others in their place. Otherwise, an "inflow of money into the economy may be described as priming the pumps but can have no effect beyond aimlessly scattering money around" (81).

This dynamic shows the severe nature of the requirement that crossovers balance. If they don't not only will the economy fail to reach its full potential (within given institutional restraints), but severe decline of recession and even depression will set in if measures are not taken by economic agents to restore the crossover balance.

Potential Problems in the Initial Phase of the Surplus Expansion

To put this within the dynamic context of expansion outlined in ECA, a particularly dangerous time for crossovers to go out of balance is in the initial phase of the major surplus expansion. Recall that during the surplus expansion more workers are being hired in the surplus sector. Part of their wages go towards their standard of living, the amount spent on basic goods equaling the crossover amount c"O". In a major surplus expansion this amount will be enormous.[47] However, since the major basic expansion has not yet taken off, there will be no additional goods available in the basic sector for these increased wages to purchase. Therefore, prices will tend to rise. Since basic enterprises had already made their outlays in the production of these goods at a lower price level, the profits received by them due to the higher price level are 'windfall' profits, that is the profits are received without any additional effort by retailers to achieve them. These increased profits are not illegitimate in Lonergan's view. What is important is how they are used.

As long as these profits are invested in the still-burgeoning surplus expansion (whether directly through the crossover i'O' or indirectly through the redistributive function), they will balance out the crossover from the surplus to the basic and the surplus expansion will be maintained. If they are not, if these increased profits are interpreted as personal income to be used by owners and managers to increase their standard of living, the surplus expansion will not be able to come to its fullest term and will begin to contract as money is drained out of the surplus circuit into the basic. Because of these consequences Lonergan termed those profits over and above normal profits the "social dividend," or more technically, "pure surplus income." This is a prime example of how Lonergan differs from the capitalist view that these profits accrue to owners and investors to be used as they desire and the Marxist view that profits belong to workers. Indeed Lonergan maintains that until his analysis, no one had an adequate view of surplus income.[48] The proportion of surplus income which heads toward purchase of additional surplus products above and beyond maintenance and replacement needs Lonergan termed pure surplus income or the social dividend because it is not supposed to go to improving individuals' standard of living but to be used in "upgrading the capital formation of society" as a whole, "shifting the probabilities of the emergence of a higher standard of living."[49]

Therefore, from the normative viewpoint of ECA these windfall profits need to be put back into the surplus expansion if in the end the overall standard of living of the economy is to increase. Otherwise, money will be drained from the surplus circuit causing the economy to contract and give up the potentially large future gains in the standard of living for all. So they are neither to be misinterpreted as personal income by their recipients and spent on improving individuals' standard of living, or invested, at this point, in anything but the surplus expansion. One advantage of the surplus expansion is that this surplus income goes to those who are most likely not to spend it on their standard of living as those of lower incomes are more likely to do, because a higher fraction of the expenditures of lower income groups tends to be spent on their standard of living. That is one reason why the surplus expansion is termed by Lonergan the "anti-egalitarian" phase of economic expansion.[50] As long as the windfall profits received by basic producers are invested back into the surplus expansion, there is more likelihood the crossovers will balance.

This analysis shows that although the price mechanism works automatically in a fashion to correct excessive basic spending following upon surplus expansion, it does not make certain that economic agents will act intelligently, reasonably and responsibly in accord with the further exigencies of the pure cycle. This is due to false expectations. In fact, despite the price mechanism working towards restoring the crossover balance as prices rise in the basic sector when the major surplus expansion takes off, rising prices increase the probability that needed further adjustments will not be made; as seen below they may give rise to unintelligent and irresponsible increases in basic production, causing prices to rise further. The importance of Lonergan's analysis is that without the prerequisite understanding of the pure cycle and the role of pure surplus income, economic agents will not be able to adjust their decisions in the required manner.

A second alternative in the major surplus expansion would be for basic enterprises to increase their own production. The first misinterpretation of the social dividend discussed was that this social dividend was personal income. This second alternative results from another misinterpretation of this increase in profits, or pure surplus income. As Lonergan wrote, an increase in the absolute price level that led to windfall profits may be falsely understood as an increase in demand for all goods (whereas a relative price increase usually signifies more is demanded of that product relative to others—that people want "more and more of everything." This misapprehension spurs basic enterprises to expand production and hire more workers, causing wage rates to increase. This in turn further increases prices and in response basic demand and production is expanded still further. In this way, the initial surplus expansion has been converted into a boom with prices and employment rising. However, those on fixed incomes do not participate in this increased prosperity; because of inflation their real incomes are going down. Since they are able to consume less and less they undergo what is termed in economics "forced savings."[51] The amount not spent or 'saved' that provides the surplus income needed to finance whatever is left of the surplus expansion. Prices will rise to continue to provide the savings required by the surplus expansion.

There are two corollaries to this type of misinterpretation of rising corporate profits; each pointing out that it is not only corporations and their owners, but also stockholders and managers that have to respect the exigencies of the pure cycle. One is that unions with strong bargaining power may seek to get 'their share' of this pure surplus income as if it becomes reflected in increased corporate profits. This also causes prices to go up with the attendant consequences for those in 'weaker unions' who are unable to negotiate higher wages and for those on fixed incomes. The second corollary is that government may be incited to force corporations receiving high profits to assume more of the burden of redistributing income to those less well off. This also can be inflationary because it adds to basic demand without increasing the amount of goods available. While it helps those on fixed income, like all the above misadventures, it stalls the surplus expansion and delays and lessens the potential major basic expansion which provides the more massive redistribution of income to workers and those on fixed income.

Sooner or later in these three types of misinterpretation of the exigencies of the pure cycle, the increased availability of basic goods reduces inflationary pressures on goods and increased pressure in labor markets increase wages. These two effects combine to reduce the basic price spread, and accordingly, high profits and the boom will end as employers start cutting back: the boom ends and moves into a recession.

Potential Problems in the Transitional Phase of the Surplus Expansion

If the major surplus expansion in its initial phase is able to avoid either contraction or boom, another critical time emerges as the transition to the major basic expansion begins. In this phase surplus sector acceleration begins to come to an end as the society achieves a new plateau of development where there are received diminishing returns to investment and more and more resources go towards maintaining and replacing products already sold to lower levels of the surplus sector and to the basic sector, instead of producing new-and-improved surplus goods. As expectations of profit in the surplus sector begin to decline, surplus investment will go down as defensive behavior sets in and producers either save excess income instead of investing it or cut back on their demand for credit. This cuts short the surplus expansion, short-circuiting an effective basic expansion and its resultant healthy effects on the standard of living.

Potential Problems in the Closing Phase of the Surplus Expansion

If the economy is able to reach this stage without a deep recession, or depression following upon boom, a risk occurs as the major surplus expansion ends and the major basic expansion begins. As the surplus expansion cools, the crossover from the surplus to the basic circuit (c"O") grows at a slower rate. As the fruits of the surplus expansion in the form of more and effective machinery and other tools of production are delivered to the basic expansion, accelerating it and increasing dramatically the amount of basic goods, inflationary pressures for these goods lessen. These two factors combine to reduce the basic price spread and thus the basic profit margin. That basic demand is growing as a result of increased wages and lower prices (restoring the real income of those on fixed income who had a lowered standard of living during the anti-egalitarian phase of surplus expansion) should stimulate further basic expansion. However, as this price spread and windfall profits received shrink in tandem, not being satisfied with this move towards "normal" profits (possibly fearing the stock market's adverse reaction to short-term profits), corporations may implement strategies designed to keep their profits high, if not increase them.[52] Normal profit in economics is the level of profits a company needs to stay in business in a normal economic situation (Lonergan's stationary state) and cover what is needed for owners and managers to purchase a proportionate standard of living.

Nevertheless, if this key distinction between normal profit and pure surplus income is not made, then falling pure surplus income in this stage might signal to owners and managers that their standard of living is falling. One way to avoid this loss of personal income is through downsizing. This results in lowering of effective demand lowering causing prices to fall and unemployment beginning to grow. The lowering of prices, profits, and demand will provoke further rounds of cutbacks and layoffs and prices will continue to spiral downward. A further complication can arise when profits are not put back into expanding basic production but are put instead into areas which are less risky since they are less vulnerable to falling profits resulting from falling prices and ineffective demand. These additional sources of pure surplus income include fixed interest bearing bonds, enormous salaries (executives often receive huge bonuses even as their firms lose money), fees, and stock options to chief executives and higher level managers. Relatively large market shares can also cushion ineffective demand,[53] and corporations may have other sources of pure surplus income in the forms of royalties, patent fees, licensing, etc., which enable them to maintain their high levels of profits in the midst of otherwise shrinking revenues in their main enterprises. The problem with some firms being sheltered in this way is that less-sheltered firms have to accept an even higher share of falling profits, reducing their receipts and their ability to maintain and replace the capital equipments and services. They eventually are driven to bankruptcy. As prices continue their downward spiral, less marginal firms also go out of business and the recession changes to a depression.

The correct maneuver, in Lonergan's view, would be for businesses to instead expand production and employment as demand becomes more effective. This would stabilize prices through keeping effective demand high. This would mean following the precept of benevolence and enterprise instead of the classical precept of thrift and enterprise. This phase marks the "egalitarian" phase of the economic expansion, a wave that metaphorically truly does raise the standard of living in all ports and of all boats.[54]

Consequences of *Macroeconomic Dynamics* for Economic Fluorishing

If it does emerge, in the major basic expansion of the pure cycle enterprises in the basic sector, in the healthy competitive drive to outdo the next firm, purchase and begin to implement into production the additional and improved technology that are the fruits of the surplus expansion, so as to increase their productivity. In doing so, they will increase outlay, hire more workers and expand production. Because more and more goods are becoming available, prices start to go down. Along with increased wages as the labor market heats up (along the way adding workers released from surplus production), lowered prices mean real basic income goes up, making basic demand become more and more effective, stimulating enterprises to expand basic production even more (as long as firms seek to maximize revenues rather than seek higher than normal profits).

On the other hand, instead of prices and increased basic production bringing on redistribution of income—the result of following precepts of benevolence and enterprise—defensive behavior in favor of high profits brings about a recession and possibly depression, accompanied by mounting obsolescence and neglect of capital formation. In the long-term (however, as Keynes pointed out, in the long run we are all dead), eventually another long-term acceleration of surplus and then basic production comes about eventuating more prosperous times. But in this case, instead of a continuous rise in the standard of living as the economy moves from one equilibrium state to a higher one, the business cycle of boom and inevitable slump sets in with no guarantee that the next expansion will even bring the standard of living up to the previous levels it enjoyed during the previous expansion, before it moved into recession.[55]

Based on this analysis, Lonergan argues that one moral of this story is that firms' attempts to maintain their high profits received in the major surplus expansion result from their failure to distinguish between a normal profit, which can be constant, and pure surplus income (social dividend), which varies depending upon what phase the economy is. For example, pure surplus income) mounts in a major surplus expansion, declines as it tapers off, and goes to zero when the expansion is finished. Just because a firm may be receiving higher than normal profits in a surplus expansion does not mean that the meaning of normal 'ratchets' up.

Instead, this social dividend, as it name implies, is not to be spent for higher standard of living to owners of basic firms, nor to be saved by them. Rather it is to be invested directly through the crossover from basic supply to surplus demand or indirectly through the redistributional area. This is crucial because, according to the exigencies of the pure cycle, the money not invested contracts surplus production, but if invested, "keeps surplus production at its attained volume." Moreover, if money keeps crossing over from the basic sector to the surplus circuit at an appropriate level interval by interval, surplus production will not taper off, but will keep accelerating. The static state of dynamic equilibrium will thus be attained and if maintained, standard of living will keep increasing.

However, it is not only firms that need to make required adjustments. Individuals must also adjust their consumption/savings decisions in line with what phase of the pure cycle the economy is in. Since the major surplus expansion requires massive amounts of funding, individuals also should put their extra income received from participation in the major surplus expansion into savings or investment. Accordingly, in this stage unions should forego wage increases that would take funds out of the surplus expansion. This is the anti-egalitarian phase, since it is more likely that individuals who have already most of their needs and wants supplied will receive surplus income. In that way, extra income created by the major surplus expansion goes back into itself so it might reach its fullest potential. On the other hand, in the basic expansion—the egalitarian phase—savings must decrease and income must be redistributed in a major way to those most likely to spend additional income on basic products, such as those on fixed incomes and the poor, who would have been most adversely especially affected by an earlier price rise in the major surplus expansion. Governments also have an important role, although they can have as deleterious a role to play as the corporations whose actions they seek to counterbalance.[56]

This deleterious role for government is discussed extensively by Lonergan under the topic of deficit spending, which, along with seeking favorable balances of trade, are examples of "superposed" circuits. These circuits represent flows to and from the redistributive function (through, for example, redistribution of income through taxation) different from flows integral to the working of the pure cycle, between the basic and surplus circuits and between the redistributive function and surplus demand and surplus supply.

Although I am not able in this book to go into depth on superposed circuits, it should be noted that in addition to the above discussed ways of misadaptation to the pure cycle, both deficit spending and favorable balances of trade are examples of governments and corporations avoiding the need for letting pure surplus income (and thus excess profits above normal) decline and go to zero. In this way not only are the short-run negative effects of the transition to the major basic expansion avoided, the basic expansion that would raise the standard of living of the population as a whole is postponed. The main common feature of these "misadventures" is that they divert attention away from and at times mitigate ineffective demand for basic goods and services.

A good historical example is the 19th century British overseas colonialization and expansion. Instead of the technological improvements of the Industrial Revolution resulting in relatively immediate prosperity for the working class (as Adam Smith envisioned), capitalists sought to increase their share of surplus income (as Marx identified) by expanding overseas markets for their goods. In this way firms involved in British overseas expansion sought to avoid, but only postponed, the requirements of eventually accepting a lower rate of return in domestic investment as the last stage of the major surplus expansion (should) leads into a major expansion of the basic stage and rising standards of living for all categories of workers. As Lonergan notes, "while England began its economic takeoff around 1790, wages in England did not begin to rise until 1870." The reason Lonergan gives for this "odd" state of affairs is it "maybe that a rise in the domestic standard of living is not a necessary consequence of a domestic surplus expansion. The surplus expansion may be directed to raising the standard of living in foreign countries"(83).

Ineffective demand for basic goods and services is, as shown above, responsible for preventing the shift from the major surplus expansion to a major basic expansion. Because of their effects on a potentially flourishing economy, the damage of misadventures and palliatives are in Lonergan's words "large and multiform" (82). In an analysis that may be compared to Pére Lebret and Pius VI's critique of colonialistic foreign development in *Populorum Progressio* that is not integral to the needs of the developing country, Lonergan also shows the damages of exporting the benefits of the major surplus expansion to the developing countries themselves.

In her analysis of ECA, the economist Elaine De Neeve brings up the possible positive role for government policy which can become more fruitful as these technical restraints are recognized. For example, there might be possible a positive role for a Keynesian-type fiscal policies to help move an economy out of a period of unemployment equilibrium or slump by increasing demand. Likewise, governments can implement enlightened monetary and tax policies and other legal and institutional changes conducive to initiate new production and trade. This would place government in the role of the redistributive function which Lonergan, in the context of discussing credit institutions, "clearly held must encourage rational behavior appropriate to whatever cycle the productive process happens to be in." [57]

Conclusion: Some Implications for Christian Ethics and Economics

Before coming to the concluding chapter comparing and contrasting ECA and Catholic social teaching, since this book concerns Christian ethics and economics, it would be appropriate in conclusion to generally but briefly relate Lonergan's economics with religious belief and ethical considerations.[58] On one hand, Lonergan's methodology and macroeconomics are regarded by him to be autonomous, that is, it does not rely on any specifically religious or scriptural basis for its analysis and precepts. The implicit economic methodology of ECA requires "merely" human attentiveness, intelligence, reason and responsibility. In this last aspect it departs from positivistic economics, and in ECA's attention to human interiority and judgment in making economic theory and decisions it departs from empiricist notions of scientific method.

More specifically, ECA is unlike some Christian economic ethics that rely explicitly on theological rationales for economic analysis and decision. Such analyses would include some aspects of Roman Catholic social teaching, arguments such as Philip Wogaman's which seeks some kind of coherence between economics and Christian doctrine, and countless other attempts to analyze economics, economic systems, and economic policy on theological or scriptural grounds.[59] While this latter type of economic ethics is very useful to alerting and conscientizing Christians and others to serious inequities in wealth distribution and oppression in our current economic systems and theory, its very basis in Christian doctrine may limit its usefulness in the public sphere, although its prophetic witness toward sinful social structures may remain strong and sometimes very effective. Nevertheless, the usefulness of Lonergan's analysis is that of providing concrete alternatives to these systems and the inequities they create.

Lonergan especially criticizes merely moralistic attempts to critique and provide remedies to complicated economic issues. Although as has been shown, concepts such as equity and the common good importantly inform Lonergan's analysis, putting him in the realm of social economics rather than economic mainstream's attempts at a "value-free" economic analysis, such attempts at integrating value questions and human freedom into economic analysis still must respect the integrity of a normative economic theory as Lonergan attempts to provide. He underscores this point in ECA:

> In equity [pure surplus income] should be directed to raising the standard of living of the whole society. The reason why it does not is not the simple-minded moralists reason: greed, but the prime cause is ignorance. Dynamics of surplus and basic production, surplus and basic expansions, surplus and basic incomes are not understood, not formulated, not taught. When people do not understand what is happening and why, they cannot be expected to act intelligently. When intelligence is a blank, first law of nature takes over: self-preservation. It is not primarily greed but frantic efforts at self-preservation that turns recession into depression, and depression into crash (82).

On the other hand, religious worldviews are essential to the economic understanding and ethic that Lonergan seeks to provide through his analysis. The desire to both seek that knowledge and implement it may require both moral and religious conversion.[60] In other words, the existence of properly functioning relationships among significant variables, and among economic agents, that Lonergan seeks to provide the requisite understanding for, needs not only the intellectual conversion that enables adequate scientific understanding but also tends to require moral, psychic, religious and affective conversion, at least among great numbers of the populace.

Therefore, Lonergan's economics, while scientifically autonomous, is integral with the larger project of religious teaching and discipleship.[61] Religious conversion is for Lonergan, "being in love [with God] in an unrestricted fashion;"[62] "since love of him is fruitful, it overflows into love of all those that he loves or might love."[63] As Byrne writes, "this type of conversion is essential for economic transformation, for such transformation requires a habitual orientation to living and thinking which acts lovingly with regard to generations to come."[64] Moral conversion is the orientation toward making one's decisions on the basis of value, not satisfaction. Since economic agents' decisions not to opt for immediate satisfaction and instead for the sacrifices required for the pure cycle to operate, moral conversion is also essential.[65]

NOTES

1. Course notes from "Macroeconomics and the Dialectic of History" taught by Lonergan in 1980 at Boston College, 3.

2. For an opposing epistemological and methodological point of view, cf. Milton Friedman, "The Method of Positive Economics," in *Essays in Positive Economics* (Chicago: University of Chicago Press, 1953). One salient difference between Lonergan and Friedman is that Lonergan argues that analysis may attain its goal without being able to predict, and on the other hand, successful predictions may be attained, say, by a Ptolemy, "without any analysis of the real grounds that make the prediction successful" (ECA, 11). Friedman instead maintains that successful prediction obviates any necessity to provide that analysis. In other words, the "black box" of economic understanding can remain dark as long as it provides successful guidance through successful prediction. Friedman's instrumentalist view of economic theory has also been critiqued for its propensity to claim more validity for its success at prediction than warranted.

3. Lonergan, "Course Notes," 3.

4. Page references in parentheses refer to this work, subsequently referred to

as ECA.

5. Cf. John Maynard Keynes, *The General Theory of Employment, Interest and Money* (New York: Harcourt, Brace, 1936). Keynes proposed governmental deficit spending to counteract ineffective demand. It will not be possible here to provide a comparison between Lonergan and Keynes, or between Lonergan and any other prominent economist and/or theory. For a comparison of ECA to certain elements in *The General Theory,* see Michael Gibbons, "Economic Theorizing: In Lonergan and Keynes," in *Religion and Culture: Essays in Honor of Bernard Lonergan, S.J.,* ed. Timothy P. Fallon, S.J. and Philip Boo Riley (Albany: State University of New York Press, 1987), 313-325. Gibbons argues that Lonergan by being a methodologist first and economist second, "was able to push his economic reflections further than Keynes because he had a firmer grasp of the essentials of effective theory." Lonergan himself wrote that his conception of the dynamic changes in velocities "underlie the Keynesian propensity to consume," (5) implying that Lonergan believes his analysis provides in some sense a better account of macroeconomic process than does Keynes.

6. This return was occasioned as well by the inability of liberation theologians like Gustav Gutierrez and German political theologians such as Johannes Metz to sufficiently use economic analysis in their theological critique of modern political economics. For example Lonergan attended a 1974 conference at which Gutierrez acknowledged that as Lawrence puts it, "the real problem with liberation theology was that none of the liberation theologians of the day had a serious knowledge of economics" (Lawrence, "Editor's Introduction," xl; Philip McShane, "Systematics, Communications, Actual Contexts," in *Religion in Context: Recent Studies in Lonergan*, ed. Timothy J. Fallon, S.J. and Philip Boo Riley (Lanham, MD: University Press of America, 1988), 139). In a 1968 letter to McShane, Lonergan wrote that the time had come for economic morality to go "beyond reflection on the family wage" as exemplified by Metz (Philip McShane, *Pastkeynes, Pastmodern Economics: A Fresh Pragmatism* (Halifax, Nova Scotia: Axial Press, 2002), 4). For more on the relationship between Lonergan's economic thought and political theology, see Frederick Lawrence, "Lonergan as a Political Theologian," in *Religion in Context: Recent Studies in Lonergan*, 1-22, and "Political Theology and 'The Longer Cycle of Decline'" in Fred Lawrence, ed. *Lonergan Workshop Volume I* (Chico, CA.: Scholars Press, 1978), 223-56.

7. Lonergan cites Joseph Alois Schumpeter's similar criticism of mainstream economics' lack of attention to these types of dynamics as found in the latter's *History of Economic Analysis*, (New York: Oxford University Press, 1954), 1125. In Lonergan and Schumpeter's view, this led the economists of their time to "miss the meaningful whole" of the relations between cyclical fluctuations and the characteristic fluctuation in the production of plant and equipment (6f.). For Schumpeter's key works on business cycle theory, cf. *The Theory of Economic Development: An Inquiry into Profits, Capital, Credit, Interest, and the Business*

Cycle, tr. Redvers Opie (Cambridge, MA: Harvard University Press, 1955 [1934]) and *Business Cycles; A Theoretical, Historical, and Statistical Analysis of the Capitalist Process* (New York: McGraw-Hill Book Company, 1939).

8. Lonergan discusses the need for new measuring instruments in accordance with new significant variables in ECA sections 19 and 23 on "Measuring Change in the Production Process (I, II)," 80-2, 107-113.

9. This aspect of Lonergan's economics is stressed by him in an earlier version of ECA, entitled *For A New Political Economy,* 5-7. Writes Gibbons: ECA "has a normative significance for the future of democratic capitalism" (Gibbons, 313).

10. As Alasdair MacIntyre writes,

> On the one side there appear the self-defined protagonists of individual liberty, on the other, the self-defined protagonists of planning and regulation, of the goods which are available through bureaucratic organization. But in fact what is crucial is that on which the contending parties agree, namely that there are only two alternative modes of social life open to us, one which the free and arbitrary choices of individuals are sovereign and one in which the bureaucracy is sovereign, precisely so that it may limit the free and arbitrary choices of individuals. Given this deep cultural agreement, it is unsurprising that the politics of modern societies oscillate between a freedom which is nothing but a lack of regulation of individual behavior and forms of collectivist control destined only to limit the anarchy of self-interest" (*After Virtue: A Study in Moral Theory* [Notre Dame: University of Notre Dame University Press, 1981], 35).

As discussed in the previous chapter, Lonergan's view of human liberty as acting intelligently, reasonably, and responsibly provides an alternative theory of human action to "the self-defined protagonists of individual liberty," described by McIntyre and also avoids the necessity for bureaucracy to be sovereign in human affairs, which works to frustrate the human ability to act intelligently, reasonably and responsibly.

11. As Gibbons notes, Lonergan's emphasis shifts from "trying to *define* the relevant variables to *searching* heuristically for the maximum extent of interconnects and interdependence." (Gibbons, 32, emphasis added).

12. The economist Elaine De Neeve argues that because Lonergan's analysis is normative rather than predictive, he does not assume that economic agents will behave in any particular way. Instead, the explanatory power of ECA reveals the possibility for rational action, not the assumption that economic agents will always act rationally in that acting according to the limitations of the technical restraint is rational economic behavior (Elaine De Neeve, "Bernard Lonergan's 'Circulation Analysis' and Macrodynamics." Ph.D. diss., McGill University,

1990, 352). On the other hand, as pointed out by Amartya Sen, the economic agents in orthodox economics are more typically "rational fools" ("Rational Fools: A Critique of the Behavioral Foundations of Economic Theory." *Philosophy & Public Affairs* 6 (1977): 317-44).

13. As Lonergan elaborates in *Insight*, ". . . in correspondence with each stage in the development of practical intelligence, there is a measure and structure of capital formation, that is, of things produced and arranged not because they themselves are desired but because they expedite and accelerate the process of supplying the goods and services that are wanted by consumers." This is justified because, "the comparatively brief time spent making spears or nets is amply compensated by the greater ease which more game or fish is taken on an indefinite series of occasions (208).

14. They are equivalent but not equal because 1) some of basic production goes to waste; 2) there is a lag between production and consumption and 3) there exists no common numerical term to compare the two because their relationship has not yet in the analysis been compared in monetary terms (31).

15. See Lonergan, *Insight*, 37-38 for a fuller discussion of implicit and functional definitions.

16. Cf. Lonergan, *Insight*, 12-13.

17. Paul Hoyt-O'Connor gives a good example of Lonergan's subtle move from description to analysis in ECA: "'Consumers' and 'producers' are no longer used to refer to groups of individuals separated out into households and firms. Rather 'consumer' and 'producer' designate for Lonergan the functional relations between the basic stage and the standard of living or between the various stages of production" (Hoyt-O'Connor, *Bernard Lonergan's Macroeconomic* Dynamics, 151).

18. Although, as will be seen it is important to establish which elements of the productive process fall into either the basic or surplus stage of production.

19. An important fact to mention is that Lonergan does not characterize the concept of surplus as correlating to "what is left over," after what is paid to workers, a conception that led to Marx's accusing the capitalist class of unjust appropriation of the labors of the workers. As Hoyt-O'Connor writes, "Rather than going down the proverbial garden path of treating first the thorny questions of who has what and whether they should, Lonergan began instead by defining basis and surplus production in terms of their functional relationships to one another and to the dynamism of the productive process as a whole" (Hoyt-O'Connor, *Bernard Lonergan's Macroeconomic Dynamics*, 152). Lonergan's concept of "pure surplus income" (discussed below) derives from this explanatory account and how it relates to acceleration of the productive process to the possibility it has for raising the standard of living for all.

20. It might be helpful to further comment on how Lonergan's views his conception of surplus income and surplus and basic acceleration in relation to

Marx's ideas of exploitation and appropriation. According to Lonergan, Marx (nor any economist) had a satisfactory view of surplus income. This led Marx in particular to ignore how part of the "surplus" goes toward significant addition of more and/or new plants and equipment. This reinvestment, if undertaken (which by no means is certain, as we will see) in turn yields additional wages paid to workers in surplus production; in time this leads to increase in demand for basic products, a demand which ends up increasing wages in the basic sector and the overall standard of living.

21. Actually anything beyond primitive fruit and nut gathering societies.

22. "For with better men, a better organization of men, and better practical ideas, it becomes possible through the short-term accelerations to introduce more efficient equipment, displace labor, devote the displaced labor to a greater quantity of equipment, and so recommence the wave or cycle of long-term advance" (34-5).

23. As he wrote in *The Wealth of Nations*, describing workers' alienation from production perhaps even more strongly than Marx, "The man whose whole life is spent in performing a few simple operations . . . has no occasion to exert his understanding, or to exercise his invention in finding out expedients for removing difficulties which never occur. . . . The torpor of his mind renders him, not only incapable of relishing or bearing a part in any rational conversation, but of conceiving any generous, noble or tender sentiment. . . ." (*An Inquiry into the Nature and Causes of the Wealth of Nations, Vol. 2* (Chicago: University of Chicago Press, 1976 [1776]), 302-303; quoted in Donald R. Stabile, "Adam Smith and the Natural Wage: Sympathy, Subsistence, and Social Distance," *Review of Social Economy* LV (1997): 292-311).

24. While he comes to different conclusions than Schumpeter, the economist Peter Burley believes "that many of Lonergan's insights [especially on the need for a dynamic economics] had their origins in Schumpeter, even if Lonergan synthesized them with numerous complementary insights" (Lonergan as a Neo-Schumpeterian," *Australian Lonergan Workshop*, ed. William J. Danaher [Lanham, MD: University Press of America, 1993], 250). McShane disagrees with this opinion, stressing ECA's independence from Schumpeter's views (personal correspondence, August 1998). Whatever the degree of independence, Lonergan's high opinion of Schumpeter's insights are indicated by his inclusion in his class handouts of a magazine article by Peter Drucker arguing that Schumpeter was a more important economist than Keynes ("Schumpeter and Keynes," *Forbes* [May 23, 1982]: 300-304).

25. For a very enlightening treatment of interdependency among regional and economic units, see Jane Jacobs, *The Economy of Cities* (New York: Random House, 1969), *Cities and the Wealth of Nations* (New York: Random House, 1984) and *The Nature of Economies* (New York: Modern Library, 2000). These in turn build upon her seminal work in urban planning, *The Death and Life of Great*

American Cities (New York: Vintage Books, 1961). For Jacobs, the most important dynamic of healthy economic growth is "import substitution," where economies continually seek to . Both Jacobs and Lonergan's analysis go very much against the grain of mainstream economic trade theory. For a brief comparison, see my "Economic Development and True Democratic Capitalism: Contrasting 'Top-Down' Economic Visions and 'Bottom-Up' Political Cultures" *Catholic Rural Life* 47:1 (Spring 2004): 25-31.

26. A very recent and pertinent example is the information revolution. For a long time companies invested in massive overhaul of their use of computers. Only after years of this, did productivity, profits and wages rise substantially. Many economists give this as part of the reason for the economic doldrums of the 1980's and early 90's and the relative prosperity and extended growth period of the economy in the later 90's. This is an excellent example of surplus acceleration being spread over hundreds of surplus products and then thousands, even millions, of basic enterprises that causes long awaited and long lasting positive acceleration throughout economy.

27. Patrick Byrne, "Economic Transformations: The Role of Conversions and Culture in the Transformation of Economies," in *Religion in Context: Recent Studies in Lonergan*, ed. Timothy J. Fallon, S.J. and Philip Boo Riley (Lanham, MD: University Press of America, 1988), 329.

28. Byrne, "Economic Transformations," 331.

29. Nicholas Kaldor, "The Irrelevance of Equilibrium Economics," *Economic Journal* 82 (December 1972): 1140-1. Quoted in Philip McShane, "Features of Generalized Empirical Method and the Actual Context of Economics," *Creativity and Method: Essays in Honor of Bernard Lonergan, S.J.*, ed. Matthew L. Lamb (Milwaukee, WI: Marquette University Press, 1984), 559.

30. On the other hand, a payment for a product of past production that was previously sold to a consumer Lonergan terms a redistributive payment, because they are not operative payments and thus are not "constitutive element[s] of current production" (43). Most members of classes of redistributive payments are obvious, such as selling a used car, garage sales, used book sales, etc. A less obvious example of a redistributive payment is a bank loan. In Lonergan's analysis, a repayment of anything above the amount of the loan such as interest is an operative payment, while the repayment of the principal is redistributive.

31. Lonergan refers to this diagram as the "baseball" diagram due to its resemblance to the bases and pitcher's mound of a baseball diamond (*Caring About Meaning: Patterns in the Life of Bernard Lonergan*, ed. Pierrot Lambert, Charlotte Tansey and Cathleen Going [Montreal: Thomas More Institute, 1982], 85). Besides being able to better illustrate these terms and functions, the benefits of a diagram include being able to better reflect the key discovery claimed by Lonergan for his analysis, "the interdependence of the whole."

32. Because of the importance of recognizing two distinct circuits and their

dynamic influence upon each other in exchange, finance, and fluctuations in the standard of living, it is critical to be able to establish which elements of the productive process fall into which stage of production. For example, the amount of electricity used in producing particular goods or aggregates of goods, whether measured in physical units or its monetary value, is usually considered as one type of factor of production. In Lonergan's more differentiated approach it is important as to determine whether what fraction of the electricity used and how much was paid for it goes to basic production and what fraction is used in some level of surplus production. Paul Hoyt-O'Connor gives a more complicated example: if an employee receives foreign language from her/his employer, part of their use could be considered to add to the individual's standard of living (basic production) while part may be used to help expand the employer's overseas production through the employee's increased proficiency in that language. This transposes into an explanatory account proprietary distinctions between households, employees and firms. As Hoyt-O'Connor notes, "Human decisions are constitutive of productive processes," not technical or proprietary concepts (*Bernard Lonergan's Macroeconomic Dynamics*, 150).

34. Money is also be added to and taken from the circuits through government fiscal policy, monetary policy, and foreign trade. While these are additional redistributions of money throughout the circuit to those of exchange and financial dealings through the redistributive function, and have significant effect on the amount and rates of money entering the circuits, they are not integral to the production process as financial dealings through the redistributive function. Thus they are dealt with as "superimposed" circuits in *ECA*. These superimposed circuits, and their potentially deleterious effect on the pure cycle are discussed below under "Misadventures."

35. This can be represented as M' = (S' - s'O') + (D' - s'I') + the crossover difference. Correspondingly, the amount of money moving into (or out of) the surplus circuit can be represented as M" = (S" - s"O") + (D" - s"I") = the crossover difference. The grouping of terms in the parentheses represents the fact that the total quantity of money added to the basic circuit is equal to the net quantity of money (per unit interval) added from the redistributive function to basic supply. plus the net quantity of money added from the redistributive function to basic demand, plus the quantity added (subtracted) from the surplus circuit to the basic circuit. Similarly, the total quantity of money added to the surplus circuit is equal to the net quantity of money added (or subtracted) from the redistributive function to surplus supply, plus the quantity of money added (or subtracted) from the redistributive function to surplus demand, minus the quantity added (or subtracted) from the surplus circuit added to the basic circuit.

36. Hoyt O'Connor, *Bernard Lonergan's Macroeconomic Dynamics*, 199.

37. For example under Federal Reserve Board Chairman Alan Greenspan's management, the economic expansion of the 1990's saw booming corporate

profits, low inflation but only a slight increase in the standard of living of the middle class.

38. As I would argue happened when in the 1990's economic boom the "overheated" (rising inflation) economy was throttled back by the Federal Reserve Board acting to raise interest rates. This resulted in the "boom" having very little effect on the standard of living of those in the middle class.

39. Lonergan's use of this somewhat normative term will be discussed further below. This term suggests one link between Lonergan's economic analysis and those relying more on the explicit use of natural law such as the Catholic moral theologian and economist John A. Ryan (1865-1945).

40. Even in a stationary state, money must flow along the path between the redistributive function and basic and surplus supply (S' - s'O' and S" - s"O") in order to counter occasional fluctuations in crossovers between the circuits. In a static state, increases in crossovers and corresponding transfers to and from the redistributive function are subsequently met with equal decreases (101).

41. Lonergan asks his readers to think of this process, though not centrally planned, in terms as analogous to the Soviet-style five-year plans intended to eventually and dramatically boost basic production (79).

42. This simultaneous occurrence of decreasing unemployment and rising real wages is contrary to the orthodox postulation of the Phillips curve in which unemployment and real wages (inflation) tend to go in opposite ways. In other words, orthodox economics holds that there tends to be a trade-off between inflation and the unemployment rate. The stagflation of the 1970's, however, where both the price level and unemployment rose at the same time threw a wrench into this analysis. Only through misadaptations to Lonergan's pure cycle do 1) real wages fall significantly or 2) real wages and employment fall together as in stagflation.

43. Hoyt-O'Connor, *Bernard Lonergan's Macroeconomic Dynamics*, 215-6.

44. In this sense, "just" distribution as elaborated in ECA takes on an immensely more differentiated, complicated, and I believe effective meaning than discussions of distributive justice found in Catholic social teaching and other theological and ethical treatments of the "social problem."

45. Lonergan's assessment of the role of the profit motive also departs from Milton Friedman's views, found for example in Friedman, "The Social Responsibility of Business is to Increase Its Profits," *New York Times* Sept. 13, 1970. Reprinted in *Twenty Questions: An Introduction to Philosophy*, ed. G. Lee Bowie, et al. (Harcourt Brace Jovanovich: San Diego, 1988), 754-759.

46. ECA illumines the channels through which the price mechanism works. In this static example, the results show the effects of these laws. However, the more dynamic analysis below from ECA shows that market mechanisms, while operative, are not determinative of the distribution of goods and payments. Instead ECA reveals the channels in which the laws of supply and demand operate

(17).

47. See above on the massiveness of the surplus expansion.

48. The editors of ECA provide a quote from a handout Lonergan gave to his students in his 1979 course based upon ECA in which Lonergan commented, "'We on the other hand, have to distinguish basic and surplus [prices and quantities] . . . For unless surplus is conceived as a distinct circuit with its own final market, the Marxists object that the basic final market is demanding payment not only for basic goods and services but also for surplus as well; hence the accusation that profit is robbing workers of part of the labor value of their contribution.'" Lonergan's alternative: "'And now with the circuits distinguished, the crossover makes it manifest that it supplements the wages paid in the basic circuit, so that profits are not robbery . . . .'" (Lawrence, et al. editors footnote 87, 71-2).

49. Hoyt-O'Connor, *Bernard Lonergan's Macroeconomic Dynamics*, 142.

50. Lonergan treats this aspect of the surplus expansion in several places in ECA. See index s.v. "anti-egalitarianism."

51. "Forced savings" is defined by *The Penguin Dictionary of Economics* as a situation in "which savings takes place because goods are not available for consumption, rather than which consumers actually wish to save" ("Forced Savings," in *The Penguin Dictionary of Economics*, ed. G. Bannock, R.E. Baxter, and R. Rees [Harmondsforth, Eng.: Penguin Books, 1976], 171). However, in Lonergan's analysis, consumers, especially those on fixed income, are unable to purchase goods in this phase not because of the unavailability of goods but because they cannot afford them, and the "savings" do not go into their bank accounts, but to the surplus expansion. But Lonergan and the *Dictionary,* which I am assuming follows mainstream economic theory, both concur that "prices will rise until the excess consumption demand is choked off.

52. As Hoyt-O'Connor points out that this process is even more unsettling "if the surplus expansion has exaggerated into a boom" (Hoyt-O'Connor, *Bernard Lonergan's Macroeconomic Dynamics*, 248), and therefore basic enterprises receive speculative losses as well. An example would be if a stereo supplier expands the number of stores as the overall price level goes up in the mistaken anticipation of increased profits from significant increased demand which then tapers off as the major surplus expansion slows.

53. In sectors of the economy where a firm or a few firms maintain a large market share (weak competition), they will be able to maintain higher profits by restricting output and keeping prices relatively high. Also cost reductions from more efficient machines, also a byproduct of weak competition may never be passed on to the consumer, so that profit rates and saving remain high in this manner. As De Neeve points out, in these cases, although there is a deceleration of crossover to the surplus sector because of declining overall profits, it is less than the deceleration through the crossover from the surplus to the basic. Thus,

while both are decelerating, the basic circuit is being drained while the surplus circuit remains too large and the downward adjustments in saving to make the basic expansion possible are not made (De Neeve, "Bernard Lonergan's 'Circulation Analysis,'" 360).

54. An example of benevolence and enterprise would be the mid-1990's strategy of Intel, the computer micro-processor manufacturer, to expand its production and lower its prices, thereby making computers more available to the public, further increasing demand. Lower prices generally mean a lower rate of return on investment. Because of the high demand for its products, it could have easily increased its profits by raising its prices and maintaining or even cutting back production. Lonergan gave his own example of benevolence in this phase of the basic expansion in an 1982 interview, that of "starting small-scale industries that employ people who really can't be taught much; including the unemployed in your economy" (*Caring About Meaning: Patterns in the Life of Bernard Lonergan*, 191). General Motors recent decision to offer lifelong employment to its workers at least on the surface may also fall into this category. In this instance, it may really be correct to say, "What is good for General Motors is good for the country."

55. To explain further, at the root of the correcting 'mechanism' that can either bring about proportionality of growth between the two circuits or spell decline, is the need for the rate of savings to correspond with the particular phase of expansion the economy is in. In the surplus expansion, the rate of saving must increase in each time period (thus accelerating) in order to assure that funds will become available (the money supply must also increase during this phase) to finance the increased outlay of surplus production. If funds are not available, money will be drained from the surplus circuit in the ways outlined above. The rate of savings needed to finance the surplus expansion will come about instead through forced savings imposed upon those with fixed or stable incomes. The need for a high rate of savings is thus accomplished through sufficient increases in the price level.

During the basic expansion, the rate of saving must decelerate, or decrease in each time period in order for the increased amount of goods produced to be purchased and for the standard of living for all to be raised up. This is accomplished through an opposite direction in the price level; prices need to go down in the basic expansion. In fact they need to go low enough that the real income of those on fixed incomes increases, even as corporate profits go down. In other words, money now needs to go into the hands of those most likely to spend it on their standard of living in the "egalitarian" phase.

56. Lonergan, as did Schumpeter analyzed business cycles in the various time-frames of pioneers of business cycle theories such as Joseph Kitchin, Clement Juglar, and N.D. Kondratieff. These range from two to four years (Kitchin) to nine to ten (Juglar), to even long-wave cycles lasting an average of 55

years (Kondratieff). For a good overview and critique of business cycle theory, see Charles K. Wilber and Kenneth P Jameson, *An Inquiry into the Poverty of Economics* (Notre Dame, IN: University of Notre Dame Press, 1983), 95-110.

57. De Neeve, "Bernard Lonergan's 'Circulation Analysis,'"363. On the other hand, Keynesian micromanagement of the economy through manipulation of interest rates is inept according to the terms of ECA. Although I do not have space to explain fully Lonergan's views on this matter, basically, shifting demand for money around a theoretical equilibrium interest rate cannot adequately attend to the concomitant demands of both the basic and surplus sectors. For example, to raise interest rates to induce savings to provide funds for investment in the surplus expansion through the redistributive function will simultaneously work to block further long-term expansion, because higher interest rates discourages capital investment by firms because it increases the annual charge of buying a piece of capital equipment (ECA, 141-144). As expressed by Lonergan: "But the requirements of the surplus phase have to encourage not only saving but also borrowing; and it would take enormous rates backed by all the propaganda techniques at our disposal to bring about the ever increasing rates of surplus income proper to the surplus expansion; and some form of magic would be needed to prevent them from discouraging all borrowing" (ECA, 141).

58. In my Conclusion, I will seek to develop a place for the implications of Lonergan's economics in wider context of Christian moral theology and social ethics, especially Catholic social teaching.

59. J. Philip Wogaman, *The Great Economic Debate: An Ethical Analysis* (Philadelphia: Westminster Press, 1977).

60. Patrick Byrne deals directly with the need for various horizon-shifts in individuals and among society, that makes Lonergan's economics a distinct paradigm in economic thought in "Economic Transformations," op. cit.

61. Lonergan put this more bluntly in the Lambert, et. al, interview. In response to the question, "Would you say that there could be such a thing as a Christian economics?," Lonergan replied, "You need Christianity to have a good one"(Pierrot Lambert, et.al., *Caring About Meaning*, 190).

62. Lonergan, *Method in Theology*, 105.

63. Lonergan, *Method in Theology*, 109.

64. Byrne, "Economic Transformations," 341

65. Byrne also adds the necessity for psychic conversion. Only the psychically converted subject, who is "the normative author of his or her own psychic rhythms," "will successfully resist the seductive rhythms of the advertising industry, the interpersonal tensions of the board room, the corrupting rhetoric of the union organizer." As Byrne points out, the necessity for widespread psychic conversion makes Lonergan's economics even more of radical transformation of economic thinking ("Economic Transformations," 342).

CONCLUSION

LONERGAN'S CONTRIBUTION TO CATHOLIC SOCIAL TEACHING AND CHRISTIAN ECONOMIC ETHICS

It remains here to address implications of Lonergan's economic thought for Christian social ethics and Catholic social teaching, especially in light of other approaches to the conjunction of ethics and economics as exemplified by the Michael Novak's neoclassical and Mary Hobgood's neo-Marxian economic critiques of Catholic social teaching delineated in Chapter Two. Placing these critiques alongside Lonergan's economics, my goal here is to elucidate new horizons of what constitutes an authentic collaboration between economics and ethics. In regards to Catholic social teaching (CST), I wish to show that Lonergan's economic analysis contributes to its understanding of the "social problem," while also pointing to consistencies of within CST and with the more adequate economic analysis I believe Lonergan provides, especially against Novak and Hobgood's highlighting of internal inconsistencies within CST from the viewpoint of their own preferred economic paradigms.

First, as pointed out above, Lonergan's economic anthropology and economic theory differs greatly from that employed by Novak and Hobgood, while at the same time essentially cohering more with the economic anthropology of Catholic social teaching (CST). Yet a key point of my argument is that Lonergan contributes greatly to both CST and secular economics by integrating CST's more adequate rendering of individual and economic agency, and his critical realist economic methodology into a new paradigm for economics. To the ethically normative, yet concretely unspecific, prescriptions of Catholic social teaching, Lonergan adds a scientifically normative macroeconomic explanation of the underlying sources of economic injustice addressed in the social encyclicals and the American bishops' economic pastoral letter. In this way Lonergan's economics critiques and complements Catholic social teaching. On the other hand, I argue that Lonergan's economic thought reciprocally requires the insights of CST to accomplish Lonergan's pastoral goal of providing adequate economic knowledge to individuals groups and governments so that they can exercise moral responsibility in their everyday economic decision making in ways that economics now does not.

A Case Study: Catholic Social Teaching, Economic Theory and the Living Wage

One way of briefly introducing the relationships among Lonergan, CST, Novak and Hobgood is to look at the example of the living wage doctrine. The living or "just" wage has been argued for in one way or another in CST since *Rerum Novarum* as a way to counter the deleterious effects of the wage contract under liberal capitalism and to provide some semblance of economic justice without resorting to collectivist management of the economy under socialism. The rationale behind the living wage doctrine criticizes underlying assumptions of liberal economic theory and has sought to provide both concrete alternatives and corrective moral guidelines to guiding the economy. Like other principles CST seeks to provide (e.g., subsidiarity), the living wage doctrine illustrates CST's view of the dialectic between the individual and social nature of property, and the potential role of the state in working to alleviate social and economic injustice.

From the viewpoint of liberal capitalism, Novak views achieving a living wage within the horizons of democratic capitalism's emphasis on individual initiative, as long as the spheres of morality and government do not succumb to the sin of envy, and hamper too much with the economic sphere's natural tendency to someday provide for all—as long as people are willing to work toward their economic welfare. As an example of his optimistic view of this dynamism, he regards only 3% of United States jobs as paying below a living wage. Those that occupy them, mostly youth, are either using them correctly as stepping stones to better jobs, which benefits employers and employees, or are using them incorrectly, substituting short-term livelihood for long-term benefits, a situation in which only employers benefit greatly.[1] However, Novak greatly downplays movements within capitalism that work to lower wages below living wage levels such as outsourcing, using temporary workers, less and less power of unions, etc. These move more and more people into the category of "working poor."[2] In addition, he makes the gross error of identifying the living wage with the minimum wage when the minimum wage does not come close to supporting an individual much less a family basic needs in our society.[3] Therefore the number of working poor that live below a decent living wage is much more than his claim of 3% of total workers. Again, though he tries to reconcile the liberal economic wage contract with CST, for example arguing especially that *Centesimus Annus* "brought economic liberty . . . into Catholic social teaching,"[4] it is clear Novak also downplays considerably CST's emphasis on the social nature of property, as reiterated clearly in *Centesimus Annus*, where John Paul II states ". . . there is a dictate of nature more imperious and more ancient than any bargain between man and man, that the remuneration must be enough to support the wage-earner in reasonable and frugal comfort." If not, "he is the victim of force and injustice" (art. 34).

In Hobgood's analysis of the living wage, CST agrees with some liberationist critiques but has always sought to ameliorate economic injustice within a market, though not capitalistic, system.[5] The living wage is a way for morality to work within that system, an approach criticized by Hobgood as not fully appreciating the power dynamics at work within capitalism and thus not moving toward necessary structural correctives. So while Novak argues that a capitalistic system will inevitably, someday rise all boats sufficiently, for Hobgood this "natural" system is wholly unnatural—the only thing natural is the in-built tension between capital and labor which can only be overcome through a radical restructuring of economic society. Although she does call for reparation to "those whose very presence in positions of underemployment, unemployment, unpaid domestic labor, and other marginalized capacities" have allowed wages to be kept down in the name of high profits and the "ongoing functioning of the society as a whole,"[6] she does not specify what a long-term Marxist-type *aufbehung* might look like that would enable good work and just remuneration to be the norm, Just that liberationist ethical principles demand it.[7] Ironically, given the tremendous differences in their approaches, both Hobgood and Novak argue against the state being able to accomplish this in a capitalist society—Hobgood because the state inevitably becomes the slave of the wealthy and Novak because capitalism will inevitably ameliorate these income differences if only the state and culture would stay out of the way (other than providing a minimal safety net).

Thus for Hobgood any other analysis than liberationist and socialist ones are either liberal or conservative readings of the neoclassical, capitalist paradigm.[8] For Novak on the other hand, any other analysis than neo-classical is socialist. They both insist that more democratic means of distributing wealth need to be achieved, but in Hobgood's case that means wresting control of the economy from capitalism's emphasis on profit, while for Novak it means wresting control from the state and misguided moral principles that don't acknowledge the role of profit and self-interest in "growing" the economy so that all might benefit. Each makes the fact/value-type error that Lonergan avoids—making *either* "science" *or* morality primarily constitutive of our collective need to understand and guide the economy. With neoclassical economics, Novak establishes "natural" economic process as constitutive of management of the economy while Hobgood, by accepting the neo-Marxist approach of praxis as foundational and regarding almost as foundational the principle that we can come to no acceptable consensus as to how the economy works, establishes morality as constitutive.[9]

Lonergan's Alternative

It is into this "in-between" world of the intersection of morality and economics, market and government that Lonergan enters with a different solution—a market "system" different from capitalism: against both Novak and Hobgood's approaches but in line with CST, that offers both morality and economics constitutive roles in understanding and guiding the economy. Although Lonergan certainly had great respect for the moral emphasis of the social encyclical tradition, like Novak and Hobgood his economics are also an implicit criticism of the potential effectiveness or concrete applications of these ideas. Agreeing with Christian Dequoc, he argues that "moral precepts that are not technically specific turn out to be quite ineffectual."[10] Instead, he wished to determine how moral precepts can be *derived from* the immanent intelligibility of economic processes themselves and in the process establishes both economic understanding and moral responsibility as intertwined and constitutive for proper economic functioning. For example, Lonergan criticizes the precept of the living wage not for its aim in alleviating the distress of the poor and oppressed, but for its method: " . . . Catholic employers who obeyed the precept went bankrupt, leaving the field to their less scrupulous rivals."[11]

Holding that "it is futile to excoriate what does exist while blissfully ignoring the task of constructing a technically viable economic system that can be put in its place,"[12] Lonergan viewed the challenge as getting to the root, "the evil influence of a mistaken economic system." Although as I've shown, concepts such as equity, the common good, and especially the social nature and responsibility of property inform Lonergan's analysis, putting him outside the realm of economic mainstream's attempts at a "value-free" economic analysis, such attempts at integrating value questions and human freedom into economic analysis still must respect the integrity of a normative economic theory as Lonergan attempts to provide. As Paul Samuelson attests, "In economics, it takes a theory to kill a theory; facts can only dent a theoretician's hide."[13]

Lonergan claims that if moral precepts grounded in proper economic analysis are understood and people are morally inclined or can be persuaded to follow them in a cooperative effort for the common good, the economy could be guided intelligently, intentionally and democratically. Interestingly, this concurs both with Novak's emphasis on personal virtue and Hobgood's stress on structural change, while at the same time disagreeing with Novak's acceptance of capitalist economic arrangements and with Hobgood's deemphasizing individual morality. But it transcends both in that in following a truly understood macroeconomics, this can be done without setting up centralized bureaucratic mechanisms and by forgoing a reliance on an illusory self-regulating market mechanism. Instead of concentrating on the role of the state, Lonergan stresses the inability of both neo-classical and Marxian economists to understand correctly the needs of the workings and requirements of economic process and therefore denying individuals and groups like companies, unions and governments the understanding needed to guide the economy. This is for Lonergan "gravely threatening to democratic liberty:"[14]

> Plainly, [rational control of the economy] can be democratic only in the measure in which economic science succeeds in uttering not counsel to rulers but precepts to mankind, not specific remedies and plans to increase the power of bureaucracies, but universal laws which men themselves administrate in the personal conduct of their lives. . . . [T]o deny the possibility of a new science and new precepts is, I am convinced, to deny the possibility of the survival of democracy.[15]

Macroeconomic Dynamics and CST: Consistencies Within and Without

I wish now to bring this conversation "full-circle" to establish the reciprocal relationships and potential for dialogue between Catholic social teaching and Lonergan's economics. My purpose will be here to highlight certain themes in the encyclicals that find affirmation in and contribute to the perspectives offered in *Macroeconomic Dynamics: An Essay in Circulation Analysis* (ECA). Along the way I will also point out the general contribution each makes to the other. To again use the comparison Lonergan suggests, Catholic social teaching provides mainly a healing emphasis, while ECA integrates that healing emphasis into a more dynamic conception of the common good based upon an expanded understanding of economic process than that attempted by Catholic social teaching. It thereby provide tools for moving toward creating the just and flourishing society aimed at by CST.

The Common Good

Both Catholic social teaching and *Macroeconomic Dynamics: An Essay in Circulation Analysis* incorporate an explicit emphasis on the common good, or more specifically, the economic good of order as a realm of cooperation, instead of the individualistic emphasis as found in mainstream economic theory.[16] For example, *Mater et Magistra* describes the good of economic order as a situation in which there is full-employment, wages and prices are balanced, and goods and services are made accessible to all. Further, this inclusive development would limit inequalities among social classes and between classes of nations as well.[17] Correspondingly, Lonergan's theory of the "pure cycle," to the extent it is adverted to and followed, avoids the slumps that cause terrible unemployment and poverty, and at times high inflation. Further as the egalitarian phase of the cycle, or the basic expansion, proceeds forward, basic or consumer goods and services are provided at lower prices, nominal wages rise causing real wages to increase even more, thus improving the standard of living of all, including those on the lower rungs of the economic ladder. Furthermore, if companies involved in foreign trade avoid the temptation of trying to maintain the heightened or surplus profits they are experiencing in the surplus expansion, this will also decrease those deleterious impacts on underdeveloped countries that *Mater et Magistra* and subsequent encyclicals condemn.

Within this tremendously enhanced conception of the common good, Lonergan's view of surplus income as existing for the sake of the basic expansion and not for the consumption of those who are experiencing or want to experience the benefits of high profits caused in the anti-egalitarian surplus expansion, is echoed in *Quadragesimo Anno.* There Pius XI argues that profits do not belong exclusively to either the capitalists, or to the workers as Marxists claim.[18] Avoiding, as does Pius, a proprietorial conception of economic exchange, Lonergan holds that surplus income/the social dividend should be directed to funding the surplus expansion. If it is not, prices will rise prematurely in the basic sector, causing a boom based on mistaken expectations that leads inexorably to a slump, and also leading to rising prices that cause those whose income is not rising, for example those on fixed incomes, to experience forced savings and a lower standard of living. It will also forestall the subsequent major basic expansion that lifts the standard of living of the economy as a whole which follows upon a intelligently, reasonably and responsibly managed successful major surplus expansion. Lonergan thus agrees with *Gaudium et Spes* which reiterates the point that reverberates throughout the history of Christian social teaching (despite Leo XIII's mistakenly attributing divine right to private property): private property has a social quality deriving from the law of the communal purpose of created goods. As the Second Vatican Council fathers declare, "if the social quality of property is overlooked, property often becomes the occasion of greed and of serious disturbances."[19] However, Lonergan maintains that it is not greed as such, but first of all ignorance of the social, macroeconomic purpose of surplus income that leads to these "serious disturbances."

Thirdly, Catholic social teaching, at least from John XXIII on, advocates economic democracy as essential to just economic relations among people. For example, *Gaudium et Spes* expresses the belief that economic development should not be left up to the judgment of a few powerful people or groups, but rather the largest possible number of people should have an active share in its direction. This theme was especially pronounced in the American bishops' pastoral letter, *Economic Justice for All*. This fully coincides with Lonergan's aim in ECA, which further argues, as noted above, that an economy "can be democratic only to the extent in which economic science succeeds in uttering not counsel to rulers but precepts to mankind."[20]

Economic Anthropology

To make the adjustments needed to avoid by distortions in theory and practice that result in the booms and slumps of the business cycle, both Catholic social teaching and Lonergan incorporate a fuller version of "economic man." For example, as noted above, Paul VI included the person's ability to self-sacrifice as necessary for true or integral economic development, contrary to the assumption of economics as people as motivated solely by self-interest. Incorporating the altruism that economic theory has no place for, Paul VI asserts that we can be fulfilled even if this imposes a personal cost to ourselves. Within this, personal frugality or limiting one's consumption is not a diminishment but a positive element of one's personal development.[21] John Paul II has stressed this point as well, emphasizing the transcendence of humanity in seeking the truth and the common good. Similarly, reinforcing John Paul II's criticisms of consumerism, limiting one's consumption is vital in certain stages of the pure cycle in ECA. This self-sacrificing is not done out of self-interest or even purely enlightened self-interest, for instance, where I realize that helping to secure the individual needs and desires of others, for example in satisfying a consumer,[22] leads to benefits for me. Instead self-sacrifice can be motivated either by moral obligation or by genuine concern for the other.[23] Lonergan calls this concern, particularly as manifested in the economic order, "enlightenment of enlightened self-interest,"[24] meaning to be fully human one must work to overcome one's biases of individual and group bias that frustrate the "the precarious attainment of intellectual and moral transcendence."[25] Lonergan thus concurs with Catholic social teaching that self-sacrifice is integral to both healthy economic development and self development.

The Search for a "Third Way": The Role of Profit

Catholic social teaching itself has been described often as a search for a "third way" between individualist capitalism and collectivist socialism. While this may be an appropriate designation for the fact that Catholic social teaching believes both political-economic systems must be corrected, on the other hand, despite possibly Pius XI's advocacy of corporatism as a distinct economic system, CST does not advocate the establishment of any particular political-economic system as alternative to capitalism and socialism.[26] Nonetheless, Catholic social teaching's very criticisms of capitalism and socialism, especially it does so on the basis of economic anthropology, point toward the need for a new economic paradigm to replace mainstream economics and the Marxian alternative.

ECA is also an attempt to move beyond capitalism and socialism, while incorporating, as does social economics, elements of both. For example, Lonergan recognizes the importance of the profit motive to a market economy, but does not place it at the center of economic motivation or his economic analysis. Like Paul VI, Lonergan condemns the profit system as the key motive for economic development, competition as the supreme law of economics, and private ownership of means of production as an absolute right that has no limits and carries no corresponding social obligation. With advocates of socialism, he has a place for ethical concerns, but does not advocate centralized planning as a way to incorporate these concerns in an economic system, agreeing with John XIII's teachings in both *Mater et Magistra* and *Pacem in Terris* that "the balance between private and public-state intervention in economic field ought not be exercised in such a way as to curtail individual freedom of personal initiative."[27] Again with capitalists, Lonergan realizes the importance of entrepreneurial efforts, but stresses that the surplus expansion that can be the fruit of such developments must be intentionally directed toward the basic expansion that is to the benefit of all. In his praise of individual initiative and creativity, Lonergan concurs with Pius XI's praise for the entrepreneurial taste for research and discovery, the ability to take calculated risk, boldness in enterprise and generosity and responsibility for the fruits of the process that modern industrialism has often evidenced.[28] He further agrees with John Paul II that the free market seems to be the "most efficient instrument for utilizing resources and effectively responding to needs" (*Centesimus Annus*, 34). However, he also agrees with both Pius XI and John Paul II's derogation of an unregulated market based on the image of the market as automatic mechanism because it lacks, as John Paul states, the "wherewithal to notice attend to, or give priority to deeper human and moral values."[29]

Like Catholic social teaching then, ECA stands in a dialectical relationship to capitalism and socialism. Lonergan's economics can be thought of as a "third way" at least between capitalism and socialism in that he believed that competing economic theories will move dialectically to a higher viewpoint and better economic theory—"towards getting one that ma[kes] sense."[30] In her analysis of Lonergan's economic thought, the economist Elaine De Neeve demonstrates how Lonergan "synthesized what are often regarded as juxtaposed viewpoints in economics in the development of his own theories."[31] For example, Like Austrian economic theory (e.g., Friedrich Hayek), monetarists, and supply-side theoreticians, Lonergan recognizes an equilibrium system underlying economic process, strong limitations to government role in the economy, and the importance of the supply side for understanding macrodynamic processes.[32] However, a crucial difference between Lonergan and mainstream economics is that he does not hold that business cycles are inevitable.

Like Keynes and the neo-Keynesians, Lonergan understands the importance of disequilibrium as well as equilibrium in the economy—"the rigidities created by price or income contracts to be factors preventing the economy from adjusting to any kind of shock" especially productivity changes that impact real investment and output. Unlike Keynesian economics he does not advocate government policies to remedy disequilibrium, but for agents to change their rational behavior in accordance with a better understanding of economic process.[33] Finally, like Marx and neo-Marxists, Lonergan appreciates both the tremendous growth provided by the free enterprise market system but also the problem capitalism has in adapting to the challenges that growth requires. Both Lonergan and Marx stress that problems will erupt (although Lonergan argues that Marx addressed this problem sociologically, not through adequate economic theory) if the pure surplus income generated by this growth is not distributed throughout the economy ending up in expansion of the standard of living for all. Again, Lonergan relies on a functional analysis to understand this, while Marx relies on a proprietorial one.

The Dialectic Between Healing and Creativity

One goal of this book has been to emphasize and to take to a higher level through Lonergan's economics the need for a concurrent integration of both healing and creating into economics and economic ethics. I have chosen to highlight Catholic social teaching because I believe among approaches to economic ethics, it has been very forthright about the need for integrating both healing and creativity, while recognizing that the creating aspect is beyond its proper bounds. Nevertheless, I agree with R. Bruce Douglass's criticism of the classicist conception of the common good present in Catholic social teaching, which is worth quoting at length because he underscores well what is at stake in the intersection of ethics and economics (here he is talking about *Economic Justice for All)*:

> "How do we bring the two [competing claims of godly living and economic efficiency]together in a way that does not entail sacrificing one for the other? The common good tradition developed, in its economic aspect at least, precisely to meet this demand, and it prevailed as long as it did because it was reasonably successful in this regard. It provided a way of acknowledging the intrinsic worth of economic pursuits without allowing them to become the be-all and end-all of human existence. It was not, however, geared to economic growth in the sense to which we have subsequently been accustomed; and this ultimately proved to be its undoing.

A key to Lonergan's analysis, and I believe a major component of its relevance to economics, and thus economic ethics, is the prescriptive power of his analysis, which is in turn based upon its explanatory power. This allows a bridge to be built between the classicist common-good tradition of the encyclical tradition and the dynamism of the market celebrated in Centesimus Annus that in This explanatory power stems from Lonergan's incorporation of functional variables, rather than merely descriptive variables such as the overall level of profits, the current rate of unemployment, wages, prices. Lonergan relies on the relationships between accelerations of such variables, but differentiates the changes in their rates according to whether they occur in the surplus or basic sectors.[35] This emphasis on acceleration and what is accelerating is the key to a dynamic view of the common good, which as the popes to their enduring credit point out, is significantly rooted in the good of the economic order. Therefore, only by paying attention to the relevant variables can a static conception of the common good that Douglass rightly decries be overcome. As Philip McShane writes,

> [O]ne does not have to call in Aristotle's view of science in potency as limited to view as off the mark, or off the wall, the reach either of Catholic social teaching or of mathematical modeling for 'just right' income distribution. The genuine reach has to be one of complex large and small negotiations of unions, managements, etc., pivoting on the enlightened self-interest . . . .[36]

For example, while John XXIII is correct that the economic order must be balanced and that wealth (or pure surplus income) generated by rapid growth must move from the wealthy to the working class and the poor,[37] Lonergan shows more concretely how this should occur when he advises that the surplus income generated be put back into the surplus expansion either through investment or plant expansion. If employees, including executives, are granted too much salary at this point or if unions demand too much this expansion is thwarted and the basic expansion required to raise the standard of living of all will be postponed or negated along with it.

Conclusion

Catholic social teaching and *Macroeconomic Dynamics: An Essay in Circulation Analysis* exist in complementary relationship with each other in that both are concerned with the common good, both have an economic anthropology rooted in the capacity of the human person to size up the facts of situations, deliberate morally, and decide beyond self-interest, in other words to transcend themselves, and both seek to move beyond the theoretical and practical deficiencies of present economic arrangements of capitalism and socialism. There are also the differences I previously outlined. While I think these differences are crucial to an adequate economic ethics, one again that Catholic social teaching does not provide, it would overstate the case for that reason to place *Essay in Circulation Analysis* over and against Catholic social teaching as I would place it over and against orthodox and Marxian economics, and economic ethics built on them.

To better understand this, I return again to the themes of healing and creativity in economic ethics. As Lonergan wrote in *Healing and Creating in History*,

> For human development is of two different kinds. There is development from below upwards, from experience to growing understanding to balanced judgment, from balanced judgment to fruitful courses of action, and from fruitful courses of action to the new situations that call forth further understanding, profounder judgment, richer courses of action. But there is also development from above downwards. There is the transformation of falling in love: the domestic love of the family; the human love of one's tribe, one's city, one's country, mankind; the divine love that orientates man in his cosmos and expresses itself in his worship. Where hatred sees only evil, love reveals values.[38]

My chapters on Lonergan's economic thought stressed mainly the "movement from below," in this case creating a more adequate economic analysis. But there is also the "movement from above" which is the movement of love and concern for the other. Both play an essential role in an adequate economic ethics and alternative economic paradigm. This approach is diametrically opposed to the neoclassical methodological individualism core assertion that all social phenomena should be traced back to the foundation in individualistic hedonistic behavior. As the neoclassical economist, James Buchanan, says explicitly, "when non-individualistic norms [such as love, solidarity, etc.] are introduced, the domain of economics as I define the discipline, is abandoned."[39]

The deeper understanding of economic life sought in ECA aims at a "further enlargement of enlightened self-interest quite different from vague Christian principles of preference for the poor, from unrealistic social yearnings for equality, from philanthropies grounded in basic injustices. It is a more distant goal, a more excellent end."[40] McShane is entirely right about the vagueness of precepts of the much of Catholic social teaching and the need to turn more to theory to address problems in the economic order.[41] However, I would argue that while Catholic social teaching points at some undefined "third way," it does so through high-lighting the importance of the enlightenment of enlightened self-interest alluded to by McShane.

Two important perspectives elaborated by Paul VI stress the complementary roles of healing and creativity. The first is his call for a "rebirth of utopias." Paul stated that while an appeal to utopia can be negative if it encourages people to "escape from concrete tasks in order to take refuge in an imaginary world," they have an important role in criticizing modern concrete political systems such as bureaucratic socialism, technocratic capitalism, and authoritarian democracy that are in their various ways trying to solve the problem of people living together in justice and equality. This role is of provoking the "forward-looking imagination both to perceive in the present the disregarded possibility hidden with in and to direct itself toward a fresh future; it thus sustains social dynamism by the confidence that it gives to the inventive powers of the human mind and heart."[42] I think this "forward-looking imagination" that contributes to the "inventive powers of the mind and heart," is exactly what Lonergan means by movements from above, and even relates the importance of correlating healing movements from above, with the creating element of the movement from below of intellectual inquiry. The second element, this time more directed at the need for adequate intellectual inquiry, is emphasized by Paul VI's call for the pursuit of the human sciences toward a truer picture of the human. Despite warranted suspicion of actual human sciences,[43] Paul VI says that the Church has confidence in this research also and urges Christians to play an active part in it." If Christians are motivated by their faith and the desire to know humanity better in a scientific way within a particular scientific discipline, they will be able to grasp a better understanding of the human person, and of dynamics of production and exchange.[44]

Therefore, Catholic social teaching although, as Hobgood rightly points out, frequently inadequate in its economic analysis, provides the images and principles necessary to incorporate the movement from above into economic life. In this way, Catholic social teaching promotes the moral, religious, psychic, and in their critique of the methods of economic science, intellectual conversion necessary to provide healthy functioning in the economic order. Also, Catholic social teaching, economic ethicists, social economists, etc, *are* economists. To an interviewer who asked him, "What do you hope to point out to people?" Lonergan replied,

> That we should get rid of the distinction between theorists in morality and theorists in economics. The moral theorists about economics are also economists; they see what's necessary for the machine to run properly. And if they don't? Well, we have to get better economists. The lesson has been drummed in for about two centuries now.[45]

Thus, to the extent that economists are not intellectually and morally converted it can be said instead that they are not doing a more adequate economics than these "non-economists."[46]

The extent that the discipline of economics as now constituted is lacking in adequate macroeconomic analysis is not the only problem. The horizon-shift required for economics goes beyond better knowledge, it requires a change in many economists themselves. Economists, in order to be able to put forth the precepts needed for people to democratically direct their economy for the common good, like all of us have to move beyond the biases involved in individual egoist morality of self-interest, and beyond the group egoist level which seeks the self-interest of the group, and undergo moral conversion if necessary.[47] As Lonergan remarked, only "Then you will get moral precepts coming out of economics."[48] This interior orientation requires both "thoughtfulness and knowing what you are doing."[49] To the extent then that Catholic social teaching promotes "thoughtfulness" in terms of reflecting about what the economy does to people, and what it could do for people, then it is invaluable.

Finally, the need for wide-spread religious, moral and intellectual conversion to appropriate the understanding provided in *Macroeconomic Dynamics: An Essay in Circulation Analysis* also goes along with the importance of religious faith for the good of the economic order in Catholic social teaching. For example, *Gaudium et Spes* adopts a more dialectical strategy that provided in earlier Catholic social teaching, in its recognition that reality is marred by social evil.[50] Lonergan's theology of history also incorporates a very nuanced approach that recognizes three vectors at work at once in persons, society and history. These are progress, decline, and redemption (human cooperation from divine activity in the world). As he writes in ECA, economic progress is "the fruit of attentiveness, intelligence, reasonableness, and responsibility." Economic decline on the other hand is "the offspring of inattention, obtuseness, unreasonableness, and irresponsibility."[51] Therefore, intellectual inquiry must be complemented with acknowledgment of our sinful human condition. But, contrary to Michael Novak and others who rely on a Niebuhrian Christian realism, that is not the end of the story. God's grace can work to remove our biases of self-centeredness and group-centeredness, and even common sense bias (which for economists, despite their ambition to be the hardest of the social sciences might be the most difficult, entrenched as they are in uncritically common sense views of human nature led by self-interest and proprietary views of circulation of money throughout the economy). As Paul Hoyt-O'Connor points out,. "For Lonergan, genuine economic recovery ultimately has its sources in divine operations through which human desiring is reoriented, and its work consists in the often incremental transformation of economic understanding and practice."[52] As a people then we have hope, but not the certainty, that more widespread moral conversion, accompanied by intellectual and religious conversion, may help us towards healing at least some of our economic woes and creating a more just and hospitable society in its place.[53]

Catholic social teaching advocates "healing from above" and a proper economic anthropology, though this approach is incomplete without an adequate alternative macroeconomic paradigm, which I've shown is integrally tied to methodological and even epistemological concerns. Lonergan's implicit economic methodology, based on his more well-known work in epistemology and cognitive science, incorporates healing (moral consciousness) and an adequate economic anthropology consonant though not explicitly derived from that of Catholic social teaching; and enables a creativity resulting in a concurrent macrodynamic paradigm necessary for full participation for all in the fruits of economic liberty. Along the way, Lonergan's economic thought points to the necessary participatory, intelligent, reasonable, responsible and even loving role for economic agents, including economists, in bringing about those fruits.

NOTES

1. Al Kresta, "Interview with Michael Novak," 4/6/2000, "Kresta in the Afternoon," Ava Maria Radio 1/7/2005 http://www.amfdn.org/ubb/Forum2/HTML /000346.html.

2. For example, in 1999 at about the time Novak is talking and at the height of the 1990's economic "boom," 26.8% of workers earned poverty-level wages, which is somewhat above a minimum wage but below a living wage. According to the Economic Policy Institute, this was an increase from 23.7% in 1979 ("Living Wage: Frequently Asked Questions," 11/2002, Economic Policy Institute, 1/7/2005 </www.epinet.org/content.cfm/issueguides_livingwage_livingwagefaq).

3. A minimum living wage level would be enough to provide enough for families to live without government assistance—this is typically over 12 times the minimum wage (Economic Policy Institute, "Living Wage: Frequently Asked

Questions").

4. Michael Novak, "Tested by Our Own Ideals," in George Weigel, ed., *A New Worldly Order: John Paul II and Human Freedom* (Washington: Ethics and Public Policy Center, c. 1992), 139. Cited in Thomas Storck, "What Does Centesimus Annus Really Teach?" Catholic.net. 1/7/2005 <http://www.catholic.net/RCC/Periodicals/Faith/2001-06/teaching.html.

5. Cf. Pope John Paul II's criticism of capitalism in *Laborem Exercens* is that it prioritizes capital over labor . That a market economy may not be "capitalistic" in this sense is argued by in *Centesimus Annus* where he praises systems which help to ensure "conditions for steady and healthy economic growth," but by not placing too much emphasis on "market mechanisms" (art. 19).

6. Mary E. Hobgood. "The Author Replies," *Journal of Religious Ethics* 25:2 (Fall 1997): 364-5.

7. Or calculate what the resulting economy would look like once those reparations were paid and the subsequent outcome for the possibility of living wages for everyone..

8. Mary E. Hobgood. "The Author Replies. 361.

9. "Rather than focusing on the failure to reach agreement . . . we approach opposing views and different positions as 'feasible contributors to creative, responsive moral discourse and agency aimed at producing justice'" (Mary E. Hobgood. "The Author Replies," 365; quoting from Marcia Riggs, "Mediating Arguments about Family Values," *Journal of Feminist Studies in Religion* 12:1 [Spring 1996]: 109).

10. Lonergan, "Healing and Creating in History," 109n14. For support, Lonergan suggests the reader consult Christian Duquoc, *Ambiguitè des thèologies de la sècularisation: essai critique* (Gembloux: Duculot, 1972), especially Duquoc's remark on Harvey Cox's *The Secular City* (67) and on *Gaudium et Spes* (103ff, 113ff).

11. Frederick E. Crowe, "Lonergan as Pastoral Theologian," in *Appropriating the Lonergan Idea*, ed. Michael Vertin (Washington, D.C.: Catholic University of America Press, 1989), 129. Lonergan's view on the family wage was that is was the closest thing moral theologians had to an economic precept, but that in practice the concept did not work because it was proposed in the Catholic social encyclicals as a precept of charity not justice, those who chose to pay the family wage would soon be pushed out of business by those who chose not to pay it. Cf. Pierrot Lambert, et. al., *Caring About Meaning*, 31, 164. One possible objection to Lonergan's objection—that the living wage doctrine does not require Catholic businesspeople to pay a family wage if it puts them out of business, only serves to underline its inefficacy as an act of charity or even "private justice." Either way the living wage is not paid—if Catholic businesses go out of business paying a family wage or do not pay it to avoid going out of business.

12. Pierrot Lambert, et.al., *Caring About Meaning.*, 108.

13. Quoted in David Card and Alan B. Krueger (contributor). *Myth and Measurement: The New Economics of the Minimum Wage* (Princeton: Princeton University Press, 1995), 155.

14. Lawrence, "Editor's Introduction," xxx. On the need for a "new political economy," see Bernard Lonergan, *For a New Political Economy*, 5-7.

15. Bernard Lonergan, "An Outline of Circulation Analysis," [3]. This is an unpublished manuscript of an earlier version of ECA, available at the Lonergan Research Centre, Toronto.

16. As discussed in Chapter Three, the good of order is the second level of the human good, built upon fulfilling individuals desires and needs, but not reducible to it.

17. *Mater et Magistra* 79, 92. The emphasis on having goods and services available to all and removing extreme differentials in income between classes and nations belongs to Lonergan's third level of the human good, in which in this case, questions of value of the economic order predominate, not just its efficient functioning. However, in ECA, efficient functioning of the economy requires conversion, questions of ultimate concern and if directed accordingly leads to providing an equitable distribution of goods and services within and among countries.

18. *Quadragesimo Anno*, 57.

19. *Gaudium et Spes*, 71.

20. Bernard Lonergan, "An Outline of Circulation Analysis," 3..

21. Lonergan, "An Outline of Circulation Analysis," 182-83.; PP 47.

22. Novak joins with Adam Smith in claiming that this exigency of the market system to please its constituents is the primary interpersonal dimension incorporated within economic theory.

23. Novak and others soften Adam Smith's reliance upon self-interest as the main component of economic activity, primarily in Smith's *The Wealth of Nations* by noting his stress upon sympathy toward others as a main organizing principle in civil society. However, the economist Amartya Sen points out how this does not necessarily correspond to transcending self-interest as CST and Lonergan's economics call for: "[Sympathy] corresponds to the case in which the concern for others directly affects one's own welfare. If the knowledge of torture makes you sick, it is a case of sympathy; if it does not make you feel personally worse off, but you think it is wrong, and you are ready to do something to stop it, it is a case of commitment." In distinction from sympathy for another's well-being, which is egoistic to the extent that sympathetic action can increase one's own utility making one happier by increasing another's pleasure (or decreasing their displeasure), Sen defines commitment in terms of a "person choosing an act that he believes will yield a lower level of personal welfare to him than an alternative that is also available to him" ("Rational Fools: A Critique of

the Behavioral Foundations of Economic Theory." *Philosophy & Public Affairs* 6 (1977): 326-7).

24. ECA, 6.

25. Hoyt-O'Connor, 313.

26. As John Paul II states, "The Church has no models to present; models that are real and truly effective can only arise within the framework of different historical situations, through the efforts of all those who responsibly confront concrete problems in all their social, economic, political, and cultural aspects" (*Centesimus Annus,* art. 43).

27. *Mater et Magistra*, 109; *Pacem in Terris*, 65.

28. In contrast to what some advocates of democratic capitalism seem to imply, Paul clearly does not assume that poverty and underdevelopment arise from purely natural causes, or from the laziness of people living in poorer parts of the world (*Populorum Progressio*, 57-60).

29. *Centesimus Annus*, 138.

30. Pierrot Lambert, Charlotte Tansey and Cathleen Going, Editors, *Caring About Meaning: Patterns in the Life of Bernard Lonergan*, ed. Pierrot Lambert, Charlotte Tansey and Cathleen Going (Montreal: Thomas More Institute, 1982), 32.

31. De Neeve, "Bernard Lonergan's 'Circulation Analysis' and Macrodynamics" (Ph.D. diss., McGill University, 1990), 228. Regarding this higher integration, I am indebted in the following paragraphs to her analysis, in which she compares *Macroeconomic Dynamics: An Essay in Circulation Analysis* to different schools of economic thought such as Austrian theory, Keynesian and neo-Keynesians, Marxian and neo-Marxian, and New Classical (supply-side) economics.

32. De Neeve, "Bernard Lonergan's 'Circulation Analysis' and Macrodynamics," 226.

33. De Neeve, "Bernard Lonergan's 'Circulation Analysis' and Macrodynamics," 227.

35. As William Matthews writes, "The real indicators of economic health are not simply income and expenditure—the budget, but rather the quantities and velocities of money and changes in those in relation to consumer and producer goods, etc., over a significant time spans" (William Matthews, S.J., "Lonergan's Economics," *Method: Journal of Lonergan Studies* 3 (March 1985): 18).

36. Philip McShane, *Economics for Everyone: Das Jus Kapital* (Edmonton, Alberta: Commonwealth Publications, 1995), 135.

37. *Mater et Magistra*, 77.

38. Lonergan, "Healing and Creating in History," 106. This stress in Lonergan's work on the "movement from above" came into prominence in the last stages in his thought, but is nevertheless a crucial element. Lonergan acknowledged this shift in "Insight Revisited," in *A Second Collection*, ed. William Ryan

and Bernard Tyrell (Philadelphia: The Westminster Press, 1974), 277. For a detailed account of this shift and its implications for understanding Lonergan's moral thought, see Frederick E. Crowe, S.J., "An Exploration of Lonergan's New Notion of Value," in *Appropriating the Lonergan Idea*, ed. Michael Vertin (Washington, D.C.: Catholic University of America Press, 1989), 51-70 and "An Expansion of Lonergan's Notion of Value" in the same volume, 344-359.

39. James Buchanan, "What Kind of Redistribution Do We Want?" *Economica* 35 (May 1968), 185; quoted in David A. Martin, "Economics in Three Paradigms: Subject, Method and Values," *Human Values and Economic Activity: The Proceedings of the 12th Conference on Value Inquiry* (Geneseo, NY: State University of New York College at Geneseo, 1978), 58-68.

40. McShane, *Economics for Everyone*, 135.

41. McShane, *Economics for Everyone*, 130.

42. *Octogesima Adveniens,* 37.

43. John Milbank in particular criticizes the use of social science for theological ethics, incorrectly I would argue, in *Theology and Social Theory* (Oxford, ENG: Basil Blackwell, 1990); "Against the Resignations of the Age" in *Things Old and New: Catholic Social Teaching Revisited*, ed. Francis P. McHugh and Samuel M. Natale (Lanham MD: University Press of America, 1993), 1-39; and "On Complex Space" in *The Word Made Strange: Theology, Language, and Culture* (Cambridge, MA: Blackwell Publishers, 1997), 268-92. D. Stephen Long takes an almost purely theological approach to economics in *Divine Economy: Theology and The Market* (London/New York: Routledge, 2000), and "Catholic Social Teaching and the Global Market" in *Wealth, Poverty and Human Destiny*, ed. Doug Bandow and David L. Schindler (Wilmington, DE: ISI Books, 2003), 77-102.

44. *Octogesima Adveniens,* 40. Also, Bellah, et. al.'s appendices to both *Habits of the Heart* and *The Good Society*, emphasize the need for a renewed human and social scientific approach to understanding economic society in terms of what is does to people.

45. Cathleen Going, ed, *Dialogues in Celebration,* Thomas More Institute Papers/80 (Montreal: Thomas More Institute, 1980), 299.

46. Going, *Dialogues in Celebration,* 299. Philip McShane rightly points out that it is not only moral theologians (and by extension liberation and political theologians) who have to work to incorporate more adequate economic theory. Taking Lonergan's definition of theology as the mediation "between a cultural matrix and the significance and role of religion in that matrix," and the task of theology as broken down into eight distinct functional specialties: research, interpretation, history, dialectic, foundations, doctrines, systematics, and communications (Lonergan, *Method in Theology*, xi), McShane writes, "The genuinely contemporary theologian has the uncomfortable task of becoming educated in the relevant invariant macrodynamic heuristic if he or she, in any

functional specialty, is to contribute to the mediation of that transposition of economic culture" (Philip McShane, "Systematics, Communications, Actual Contexts," in *Religion in Context: Recent Studies in Lonergan*, ed. Timothy J. Fallon, S.J. and Philip Boo Riley (Lanham, MD: University Press of America, 1988), 70).

47. Going, *Dialogues in Celebration*, 302.

48. However, there is no need for whole-scale intellectual and moral conversion in the economics community in Lonergan's view. As he remarked, "If we get 5 or ten percent of the economists to recognize a moral obligation to what is really good, we can get somewhere" (Going, *Dialogues in Celebration*, 305).

49. Going, *Dialogues in Celebration*, 305.

50. *Gaudium et Spes*, 69.

51. ECA, 94.

52. Hoyt O'Connor, 298.

53. Cf. Daniel C. Maguire, *The Moral Core of Judaism and Christianity: Reclaiming the Revolution* (Minneapolis: Fortress Press, 1993), especially Part II, "Scripting a New Humanity," for a cogent and inspired account of the power of biblically-immersed theology can inform the economic anthropology necessary for well-grounded economic theory.

WORKS CONSULTED

Anderson, Bruce and Philip McShane. *Beyond Establishment Economics: No Thank-you Mankiw*. Halifax, Nova Scotia: Axial Press, 2002.

Atherton, John. *Christianity and the Market: Christian Social Thought for Our Times.* London: SPCK, 1992.

Bannock, G., R.E. Baxter, and R. Rees, ed. "Forced Savings." P. 171 in *The Penguin Dictionary of Economics*. Harmondsforth, Eng.: Penguin Books, 1976.

Baum, Gregory. *The Priority of Labor: A Commentary on "Laborem Exercens," Encyclical Letter of Pope John Paul II.* New York: Paulist Press, 1982.

——. "John Paul's Encyclical on Labor." Pp. 233-40 in *Readings in Moral Theology No. 5: Official Catholic Social Teaching,* ed. Charles E Curran and Richard A. McCormick. New York: Paulist Press, 1986.

——. "Liberal Capitalism." Pp. 75-89 in *The Logic of Solidarity: Commentaries on Pope John Paul II's Encyclical "On Social Concern,"* ed. Gregory Baum and Robert Ellsberg. Maryknoll, NY: Orbis Books, 1989.

——. "Structures of Sin." Pp. 110-26 in *The Logic of Solidarity: Commentaries on Pope John Paul II's Encyclical "On Social Concern,"* ed. Gregory Baum and Robert Ellsberg. Maryknoll, NY: Orbis Books, 1989.

——. "The Originality of Catholic Social Teaching." Pp. 55-62 in *Rerum Novarum: A Hundred Years of Catholic Social Teaching.* Ed. John Coleman and Gregory Baum. London: SCM Press; Philadelphia: Trinity Press International, 1991.

——. "The Ethical Foundations of Worker's Co-ops." Pp. 223-44 in *Essays in Critical Theology*. Kansas City: Sheed and Ward, 1994.

——. *Karl Polanyi: On Ethics and Economics.* Montreal: McGill Queens University Press, 1996.

Beckley, Harlan. "Social Science and Theological Ethics: A Response to Mary E. Hobgood." *Journal of Religious Ethics* (Fall 1997): 343-50.

Bell, Daniel. *The Cultural Contradictions of Capitalism.* New York: Basic Books, 1976.

Bellah, Robert et al. *Habits of the Heart: Individualism and Commitment in American Life.* Berkeley/Los Angeles: University of California Press, 1985.

Benne, Robert. *The Ethic of Democratic Capitalism: A Moral Reassessment.* Philadelphia: Fortress Press, 1981.

Bernstein, Richard J. *Beyond Objectivism and Relativism: Science, Hermeneutics, and Praxis*. Philadelphia: University of Pennsylvania Press, 1983.

Birnbaum, Norman. "The Bishops in the Iron Cage: The Dilemmas of Advanced Society." Pp. 153-78 in *The Catholic Challenge to the American Economy: Reflections on the U.S. Bishops' Pastoral Letter on Catholic Social Thinking and the U.S. Economy*, ed. Thomas M. Gannon, S.J. New York: MacMillan Publishing Company, 1987.

Burley, Peter. "A Summary of Lonergan's Economic Diagram." Pp. 3-11 in *Australian Lonergan Workshop*, ed. W.J. Danaher. Lanham, MD: University Press of America, 1993.

——. "Lonergan as a Neo-Schumpeterian." Pp. 249-57 in *Australian Lonergan Workshop*, ed. William J. Danaher. Lanham, MD: University Press of America, 1993.

Byrne, Patrick "Economic Transformations: The Role of Conversions and Culture in the Transformation of Economics." Pp. 327-48 in *Religion in Context: Recent Studies in Lonergan*, ed. Timothy J. Fallon, S.J. and Philip Boo Riley. Lanham, MD: University Press of America, 1988.

——. "*Ressentiment* and the Preferential Option for the Poor." *Theological Studies* 54 (1993): 214-41.

Caporaso, James A. and David P. Levine. *Theories of Political Economy.* Cambridge, UK: Cambridge University Press, 1992.

Card, David and Alan B. Krueger (contributor). *Myth and Measurement: The New Economics of the Minimum Wage.* Princeton: Princeton University Press, 1995.

Cobb, Jr., John B. "Christianity, Political Theology and the Economic Future." Pp. 207-23 in *Civil Religion and Public Theology.* Ed. by Leroy C. Rouner. Notre Dame, IN: University of Notre Dame Press, 1986.

——. "Foreword." Pp. ix-x in *The Wealth or Health of Nations: Transforming Capitalism from Within,* by Carol A. Johnston. Cleveland: The Pilgrim Press, 1998.

Coleman, S.J., John A. "Neither Liberal nor Socialist." Pp. 25-43 in *One Hundred Years of Catholic Social Thought: Celebration and Challenge,* ed. by John A. Coleman, S.J. Maryknoll: Orbis Books, 1991.

Collier, Jane. *The Culture of Economism: An Exploration of Barriers to Faith-as-Praxis.* Frankfurt am Main: Peter Lang, 1990.

Copeland, M. Shawn. "The Interaction of Racism, Sexism, and Classism in Women's Exploitation." Pp. 19-27 in *Women, Work and Poverty,* ed. Elisabeth Schussler Fiorenza and Anne Carr. Concilium: Theology for the Eighties, vol. 194, 1987.

——. "A Genetic Study of the Human Good in the Thought of Bernard Lonergan." Ph.D. diss., Boston College, 1991.

Crowe, Frederick E. *The Lonergan Enterprise.* Cambridge, MA: Cowley Press, 1980.

——. "An Exploration of Lonergan's New Notion of Value." Pp. 51-70 in *Appropriating the Lonergan Idea*, ed. Michael Vertin. Washington, DC: The Catholic University of America Press, 1989.

——. "Lonergan as Pastoral Theologian." Pp. 451-70 in *Appropriating the Lonergan Idea*, ed. Michael Vertin. Washington, DC: The Catholic University of America Press, 1989.

——. *Lonergan*, in *Outstanding Christian Thinkers Series*, series ed. Brian Davies, O.P. Collegeville, MN: The Liturgical Press, 1992.
——. "Editor's Introduction," to "Lonergan's 'Moral Theology and the Human Sciences.'" *Method: Journal of Lonergan Studies* 15 (1997): 5-20.
Curran, Charles E. *American Catholic Social Ethics*. Notre Dame, IN: University of Notre Dame Press, 1982.
——. "The Changing Anthropological Bases of Christian Social Ethics." Pp. 188-218 in *Readings in Moral Theology, No. 5: Official Catholic Social Teaching*, ed. Charles E. Curran and Richard A. McCormick. New York: Paulist Press, 1986.
——. "Relating Religious-Ethical Inquiry to Economic Inquiry." Pp. 42-54 in *The Catholic Challenge to the American Economy: Reflections on the U.S. Bishops' Pastoral Letter on Catholic Social Thinking and the U.S. Economy*, ed. by Thomas M. Gannon, S.J. NY: MacMillan Publishing Company, 1987.
Dallmayr, Fred. R. and Thomas A. McCarthy, ed. *Understanding and Social Inquiry*. Notre Dame, IN: University of Notre Dame Press, 1977.
Daly, Herman, and John B. Cobb, Jr. *For the Common Good: Redirecting the Economy Toward Community, the Environment and a Sustainable Future*. Boston: Beacon Press, 1989.
Davis, Charles. *Theology and Political Society*. New York: Cambridge University Press, 1980.
——. "Lonergan's Appropriation of the Concept of Praxis." *New Blackfriars* (1981): 114-126.
Davis, John B. "Introduction." Pp. vii-xxix in *The Social Economics of Human Material Need*, ed. John B. Davis and Edward J. O'Boyle. Carbondale, IL: Southern Illinois University Press, 1994.
De Neeve, Elaine. "Bernard Lonergan's 'Circulation Analysis' and Macrodynamics." Ph.D. diss., McGill University, 1990.
——. "Suspicion and Recovery: Ethical Approaches to Economics." *Method: A Journal for Lonergan Studies* 15 (1995): 29-50.
Dionne, E.J. "Capitalism With Soul. Novak on the Catholic Ethic. Review of Michael Novak, *The Catholic Ethic and the Spirit of Capitalism*." *Commonweal* 21 (May 21, 1993): 9-11.
Doran, Robert. *Theology and the Dialectics of History*. Toronto: University of Toronto Press, 1990.
Dorr, Donal. *Option for the Poor: A Hundred Years of Catholic Social Teaching*. Rev. ed. Maryknoll, N.Y.: Orbis Books, 1992.
Dorrien, Gary. *The Democratic Socialist Vision*. Totowa, NJ: Rowman and Littlefield, 1986.
——. *Soul in Society: The Making and Renewal of Social Christianity*. Minneapolis: Fortress Press, 1995.
——. *Reconstructing the Common Good: Theology and the Social Order*. Maryknoll: Orbis Books, 1990.
Drucker, Peter. "Schumpeter and Keynes." *Forbes* (May 23, 1982): 300-304.

Dunne, T.A. "Lonergan on Social Process and Community." Th.D. diss., Regis College, Toronto, 1975.

Economic Policy Institute. "Living Wage: Frequently Asked Questions." 11/2002. Economic Policy Institute. <http://www.epinet.org/content.cfm/issueguides_livingwage_living-wage faq. > 1/7/2005

Finn, Daniel Rush. "Review of Mary E. Hobgood, *Catholic Social Teaching and Economic Theory*." *Horizons* 20 (Spring 1993): 185-6.

——. "Monologue and Dialogue in Christian Economic Ethics: A Response to Mary E. Hobgood." *Journal of Religious Ethics* (Fall 1997): 335-41.

Friedman, Milton. "The Methodology of Positive Economics." In *Essays in Positive Economics*. Chicago: University of Chicago Press, 1953.

——. "The Social Responsibility of Business is to Increase Its Profits," *New York Times* Sept. 13, 1970. Reprinted pp. 754-59 in *Twenty Questions: An Introduction to Philosophy*, ed. by G. Lee Bowie, et al. Harcourt Brace Jovanovich: San Diego, 1988.

Gaburro, Giuseppe. "Christian Anthropology as a Foundation for a New Economics." Pp. 43-53 in *On the Condition of Labor and the Social Question One Hundred Years Later: Commemorating the 100th Anniversary of Rerum Novarum and the Fiftieth Anniversary of the Association for Social Economics*, ed. by Thomas O. Nitsch, et al. Lewisport, NY: The Edwin Mellen Press, 1994.

Gay, Craig M. *With Liberty and Justice for Whom?: The Recent Evangelical Debate Over Capitalism*. Grand Rapids, MI: William P. Eerdmans, 1991.

George, David. "Social Economics in the Years Ahead: An Economist's Perspective." *Review of Social Economy* 51 (1993): 476-89.

Goodzwaard, Bob. *Capitalism and Progress: A Diagnosis of Western Society*. Trans. and ed. by J. van Nuis Zylstra. Grand Rapids, MI: William P. Eerdmans, 1979.

Gower, Joseph F. "Introduction." Pp. [ix]-xxvi in *Religion and Economic Ethics*, ed. Joseph F. Gower. Lanham, MD: University Press of America, 1990.

Griffiths, Brian. *The Creation of Wealth: A Christian's Case for Capitalism*. Downers Grove, IL: Intervarsity Press, 1984.

Hammond, David M. "The Influence of Newman's Doctrine of Assent on the Thought of Bernard Lonergan: A Genetic Study." *Method: Journal of Lonergan Studies* 7/2 (October 1989): 95-115.

Harrison, Beverly W. "The Role of Social Theory in Religious Social Ethics." Pp. 58-72 in *Making the Connections: Essays in Feminist Social Ethics*, ed. Carol S. Robb. Boston: Beacon Press, 1985.

——. "The Fate of the Middle Class in Late Capitalism." In *God and Capitalism*, ed. J. Mark Thomas and Vernon Visick. Madison, WI: A-R Editions, 1991. 53-71.

Hay, Donald. *Economics To-day: A Christian Critique*. Grand Rapids, MI: William P. Eerdmans, 1989.

Hobgood, Mary E. "Conflicting Paradigms in Social Analysis." Pp. 167-85 in *The Logic of Solidarity: Commentaries on Pope John Paul II's Encyclical "On Social Concern,"* ed. Gregory Baum and Robert Ellsberg. Maryknoll, NY: Orbis Books, 1989.

——. *Catholic Social Teaching and Economic Theory: Paradigms in Conflict.* Philadelphia: Temple University Press, 1991.

——. "Poor Women, Work, and the U.S. Catholic Bishops: Discerning Myth from Reality in Welfare Reform." *Journal of Religious Ethics* (Fall 1997): 307-329.

——. "The Author Replies." *Journal of Religious Ethics* (Fall 1997): 361-2.

Hollenbach, David, S.J. *Claims in Conflict: Retrieving and Renewing the Catholic Human Rights Tradition.* New York: Paulist Press, 1983.

——. "Human Work and the Story of Creation: Theology and Ethics in *Laborem Exercens.*" Pp. 59-77 in *Co-Creation and Capitalism: John Paul II's "Laborem Exercens,"* ed. John Houck and Oliver Williams. Washington, D.C.: University Press of America, 1983.

____. "The Pope and Capitalism." *America* 164 (June 1, 1991): 590-1.

Hoyt-O'Connor, Paul E. "Lonergan and Bellah: Social Science and Public Philosophy." *Proceedings of the American Catholic Philosophical Association* 68 (1994): 259-70.

——. *Bernard Lonergan's Macroeconomic Dynamics.* Lewiston, NY: Edwin Mellen Press, 2004.

Jacobs, Jane. *The Economy of Cities.* New York: Vintage Books, 1979.

——. *Cities and the Wealth of Nations.* New York: Random House, 1984.

——. *The Nature of Economies.* New York: Modern Library, 2000.

Kaldor, Nicholas. "The Irrelevance of Equilibrium Economics." *Economic Journal* 82 (December 1972): 1237-52.

Katouzian, Homa. *Ideology and Method in Economics.* New York: New York University Press, 1980.

Kresta, Al. "Interview with Michael Novak." 4/6/2000. Al Kresta in the Afternoon," Ava Maria Radio. <http://www.amfdn.org/ubb/Forum2/HTML/000346.
html> 1/7/2005.

Lakeland, Paul. *Theology and Critical Theory.* Nashville: Abingdon Press, 1990.

Lamb, Matthew. "The Relationship between Theory and Praxis in Contemporary Christian Theologies." *C.T.S.A. Proceedings* 31 (1976):149-78.

——. *History, Method and Theology: A Dialectical Comparison of Wilhelm Dilthey's Critique of Historical Reason and Bernard Lonergan's Meta-Methodology*, AAR Dissertation Series, no. 25. Missoula, MT: Scholars Press, 1978.

——. *Solidarity with Victims: Toward a Theology of Social Transformation.* New York: Crossroad, 1982.

——. "Modernism and Americanism Revisited Dialectically: A Challenge for Evangelization." *Communio* 21 (Winter 1994): 167-85.

Lawrence, Frederick. "Political Theology and 'The Longer Cycle of Decline.'" Pp. 223-55 in *Lonergan Workshop*, Volume I, ed. by Frederick Lawrence. Missoula, MT: Scholars Press, 1978.

——. "Lonergan as a Political Theologian." Pp. 1-22 in *Religion in Context: Recent Studies in Lonergan*, ed. Timothy P. Fallon and Philip Boo Riley. College Theology Society Resources in Religion 4. Lanham, MD: University Press of America, 1988.

——. The Human Good and Christian Conversation." In *Communication and Lonergan: Common Ground for Forging the New Age*, ed. Thomas J. Farrell and Paul A. Soukup, 248-68. Kansas City: Sheed & Ward, 1993.

Lawrence, Frederick and Charles Hefling and Patrick Byrne. "Editor's Introduction." Pp. [xxv]-lxxii in Bernard Lonergan, *Macroeconomic Dynamics: An Essay in Circulation Analysis*, ed. Frederick G. Lawrence, Patrick H. Byrne, and Charles Hefling, Jr., Vol. 15 of *Collected Works of Bernard Lonergan*, ed. Frederick E. Crowe and Robert M. Doran. Toronto: University of Toronto Press, 1999.

Lay Commission on Catholic Social Teaching and the U.S. Economy. *Toward the Future: Catholic Social Thought and the U.S. Economy: A Lay Letter.* Notre Dame, IN: Quodlibetal Publications, 1984.

Loewe, William. "Dialectics of Sin: Lonergan's *Insight* and the Critical Theory of Max Horkheimer." *Anglican Theological Review* 61 (April 1979): 224-45.

Lonergan, S.J. Bernard J.F. "An Outline of Circulation Analysis [c1944]." Unpublished manuscript available at the Lonergan Research Centre, Toronto.

——. *Method in Theology.* New York: Seabury Press: 1972.

——. "An Interview with Fr. Bernard Lonergan, S. J." Pp. 209-30 in *A Second Collection.* Ed. William Ryan and Bernard Tyrell. Toronto: University of Toronto Press, 1996 [1974].

——. "Insight Revisited." Pp. 263-78 in *A Second Collection.* Ed. William Ryan and Bernard Tyrell. Toronto: University of Toronto Press, 1996 [1974].

——. "The Response of the Jesuit as Priest and Apostle in the Modern World." Pp. 165-87 in *A Second Collection.* Ed. William Ryan and Bernard Tyrell. Toronto: University of Toronto Press, 1996 [1974].

——. "Course notes from 'Macroeconomics and the Dialectic of History'" Boston College, 1980. Available from the Lonergan Research Institute, Toronto.

——. *Caring About Meaning: Patterns in the Life of Bernard Lonergan.* Interviewed by Pierrot Lambert, Charlotte Tansey and Cathleen Going. Montreal: Thomas More Institute, 1982.

——. "Healing and Creating in History." Pp. 100-109 in *A Third Collection*, ed. Frederick E. Crowe, S.J. New York/Mahwah, NJ: Paulist Press, 1985.

——. "Cognitional Structure." Pp. 221-39 in *Collection.* Vol. 4 of *Collected Works of Bernard Lonergan,* ed. Frederick E. Crowe and Robert M. Doran. Toronto: University of Toronto Press, 1988.

——. "The Role of The Catholic University in the Modern World." Pp. 114-20 in *Collection.* Vol. 4 of *The Collected Works of Bernard Lonergan,* ed. Frederick E. Crowe and Robert M. Doran. Toronto: University of Toronto Press, 1988.

——. *Collected Works of Bernard Lonergan.* Ed. Frederick E. Crowe and Robert M. Doran. Vol. 5, *Understanding and Being: An Introduction and Companion to "Insight,"* ed. Elizabeth A. Morelli and Mark D. Morelli. Toronto: University of Toronto, 1990.

——. *Collected Works of Bernard Lonergan.* Vol. 3, *Insight: A Study of Human Understanding,* ed. by Frederick E. Crowe and Robert M. Doran. Toronto: University of Toronto Press, 1992.

——. "Moral Theology and the Human Sciences [1974]." Method: Journal of Lonergan Studies 15 (1997):5-20.

——. *Collected Works of Bernard Lonergan.* Ed. by Frederick E. Crowe and Robert M. Doran. Vol. 21, *For a New Political Economy*, ed. Philip McShane. Toronto: University of Toronto Press, 1998.

——. *Collected Works of Bernard Lonergan.* Ed. by Frederick E. Crowe and Robert M. Doran. Vol. 15, *Macroeconomic Dynamics: An Essay in Circulation Analysis*, ed. Frederick Lawrence, Charles Hefling and Patrick Byrne. Toronto: University of Toronto Press, 1999.

Long, D. Stephen. *Divine Economy: Theology and The Market.* London/New York: Routledge, 2000).

——. *The Goodness of God: Theology, Church and the Social Order.* Grand Rapids: Brazos, 2001).

——. "Catholic Social Teaching and the Global Market." Pp. 77-102 in *Wealth, Poverty and Human Destiny*, ed. Doug Bandow and David L. Schindler. Wilmington, DE: ISI Books, 2003.

MacKinnon, Edward. "Cognitional Analysis and the Philosophy of Science." *Continuum* 2 (Fall 1964): 343-68.

Maguire, Daniel C. *The Moral Choice.* Garden City, NY: Doubleday: 1978.

——. *The Moral Core of Judaism and Christianity: Reclaiming the Revolution.* Minneapolis: Fortress Press, 1993.

Martin, David. *The Dilemmas of Contemporary Religion.* Oxford: Basil Blackwell, 1978.

Martin, David A., "Economics in Three Paradigms: Subject, Method and Values." Pp. 58-68 in *Human Values and Economic Activity: The Proceedings of the 12th Conference on Value Inquiry* (Geneseo, NY: State University of New York College at Geneseo, 1978).

Martin, Stephen L. "Economic Development and True Democratic Capitalism: Contrasting 'Top-Down' Economic Visions and 'Bottom-Up' Political Cultures." *Catholic Rural Life* 47:1 (Spring 2004): 25-31.

Matthews, S.J., William. "Explanation in the Social Sciences." Pp. 245-60 in *Religion and Culture: Essays in Honor of Bernard Lonergan*, ed. Timothy P.

Fallon and Phillip Boo Riley. Albany: State University of New York Press, 1987.
Mayer, Herbert T. "Review of Michael Novak, *Freedom With Justice: Catholic Social Thought and Liberal Institutions*." *Currents in Theology and Mission* 13 (June 1986): 177-8.
McCool, Gerald A. "The Tradition of Saint Thomas in North America: At 50 Years." *The Modern Schoolman* 65 (March 1988): 185-206.
McCormick, Patrick T. "Centesimus Annus." Pp. 132-43 in *The New Dictionary of Catholic Social Thought*, ed. Judith Dwyer. Collegeville, MN: The Liturgical Press, 1994.
McShane, Philip. "Generalized Empirical Method and the Actual Context of Economics." Pp. 543-71 in *Creativity and Method: Essays in Honor of Bernard Lonergan, S.J.*, ed. Matthew L. Lamb. Milwaukee: Marquette University Press, 1981.
——. "Systematics, Communications, Actual Contexts." Pp. 59-86 in *Religion in Context: Recent Studies in Lonergan*, ed. Timothy J. Fallon, S.J. and Philip Boo Riley. Lanham, MD: University Press of America, 1988.
——. *Economics for Everyone, "Das Jus Kapital": A Book to Enlighten Beginning and Master Economists Alike.* Edmonton, Alberta: Axial Press, 1998.
——. *Pastkeynes, Pastmodern Economics: A Fresh Pragmatism*. Halifax, Nova Scotia: Axial Press, 2002.
Melchin, Kenneth. *History, Ethics and Emergent Probability: Ethics, Society and History in the Work of Bernard Lonergan*. Lanham, MD: University Press of America, 1987.
——. *Living With Other People: An Introduction to Christian Ethics based on Bernard Lonergan*. Collegeville, MN: The Liturgical Press, 1998.
Meynell, Hugo. "Lonergan's Theory of Knowledge and the Social Sciences." *New Blackfriars* 56 (Sept. 1985): 388-98.
Milbank, John. *Theology and Social Theory: Beyond Secular Reason.* Oxford: Basil Blackwell, 1990.
——. "Against the Resignations of the Age." Pp. 1-39 in *Things Old and New: Catholic Social Teaching Revisited*, ed. Francis P. McHugh and Samuel M. Natale. Lanham MD: University Press of America, 1993.
——. "On Complex Space." Pp. 268-92 in *The Word Made Strange: Theology, Language, and Culture* (Cambridge, MA: Blackwell Publishers, 1997). This is a slightly revised version of "Against the Resignations of the Age."
Misner, Paul. "The Predecessors of *Rerum Novarum* within Catholicism." *Review of Social Economy* 49 (1991): 444-64.
——. *Social Catholicism in Europe: From the Onslaught of Industrialization to the First World War.* New York: Crossroad, 1991.
Nessan, Craig. "Review of Michael Novak, *Freedom With Justice: Catholic Social Thought and Liberal Institutions*." *Dialog* 25 (Spring 1988): 154-6.

Niebuhr, Reinhold. *Moral Man and Immoral Society: A Study in Ethics and Politics*. New York: Charles Scribner's Sons, 1932.

Niebuhr, H.R. *Christ and Culture*. New York: Harper & Row, 1951.

Nitsch, Thomas. "Social Economics: The First 200 Years." Pp. 5-90 in *Social Economics: Retrospect and Prospect*, ed. Mark A. Lutz. Boston: Kluwer Academic Publishers, 1990.

Nordquest, David A. "Lonergan's Cognitional Theory: Toward a Critical Human Science." *Review of Politics* 56 (Winter 1994): 71-99.

Novak, Michael. *The Spirit of Democratic Capitalism*. New York: Simon & Schuster/American Enterprise Institute, 1982.

——. *Freedom with Justice: Catholic Social Thought and Liberal Institutions*. San Francisco: Harper & Row, 1984.

——. *Catholic Social Thought and Liberal Institutions: Freedom with Justice*. New Brunswick NJ: Transaction Publishers, 1989. Rev. ed. of *Freedom with Justice: Catholic Social Thought and Liberal Institutions*, with new introduction by the author.

——. *The Catholic Ethic and the Spirit of Capitalism*. New York: Free Press, 1993.

——. "Catholic Social Teaching, Markets and the Poor." Pp. 51-75 in *Wealth, Poverty & Human Destiny*, ed. Doug Bandow and David L. Schindler. Wilmington, DE: ISI Books, 2003.

O'Boyle, Edward J. "Catholic Social Economics: A Response to Certain Problems, Errors and Abuses of the Modern Age." In *Social Economics: Retrospect and Prospect*, ed. by Mark A. Lutz. Boston: Kluwer Academic Publishers, 1990. 121-44.

——. "Challenges Facing Social Economists in the Twenty-first Century: A Catholic's Perspective." *Review of Social Economy* 51 (1993): 426-40.

——. "*Homo Socio-economicus*: Foundational to Social Economics and the Social Economy." *Review of Social Economy* 52 (1994): 286-313.

O'Brien, David. J. and Thomas A. Shannon, ed. *Catholic Social Thought: The Documentary Heritage*. Maryknoll, NY: Orbis Books, 1992.

Pemberton, Prentiss L. and Daniel Rush Finn. *Toward a Christian Economic Ethic*. Minneapolis: Winston Press, 1985.

Preston, Ronald H. *Religion and the Persistence of Capitalism*. London: SCM Press, 1979.

——. *Religion and the Ambiguities of Capitalism*. Cleveland: The Pilgrim Press, 1979.

Rhodes, Royal W. and George E. McCarthy. *Eclipse of Justice: Ethics and Economics and the Lost Traditions of American Catholicism*. Maryknoll NY: Orbis Books, 1992.

Ryan, John A. *A Living Wage: Its Ethical and Economic Aspects*. New York: Macmillan, 1906.

——. *Distributive Justice: The Right and Wrong of Our Present Distribution of Wealth*. New York: MacMillan, 1916.

Schindler, David L. "The Church's 'Worldly' Mission." *Communio* 18 (Fall 1991): 365-97.

——. "Christology and the Church's Worldly' Mission: Response to Michael Novak." *Communio* 19 (Spring 1992): 164-78.

Schuck, Michael. *That They May Be One: The Social Teaching of the Papal Encyclicals, 1740-1989.* Washington, DC: Georgetown University Press, 1991.

Schumpeter, Joseph A. *History of Economic Analysis.* Ed. by Elizabeth Moody Schumpeter. New York: Oxford University Press, 1954.

Sen, Amartya. "Rational Fools: A Critique of the Behavioral Foundations of Economic Theory." *Philosophy & Public Affairs* 6 (1977): 317-44.

Shute, Michael. *The Origins of Lonergan's Notions of the Dialectic of History: A Study of Lonergan's Early Writings on History.* Lanham, MD.: University Press of America, 1993.

Stabile, Donald R. "Adam Smith and the Natural Wage: Sympathy, Subsistence, and Social Distance." *Review of Social Economy* LV (1997): 292-311.

Storck, Thomas. "What Does Centesimus Annus Really Teach?" Catholic.net. <http://www.catholic.net/RCC/Periodicals/Faith/2001-06/teaching.html> 01/07/ 2005.

Tekippe, Terry J. "The Crisis of the Human Good." In Pp. 313-30 in *Lonergan Workshop*, Vol. 7, ed. Frederick E. Lawrence. Atlanta, GA: Scholars Press, 1988.

Tiemstra, John P., et. al. *Reforming Economics: Calvinist Studies on Methods and Institutions*, vol. 48 of *Toronto Studies in Theology*, ed. John P. Tiemstra. Lewiston, NY: The Edwin Mellen Press, 1990.

Tolkien, J.R.R. *Lord of the Rings Trilogy.* London: Allen and Unwin, 1954-55.

Tracy, David. *The Achievement of Bernard Lonergan.* New York: Herder and Herder, 1970.

Varacelli, J.A. "Review of Michael Novak, *Freedom With Justice: Catholic Social Thought and Liberal Institutions.*" *Religious Studies and Theology* 6 (Jan.-May 1986): 51-3.

Wilber, Charles K. and Robert P. Jamison. *An Inquiry into the Poverty of Economics.* Notre Dame, IN: University of Notre Dame Press, 1983.

Winch, Peter. *The Idea of a Social Science and its Relation to Philosophy.* London: Routledge, 1963.

Winter, Gibson. "Introduction." In *Social Ethics: Issues in Ethics and Society*, ed. Gibson Winter. New York: Harper & Row, 1968.

Wogaman, J. Philip. *The Great Economic Debate: An Ethical Analysis.* Philadelphia: Westminster Press, 1977.

Wolff, Edward N. "Recent Trends in Wealth Ownership, 1983-1998." Jerome Levy Economics Institute. <http://www.levy.org/docs/wrkpap/papers/300.html> April 2000.

INDEX

ABOUT THE AUTHOR

Dr. Stephen Martin is Assistant Professor of Catholic moral theology at Seton Hall University in the Department of Religious Studies. He received his B.S. in Economics from Bradley University, and Ph.D. in Theology and Society from Marquette University, specializing in economic ethics. He has published articles on Bernard Lonergan's macroeconomics and presented different perspectives on Lonergan's economic thought at the Society of Christian Ethics, Catholic Theological Society of America, College Theology Society, American Academy of Religion and the Woodstock Theological Institute at Georgetown University. Stephen and his wife Elaine live with their two daughters in Bethlehem, PA.

www.ingramcontent.com/pod-product-compliance
Ingram Content Group UK Ltd.
Pitfield, Milton Keynes, MK11 3LW, UK
UKHW041104150926
475561UK00001BA/27

9 780761 837657